I0793594

IMAGES
of Rail

Pittsburg, Shawmut & Northern Railroad

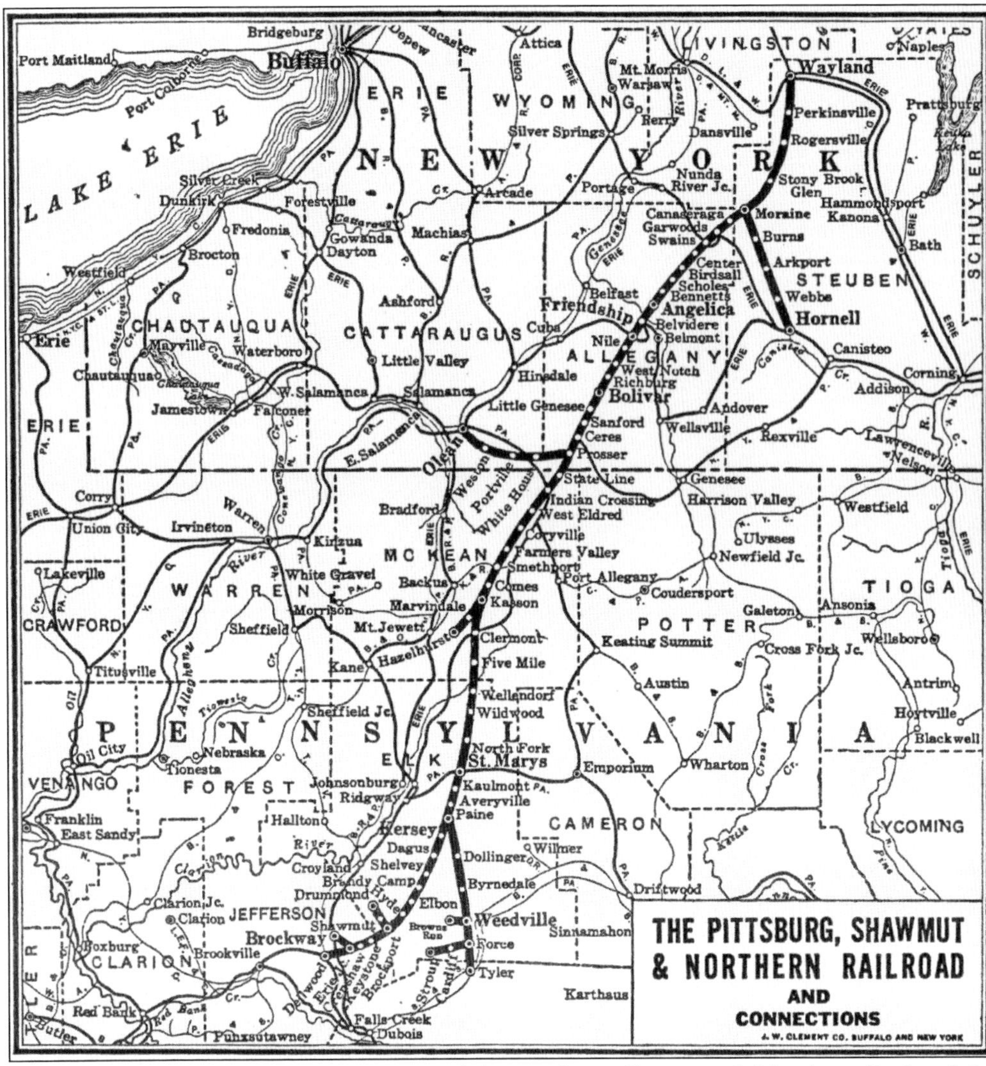

This 1920s system map shows the extent of the Pittsburg, Shawmut & Northern Railroad. Its southern terminus was Brockway, Pennsylvania, where it interchanged with the Erie Railroad, the Pittsburg & Shawmut Railroad, and the Buffalo, Rochester & Pittsburgh Railway. Its northern terminus was in Wayland, New York, where it connected with the Delaware, Lackawanna & Western Railroad. Two major branch lines included the one to Olean, New York, where it connected with the Pennsylvania Railroad, and the branch to Hornell, New York, where it again connected with the Erie Railroad. (Pittsburg, Shawmut & Northern Railroad Historical Society.)

ON THE COVER: This photograph, taken about 1905, shows linemen who installed and maintained the line-side telegraph poles and wires. The pump-style handcart carries spools of telegraph wire. Notice that all the men are wearing pole spikes on their boots. This allowed them to climb up the poles. (Pittsburg, Shawmut & Northern Railroad Historical Society.)

IMAGES
of Rail

Pittsburg, Shawmut & Northern Railroad

Ken Clark

ARCADIA
PUBLISHING

ISBN 978-1-4671-1726-5

Published by Arcadia Publishing
Charleston, South Carolina

Printed in the United States of America

Library of Congress Control Number: 2016937259

For all general information, please contact Arcadia Publishing:
Telephone 843-853-2070
Fax 843-853-0044
E-mail sales@arcadiapublishing.com
For customer service and orders:
Toll-Free 1-888-313-2665

Visit us on the Internet at www.arcadiapublishing.com

This book is dedicated to Wilford Keller Clark, my father, who regaled me with stories of the Shawmut Line when I was a child. Thanks, Dad, for this lifelong journey.

Contents

ACKNOWLEDGMENTS

I wish to thank John M. Muchler, treasurer and newsletter editor of the Pittsburg, Shawmut & Northern Railroad Historical Society, for his encouragement and support of me during this project. John provided me with unlimited access to the society's archives and also helped me hunt down the elusive photograph from time to time. I consider John to be one of my closest friends.

I also wish to thank Prof. Carole McNall, Esq., from St. Bonaventure University, who proofread my manuscript. Carole was my first editor way back in the day when I worked for her on the Pennsylvania bureau desk at the *Olean Times Herald*. Our friendship has remained strong though the many years and many miles.

Unless otherwise noted, all images appear courtesy of the Pittsburg, Shawmut & Northern Railroad Historical Society (PS&NRRHS) and the St. Marys Historical Society (SMHS).

Introduction

The Pittsburg (no *h*), Shawmut & Northern (PS&N) Railroad Company, also known as the "Shawmut Line," was a standard-gauge, Class I railroad that operated both freight and passenger service from 1899 to 1947. Trackage extended from Wayland, New York, to Brockway (née Brockwayville), Pennsylvania—a distance of approximately 190 miles. In addition, the railroad operated branches to Olean and Hornell, New York, and to Hazelhurst (now Hazel Hurst), Cardiff, Drummond, and Tyler, Pennsylvania.

The Pittsburg, Shawmut & Northern Railroad started on August 2, 1899, as the combination of five smaller financially troubled railroads in New York State and Pennsylvania. The purpose of the railroad was to haul coal from the mines of Elk (and later Jefferson) Counties in Pennsylvania to the Buffalo, Rochester, and New York City areas in New York State.

The first railroad that would eventually become part of the PS&N started as the narrow-gauge Olean Railroad. This line, chartered on May 2, 1881, was financed by Olean businessmen. It was constructed from Olean, New York, east to Bolivar, New York. Most of the railroad was built on the towpath of the abandoned Genesee Valley Canal. This railroad was built to serve the oil boom then happening in Bolivar and nearby Richburg.

Soon to follow was the Friendship Railroad. Chartered on May 10, 1881, this endeavor started in Friendship, New York, and headed south to Bolivar. It was financed by Asher Miner, a Friendship banker, and Abijiah Wellman, a Friendship lumberman. Like the Olean Railroad, it was also constructed as a three-foot narrow-gauge line.

Third was the Allegany Central Railroad. This railroad was chartered to start in Friendship, New York, at a connection with the Friendship Railroad and head east through Belvidere, Angelica, and on to Swainsville, New York. Swainsville was later renamed Swain but was always referred to as Swains by the railroad. This railroad was financed by Frank Sullivan Smith, an Angelica attorney, and Archer Martin, a vice president at the railroad syndicate of Clark, Post & Martin. The little Olean and Friendship Railroads did not go unnoticed by Clark, Post & Martin. On November 21, 1881, they were purchased outright and consolidated into the (second) Allegany Central Railroad.

In late 1882, plans were taking shape to construct a new bridge line railroad that would link the Delaware, Lackawanna & Western Railroad in Perkinsville, New York, with the Buffalo, New York & Philadelphia (BNY&P) Railroad at Belfast, New York. The BNY&P had been purchased by Clark, Post & Martin in 1881 at the same time they had purchased the narrow-gauge lines. This new line would offer competition to the existing east-west railroads: the New York Central, the Erie, and the Pennsylvania. This line was to make use of the Allegany Central between Angelica and Swain.

This new line, chartered on November 1, 1882, was named the Lackawanna & Pittsburgh. It converted the portion of the Allegany Central north of Angelica to standard gauge. It also constructed new trackage from Swain north to Perkinsville and from Angelica east to Belfast. On July 1, 1883, the Allegany Central was officially consolidated into the Lackawanna & Pittsburgh. The original portion of the Allegany Central south of Angelica remained narrow gauge.

The bridge line operations of the Lackawanna & Pittsburgh never amounted to much, and the railroad was constantly plagued by financial troubles. Over the next six years, it operated in an on-again, off-again fashion. Trains operated only when funds were available and strikes were common when payrolls were missed. The only portion of the line that was in good financial shape was the narrow-gauge portion serving Bolivar. This success was due to the high levels of both passenger and freight traffic stemming from the oil boom in Bolivar and surrounding areas.

The next railroad that would become part of the Shawmut—the Rochester, Hornellsville & Lackawanna Railroad—was chartered in June 1886. This railroad was built from a connection on the Lackawanna & Pittsburgh just east of Canaseraga, New York, south to the city of Hornellsville (now Hornell), New York, a distance of 10 miles. Another Clark, Post & Martin investment, this railroad was constructed to increase freight traffic on the ailing Lackawanna & Pittsburgh.

Financial troubles for the Lackawanna & Pittsburgh came to a head on April 27, 1889, when it was sold at foreclosure on behalf of the bondholders. The bondholders then organized the Lackawanna & Southwestern Railroad. In October of that year, they merged that line with the Rochester, Hornellsville & Lackawanna, forming the second Lackawanna & Southwestern Railroad.

The finances of the new Lackawanna & Southwestern were no better than the previous Lackawanna & Pittsburgh. To head off abandonment, Frank Sullivan Smith enticed John Byrne, an attorney from New York City, to purchase the railroad. Byrne named it the Central New York & Western. In an interesting twist of fate, the old Rochester, Hornellsville & Lackawanna (RH&L) Railroad was purchased separately by Smith and Byrne, then leased to the Central New York & Western. The RH&L would remain a separate railroad through the entire existence of the Pittsburg, Shawmut & Northern.

In Pennsylvania, the first line that would become the Pittsburg, Shawmut & Northern began in the 1860s when investors from Boston, Massachusetts, purchased coal lands in the Mead Run valley northeast of Brockwayville. These investors were financed by the Shawmut Bank of Boston. The name *Shawmut* comes from the Native American name for a hill overlooking the city of Boston.

This endeavor was not a financial success. The bank panic in the summer of 1893 permitted Andrew Kaul and James K.P. Hall of St. Marys, Pennsylvania, to acquire this operation. On June 19, 1893, they chartered the St. Marys & Southwestern Railroad to link their new holdings with St. Marys and a connection with the Philadelphia & Erie Railroad.

On June 5, 1895, Kaul and Hall organized the Buffalo & St. Marys Railroad. Starting in St. Marys, the line headed north to Clermont, Pennsylvania, and a connection with the McKean & Buffalo branch of the Western New York & Pennsylvania (WNY&P) Railroad. This railroad operated as one line with the St. Marys & Southwestern. Coal that was mined in Shawmut and Elbon was shipped north to Clermont and turned over to the WNY&P. On January 29, 1897, Kaul and Hall officially merged the two lines, forming the Buffalo, St. Marys & Southwestern Railroad.

The last railroad in Pennsylvania to become part of the Shawmut was the Mount Jewett & Smethport Railroad. This line was constructed from Mount Jewett, Pennsylvania, at a connection with the Buffalo, Rochester & Pittsburgh Railway east to the hamlet of Hazelhurst (now Hazel Hurst). At the time, Hazelhurst was home to several lumber mills and a glass plant. This railroad would be consolidated with the Emporium & Mount Jewett Railroad to form the Mount Jewett, Clermont & Northern on May 26, 1897.

As stated, these five separate railroads were consolidated on August 2, 1899, to form the Pittsburg, Shawmut & Northern Railroad. However, at the time of consolidation, they were isolated from each other and included a mixture of both narrow and standard gauges. The company put together an ambitious and costly plan to unite the route and convert the entire line to standard gauge; this feat was not completed until 1910. The financial burden of this endeavor combined with lackluster freight business forced the company into receivership (a form of bankruptcy) in 1905. The bankruptcy laws in the United State at that time stated that "companies operating in the public interest shall not be foreclosed, but instead shall have a court-appointed receiver to operate the property." This state of receivership lasted for the remainder of the Shawmut's 42 years of existence—one of the longest in American railroading history.

The principal shops of the railroad were divided between Angelica, New York, and St. Marys, Pennsylvania. The Angelica shops were used mostly as car repair, painting, and maintenance-of-way work with some repairs on locomotives. The major locomotive shop was in St. Marys. The Angelica shops burned on May 23, 1918, and the St. Marys shops burned on March 20, 1941; both were replaced.

The same officers who put together the PS&N started building a route toward Pittsburgh, Pennsylvania. It was to operate from Brockway, Pennsylvania, (and a connection with the PS&N) to Freeport, Pennsylvania. The officers initially named their line the Brookville & Mahoning

Railroad, hoping to entice local investors in the Brookville area, but their goal was always to merge this line into the PS&N.

In 1909, when the company issued its first public offering of stock, the name was changed to the Pittsburg & Shawmut (P&S) Railroad to make the stock more enticing to buyers. This stock offering was part of an overall plan to provide funding for the continued expansion of the P&S, to eventually lift the Pittsburg, Shawmut & Northern out of receivership, and, finally, to merge the two into a unified system.

An often repeated (but incorrect) legend claims the name change was done because of confusion with the Boston & Maine Railroad. However, the Brookville & Mahoning never owned a single piece of rolling stock, suggesting the idea of confusion with the reporting markings on freight cars was indeed a legend.

The P&S was under lease to the PS&N from 1906 to 1916. However, the poor finances of the PS&N and its state of receivership precluded a merger. In 1916, after a consulting firm evaluated the financial state of both roads, the backers of the P&S terminated the lease; the two companies operated separately from then on.

The same financial analysis also determined that the P&S was receiving a disproportionally low portion on the division of rates it received from coal traffic being handed over to the PS&N at Brockway. As a result, the P&S elected to turn over most of its coal traffic to the Erie Railroad at Brockway and earn more money on the very same traffic. The only coal turned over to the PS&N after this revelation was coal contracted by the Delaware, Lackawanna & Western Railroad for its own locomotive use.

The PS&N has been described as "a railroad that started nowhere and ended no place with a lot of nothing in between." It connected the mines with markets to the north, yet it did not touch upon any major industrial cities. After World War II, the demand for coal began to decrease. The strengthening labor movement in the mines caused many disruptive strikes. Nothing was being done to improve living conditions in the mining towns. The Shawmut Mining Company (a wholly owned subsidiary of the railroad) had strikes and labor problems.

In August 1945, the sole "company doctor," Betty Hayes, started investigating the sanitary conditions at the company-owned mining villages of Force, Byrnedale, and Hollywood, Pennsylvania. The conditions were so bad that the water had to be boiled before drinking and sewage overflowed into the streets, causing mud bogs. The doctor confronted the Shawmut Mining Company officials with these deplorable conditions. The officials replied that there was nothing that they could do, especially since the mines would be worked out and abandoned in only five or six years. We know now that this was not the case, as some mines lasted well into the 1950s and 1960s.

With the help of Dr. Hayes, the issue came before federal judge Guy K. Bard, who had jurisdiction over the receiver and who then ordered an investigation. The receiver at the time, John D. Dickson, was removed.

In late November 1945, the court appointed two new receivers: Thomas C. Buchanan and Robert C. Sproul Jr. Judge Bard instructed them to investigate the situation. However, taking the extreme length of the receivership into consideration, he also instructed the new receivers to "wrap things up, quickly!"

What the new receivers found was a company that was about $30 million in the red. There was not enough money on hand to meet their first payroll. There were not even enough serviceable locomotives on the property to operate the entire length of the line.

On May 21, 1946, an emergency request to the bankruptcy court was granted to embargo all traffic north of Bolivar, New York. This, combined with other cost-saving measures, gave the receivers time to figure out how to operate the properties at a profit. But they could come up with no way to do so.

The mining subsidiaries (the Shawmut Mining Company and the Kersey Mining Company) were at first leased to and eventually sold to the New Shawmut Mining Company. This company also acquired the mines of the former Buffalo & Susquehanna Coal and Coke Company in the Tyler, Pennsylvania, area and several mines in Jefferson County, Pennsylvania. This company was financially successful and lasted into the 21st century. Most of the original Shawmut mines were operated into the late 1960s, when they were finally closed.

Faced with the reality that there was no way to save the railroad and with the court's blessing, the PS&N Railroad and the wholly owned Kersey Railroad Company were sold at an auction presided over by Judge Bard on March 4, 1947. When the final gavel struck, the winner (for $1,505,000) was Harry W. Findley, a scrap dealer, of Carnegie, Pennsylvania. The last train of the Pittsburg, Shawmut & Northern Railroad ran on April 1, 1947, at which time the Class I common carrier ceased to exist.

The unique spelling of Pittsburg (without the *h*) comes from 1891, when the US Post Office Department enacted a plan to standardize the spelling of place-names within the United States. All places ending in "burgh" or "burg" were standardized as "burg." Thus, during the time that the Pittsburg, Shawmut & Northern Railroad and its affiliated Pittsburg & Shawmut Railroad were chartered, the correct spelling of the name was Pittsburg. This caused great consternation for the residents of Pittsburgh. It would take 20 years, but on July 19, 1911, the previous decision with regard to the spelling of Pittsburgh without a final *h* was rescinded. However, the charters of the affected railroads were never changed, thus leaving us with these unique spellings and an interesting piece of trivia.

One

The Shawmut in New York State

The Pittsburg, Shawmut & Northern Railroad in New York State began in Wayland, New York, at milepost (MP) 0.0. It extended south to the town of Portville, New York, where it crossed into Pennsylvania at MP 70.5. Wayland was a key interchange point between the Shawmut and the Delaware, Lackawanna & Western Railroads.

The focal point of activity on the Shawmut in New York State was at Angelica, New York, located at MP 35.8. Angelica was home to the Maintenance of Way Department and the Office of the Receiver. It was the location of one of the two principal yards and shops of the railroad; the other was located in St. Marys, Pennsylvania (see chapter 2).

During the railroad's formative years, the Angelica shops included an engine house, a coach house, and an extensive carpentry shop. Until the advent of steel railroad cars in the 1920s, this carpentry shop constructed many of the freight cars and cabooses operated by the Shawmut. Angelica's importance as a railroad center would eventually wane, matching the overall fortunes of the Shawmut.

North of Angelica at MP 10.9 was Moraine Junction, the location of the branch to Hornell, New York. This branch line was, in fact, a separate railroad: the Rochester, Hornellsville & Lackawanna Railroad. This railroad was owned by the Shawmut's first president, Frank Sullivan Smith, and simply leased by the Shawmut. Upon Smith's death, it was willed to his widow Clara Higgins Smith. She eventually willed the branch to the American Red Cross. With the demise of the Shawmut in 1947, the Red Cross went on to sell the line for scrap, except for the Hornell terminal properties, which were sold to the Erie Railroad and operated until the early 1980s.

Near the Pennsylvania state line at MP 67.9 was Prosser Junction, the location of the branch to Olean, New York. This branch can trace its history back to the narrow-gauge Olean Railroad and was constructed on top of the towpath of the old Genesee Valley Canal. Olean was a key interchange point between the Shawmut and the Pennsylvania Railroad.

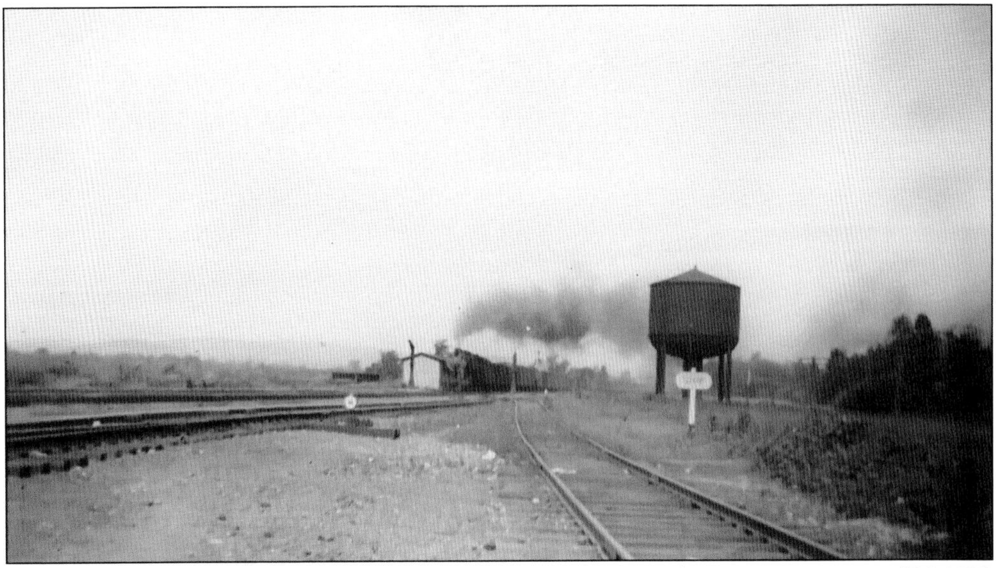

This 1944 photograph shows the far east end of the Delaware, Lackawanna & Western (DL&W) yard at Wayland, New York. This was MP 0.5 on the Shawmut's main line. Milepost 0.0 was another half mile distant at the Lackawanna's depot on South Lackawanna Avenue. The approaching westbound DL&W freight is about to pass the water columns fed by the DL&W's steel water tank at right. (SMHS.)

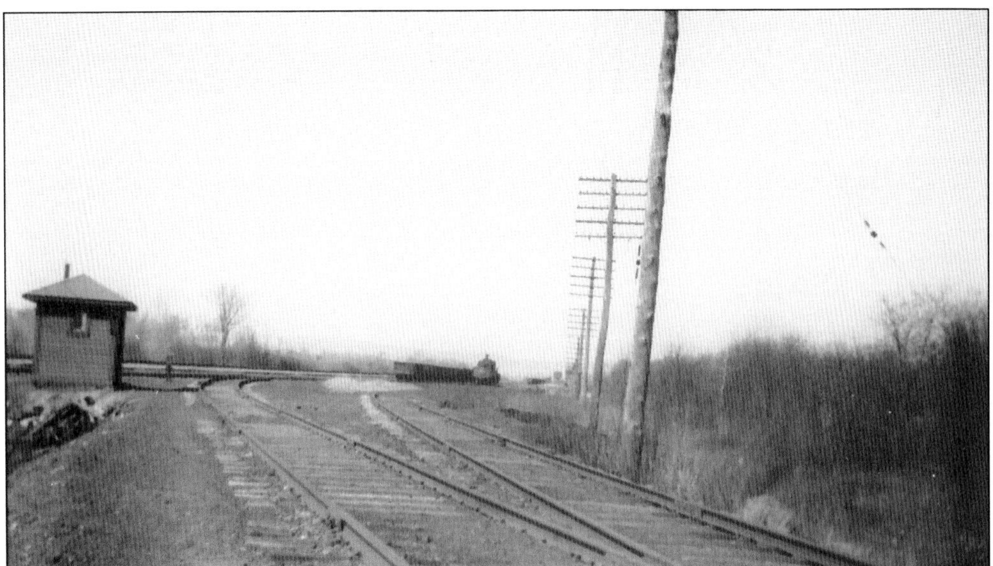

The west end of the yard in Wayland, New York, was named Wayland Junction. Located at MP 1.2, the building at the left was named "WA Office." It contained a railroad telephone that connected with the dispatcher in St. Marys, Pennsylvania. This is the point where the Shawmut main line (in the foreground) veered away from the DL&W tracks and began its journey south. (SMHS.)

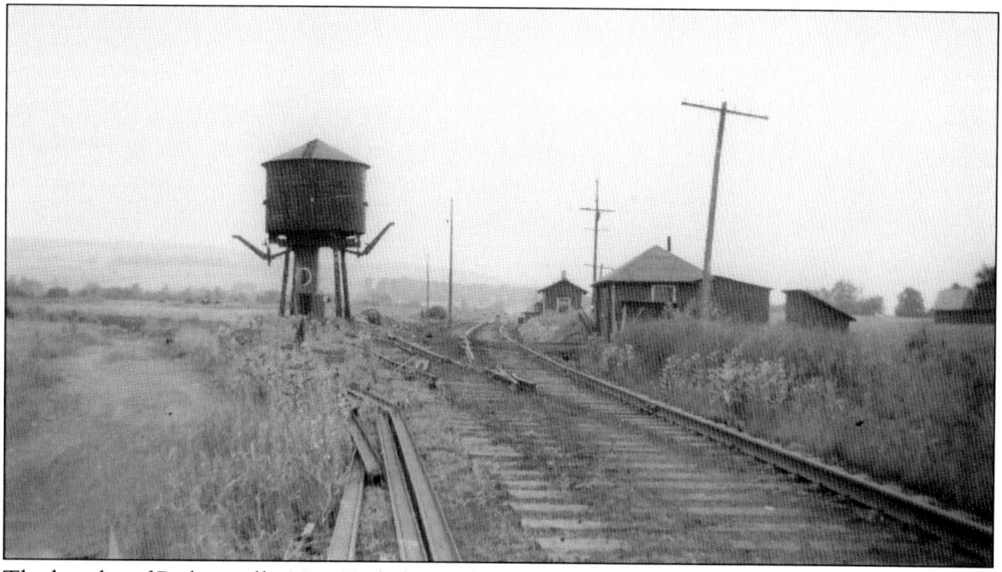

The hamlet of Perkinsville, New York, located at MP 1.5, was where the Shawmut maintained its own engine servicing facilities. The view in this 1947 photograph is looking south and shows the rails being taken up. The north leg of the wye veers off to the left. Engines could take on water from the 50,000-gallon tank from both the wye and the ash pit track. The bunkhouse stands at the right. (SMHS.)

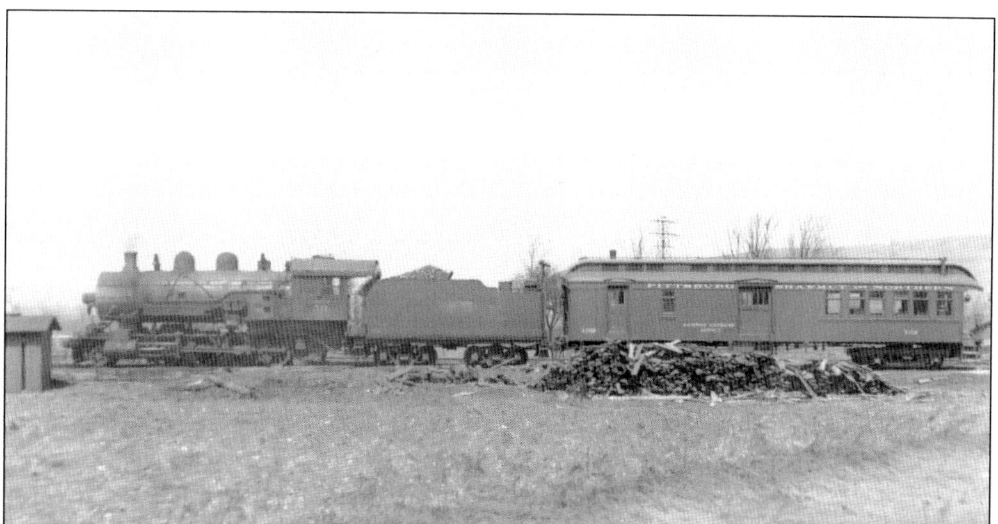

Engine No. 50 is shown arriving at Perkinsville, New York, pulling combination car No. 132. The car was a unique combination railway post office, baggage/express, and passenger car. By combining all services into a single car, the Shawmut was able to minimize expenses compared to operating three separate cars. (PS&NRRHS.)

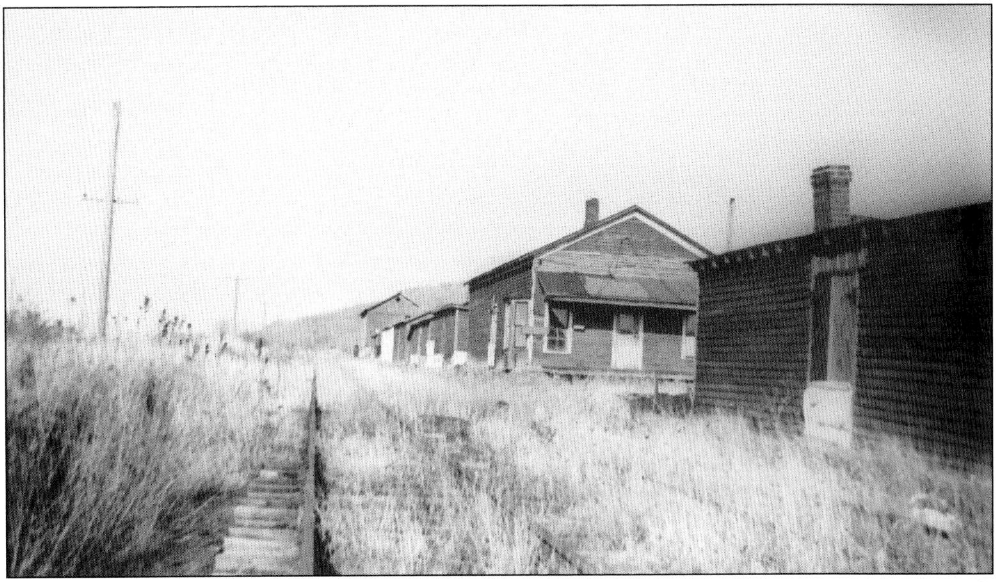

The hamlet of Rogersville, New York, was located at MP 5.0. The view in this 1947 photograph is looking east (timetable north) after the railroad was abandoned but before the rails were removed. Rogersville hosted six commercial produce warehouses. The large building (center) is the Shawmut passenger depot. At one time, tons of potatoes were shipped from here. Today, Rogersville is a ghost town. (SMHS.)

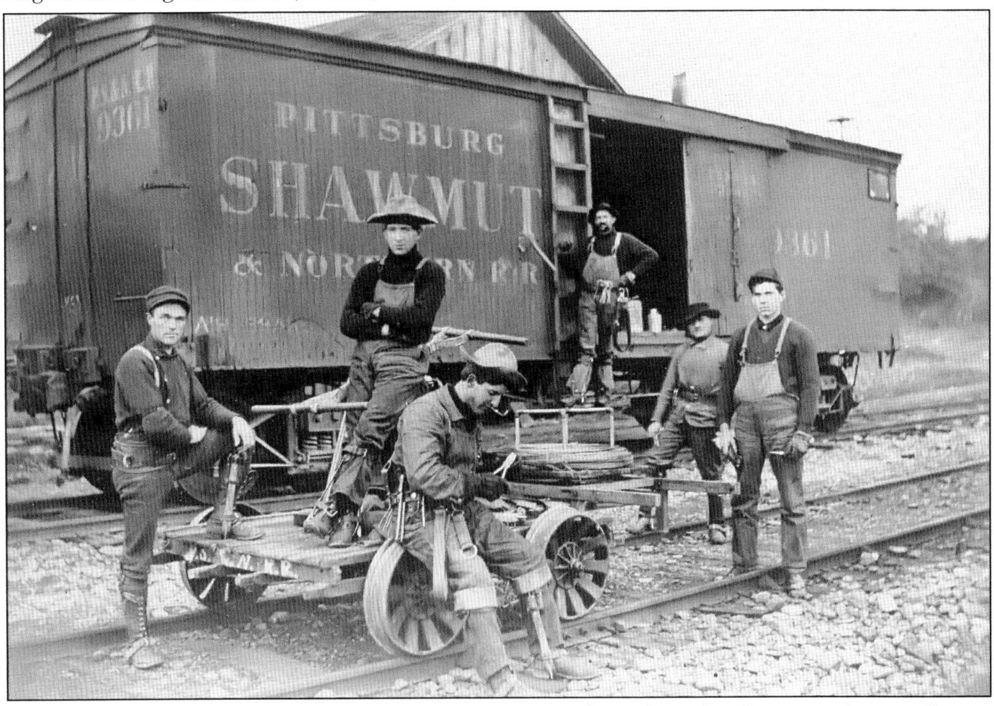

Besides laying ties and rails, the other major construction along the right-of-way was the installation of telegraph wires. This photograph was taken about 1905. The pump-style handcart carries spools of telegraph wire. Notice that all the men, except the one at the right, are wearing pole spikes on their boots. This allowed them to climb up the poles. (PS&NRRHS.)

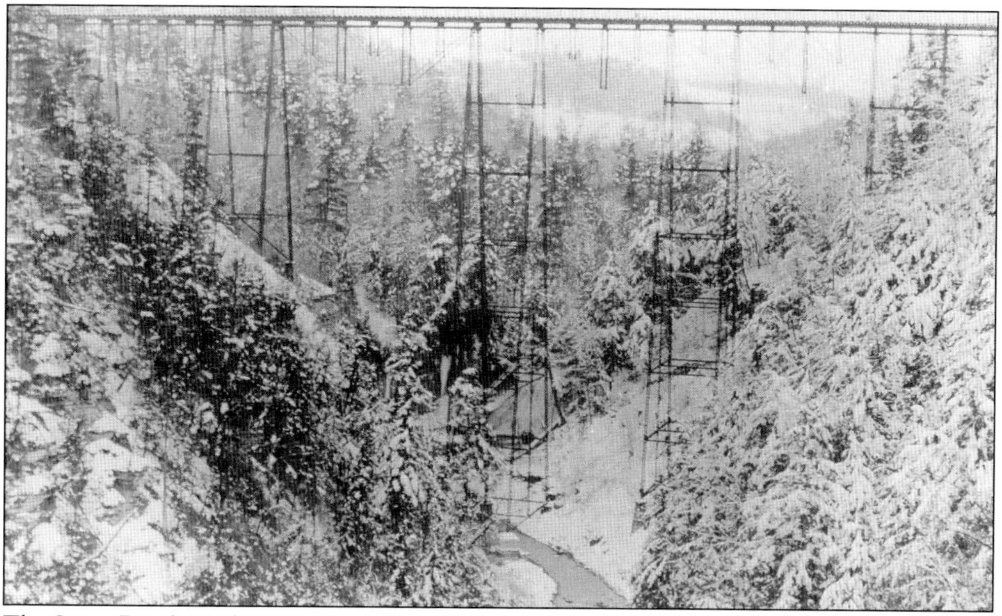

The Stony Brook Viaduct stood at MP 5.9. This viaduct was built in 1883 by the Lackawanna & Pittsburgh Railroad. This spiderweb-looking iron viaduct was constructed by the Delaware Bridge Company of Trenton, New Jersey, at a cost of $75,000. At 700 feet long and 240 feet high, it was the highest railroad bridge in New York State. (PS&NRRHS.)

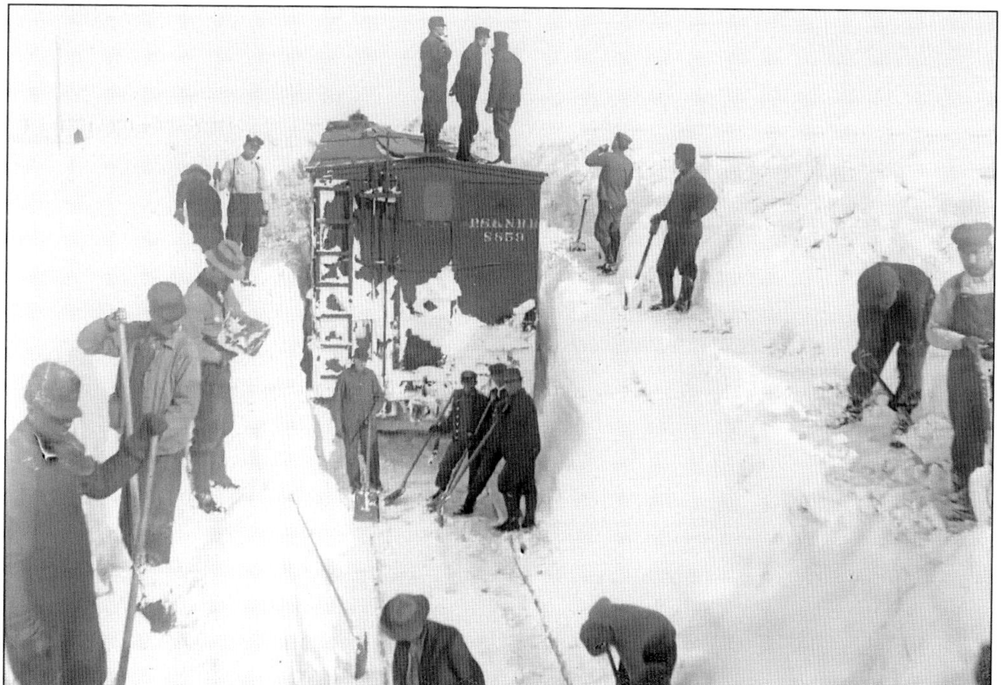

The Shawmut in New York State typically did not suffer from lake-effect snow. However, in 1910, a train became snowbound and buried south of the Stony Brook Viaduct. Snowplows and other trains were unable to rescue the stranded train. Section crews had to dig the train out by hand. (PS&NRRHS.)

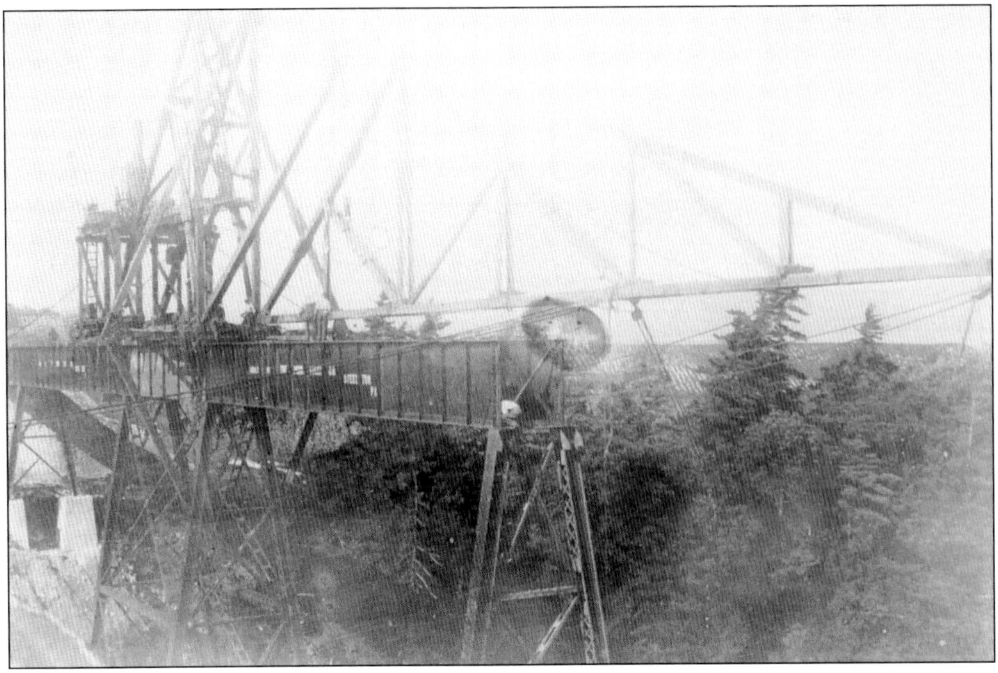

The financially troubled Lackawanna & Pittsburgh lacked the funds to perform any maintenance on the original Stony Brook Viaduct. Twice, in 1894 and 1895, New York State inspectors nearly condemned it. By 1903, the state recommended a total replacement. By 1906, the relatively young Shawmut was able to obtain approval from the bankruptcy court to construct a replacement bridge next to the old one. (SMHS.)

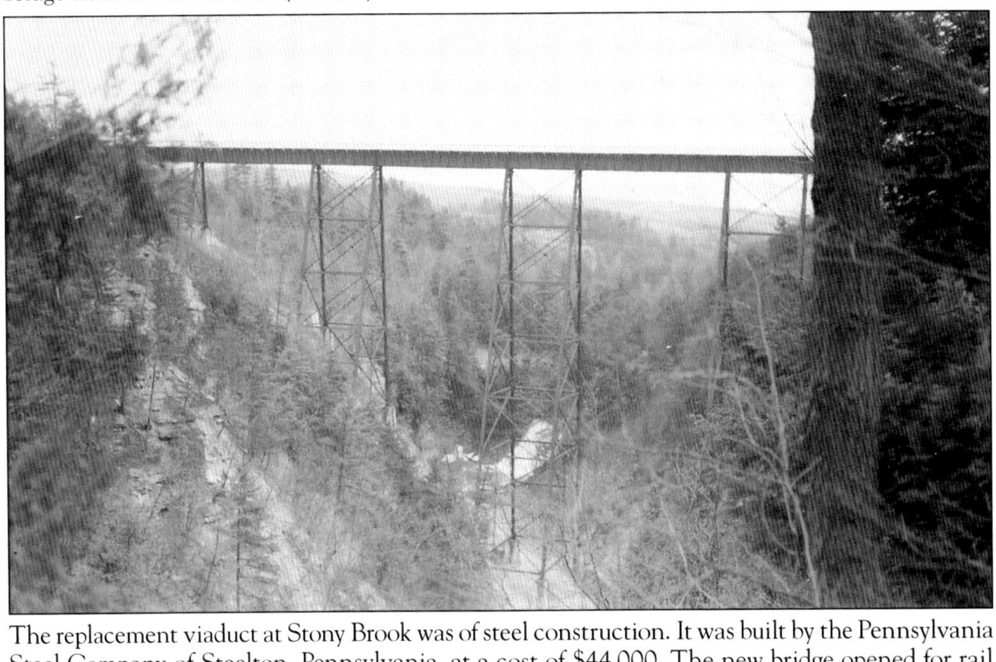

The replacement viaduct at Stony Brook was of steel construction. It was built by the Pennsylvania Steel Company of Steelton, Pennsylvania, at a cost of $44,000. The new bridge opened for rail traffic on Tuesday, November 28, 1907. A test train consisting of engines No. 53 and No. 54 hauling 17 loaded coal cars and a caboose was used to test the new bridge. (PS&NRRHS.)

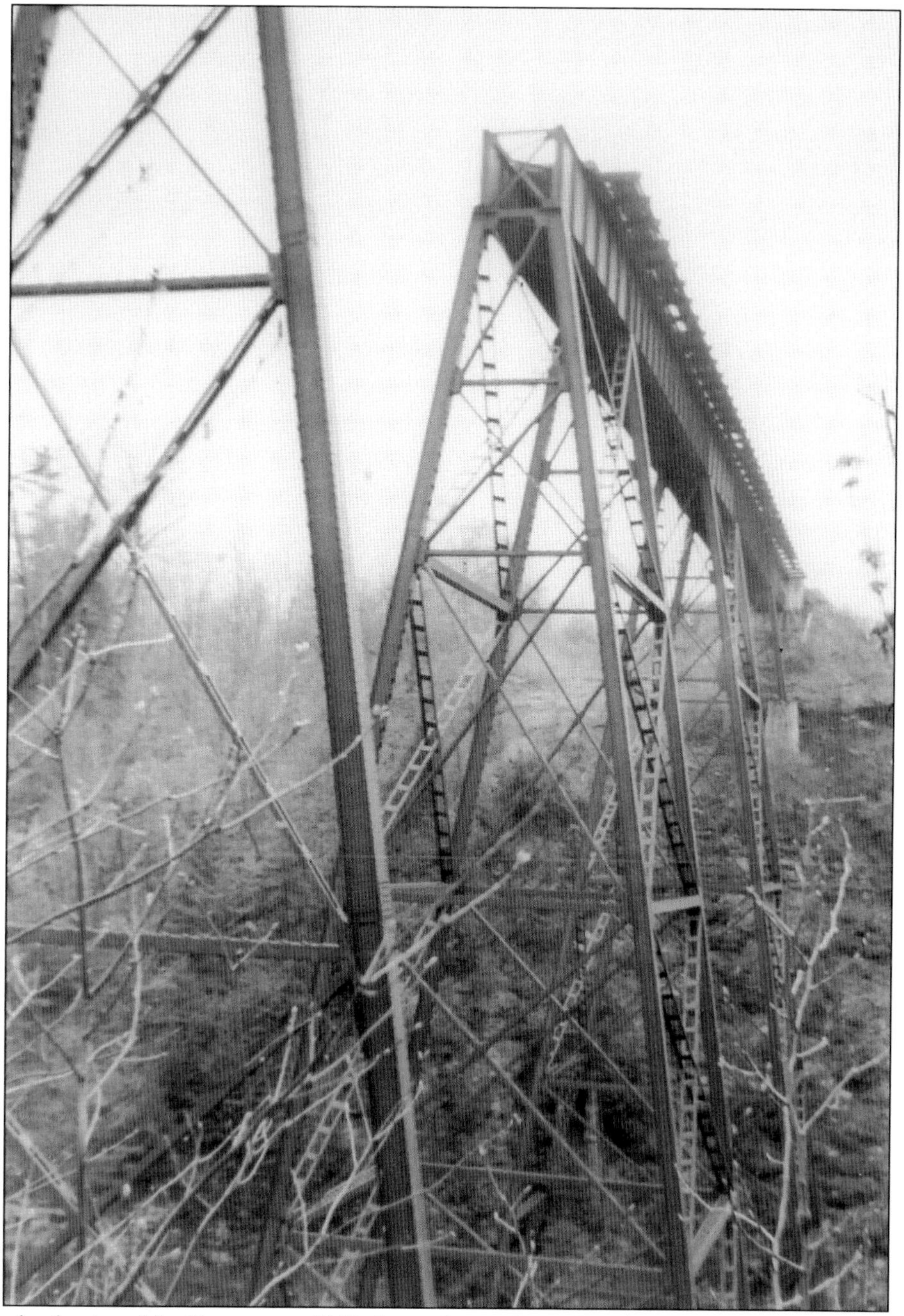

With the demise of the Shawmut in 1947, the viaduct at Stony Brook was cut up for scrap beginning in April 1948. Every bridge, be it modern or old, has a fixed (or anchored) end and a loose end on rollers. This permits the bridge to expand and contract with the weather. Unfortunately, the scraper failed to take this into account and cut the anchored end loose first. As a result of the high winds in the valley, all of the remaining towers swayed about a foot in all directions until they were cut down one by one. Today, this is the location of Stony Brook State Park, part of the New York State Parks system. Park visitors who walk up the gorge past the wading pool and waterfalls will come to the footings of both the original and replacement bridges. (SMHS.)

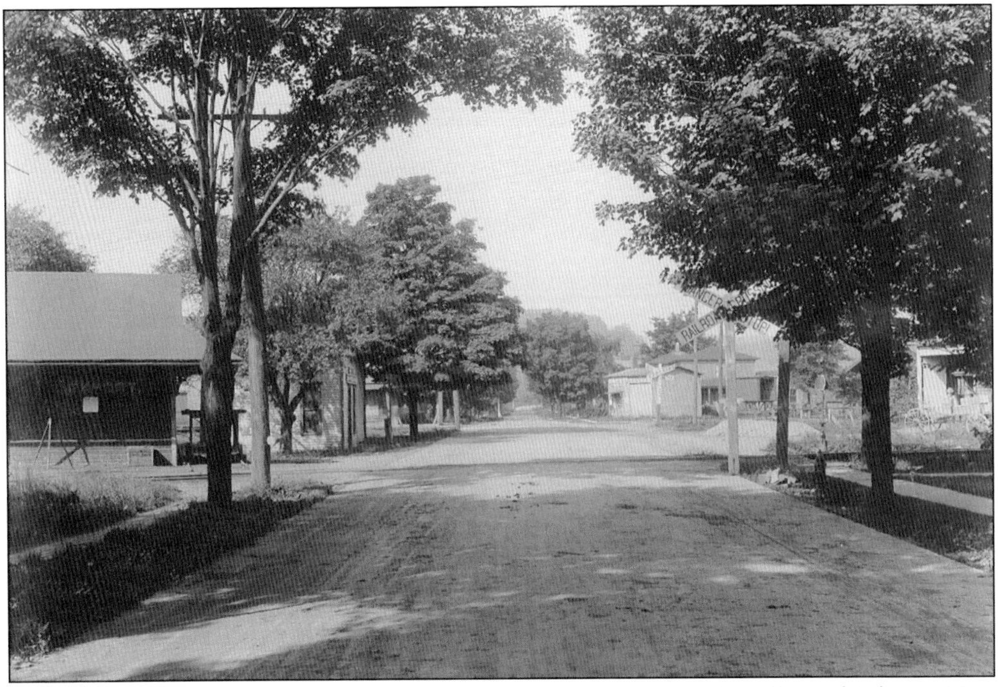

The view in this 1910 photograph looks west down West Avenue in the village of Arkport, New York. The Shawmut depot, located at MP 15.4 on the Hornell Branch, is seen at the left of the photograph. The Shawmut tracks cross in the foreground. Beyond the depot is the Taylor Produce Company. The second railroad crossing in the background is the main line of the Erie Railroad's Buffalo Division. (PS&NRRHS.)

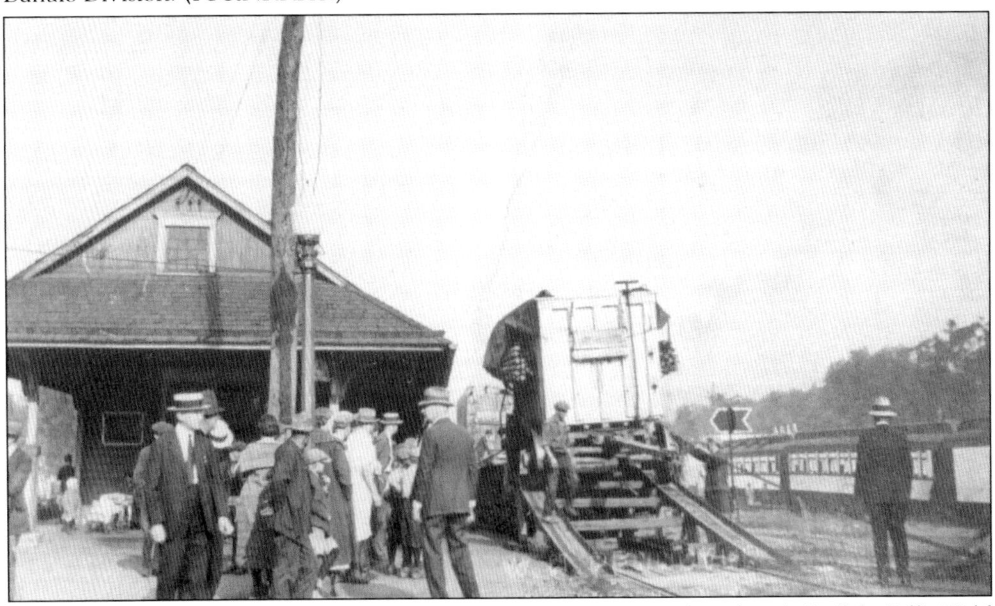

On Saturday morning, June 26, 1926, the Sells-Floto Circus, combined with Buffalo Bill's Wild West show, unloaded circus carts and wagons next to the Shawmut depot in Hornell, New York. Located on Seneca Street in the north end of town, the depot was at MP 20.0 on the Shawmut's Hornell Branch. The circus headed to Olean, New York, the next day. (PS&NRRHS.)

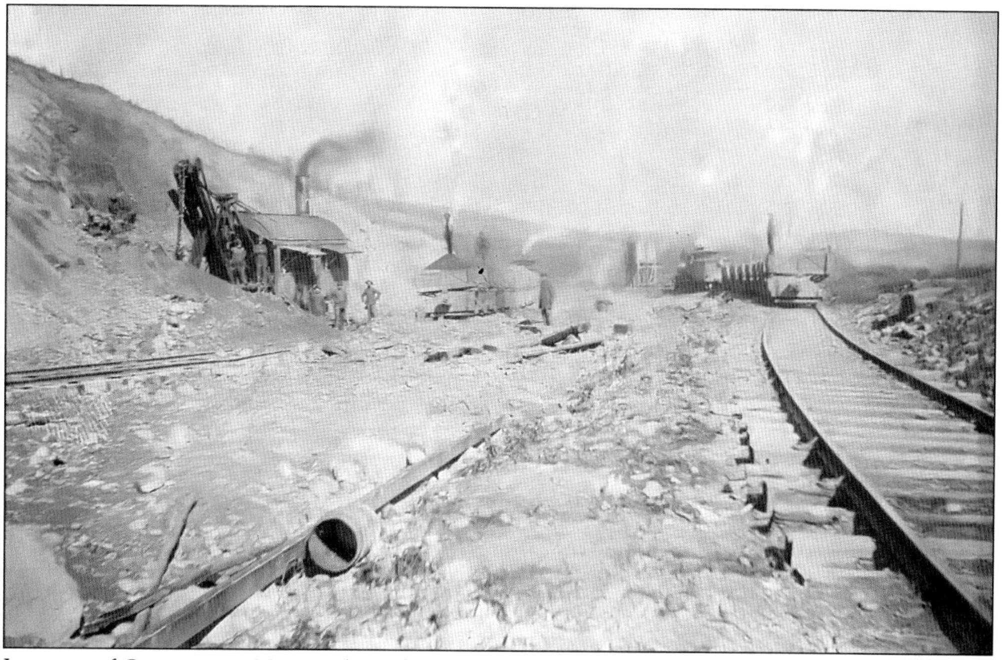

Just east of Canaseraga, New York, and near where the Rochester, Hornellsville & Lackawanna Railroad connected with the Lackawanna & Pittsburgh Railroad at Moraine, New York, was a place known as Camp Way. This 1897 photograph shows excavation being done by the (then) Central New York & Western Railroad. (SMHS.)

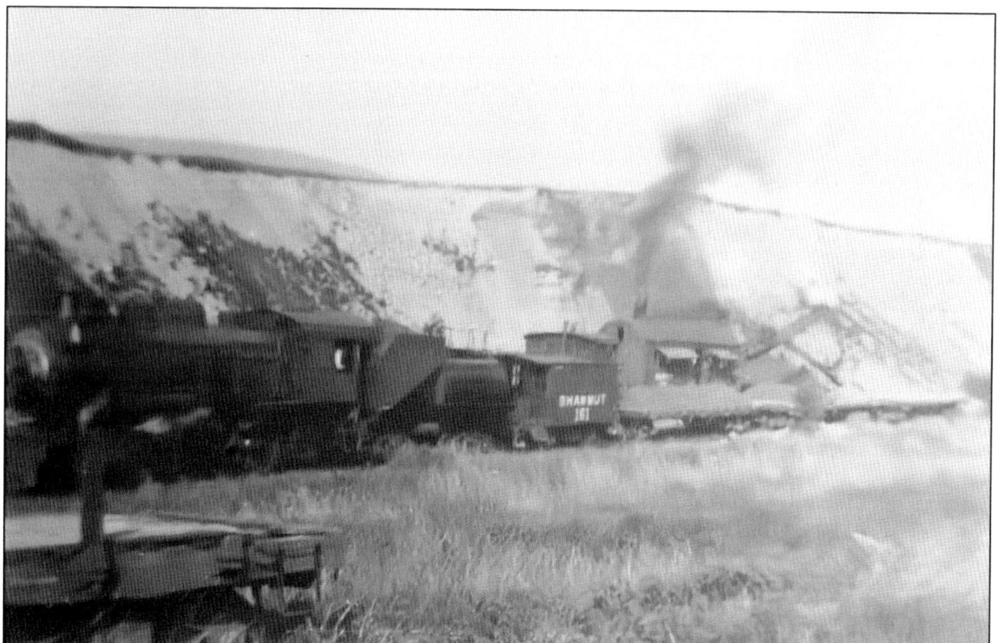

Camp Way, located at MP 11.5, was where the Shawmut contracted with property owner Stephen N. Bennett to dig gravel for use in ballasting its tracks. This 1922 photograph shows the excavation in progress. The contract permitted the Shawmut to extract gravel up to 10 feet below the level of the main track. (SMHS.)

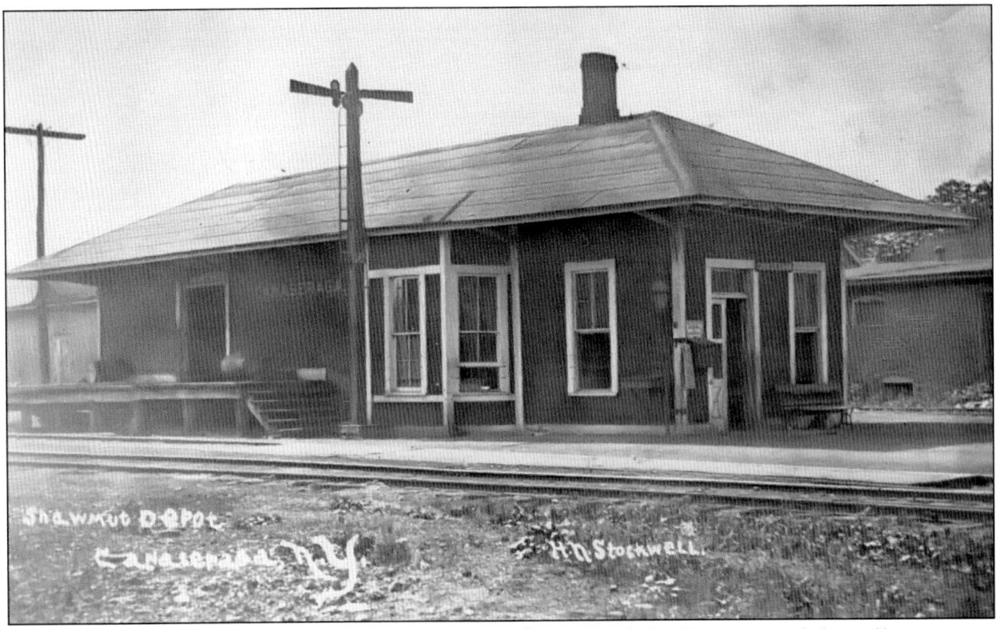

The village of Canaseraga, New York, was located at MP 13.6. The name of the village comes from the Seneca language and means "lying among milk-weeds." The letters "RA" on the signal mast to the left of the bay window are the telegraph call sign for this station. These 19th-century call signs were the equivalent of today's phone number or e-mail address. This station has been preserved. (PS&NRRHS.)

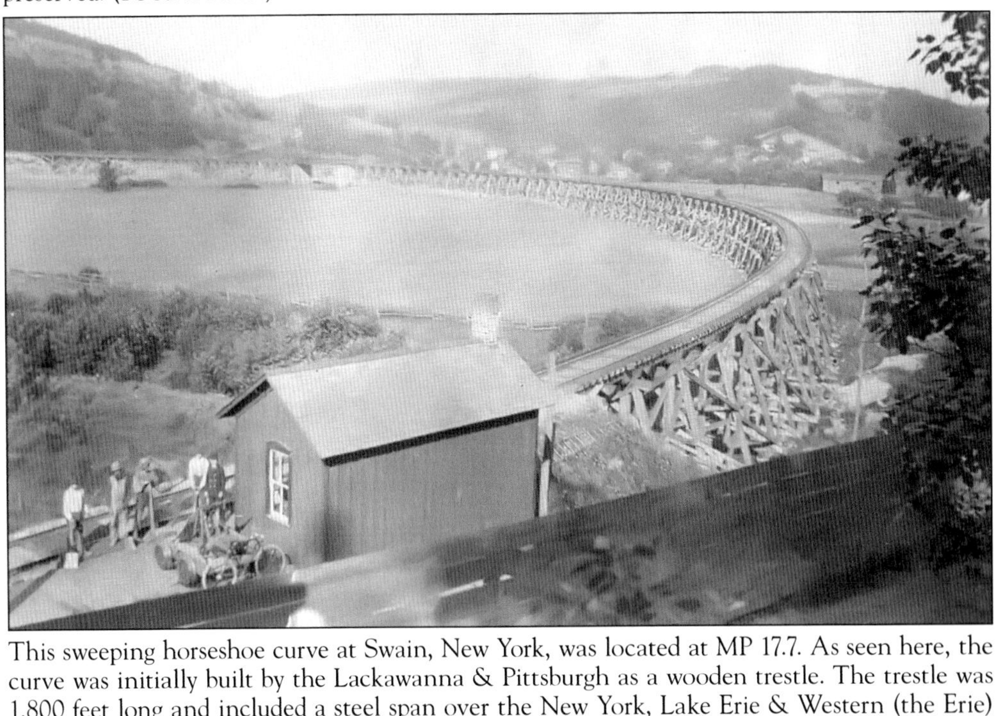

This sweeping horseshoe curve at Swain, New York, was located at MP 17.7. As seen here, the curve was initially built by the Lackawanna & Pittsburgh as a wooden trestle. The trestle was 1,800 feet long and included a steel span over the New York, Lake Erie & Western (the Erie) Railroad in the middle. Originally named Swainsville, this location was called Swains by the railroad. (PS&NRRHS.)

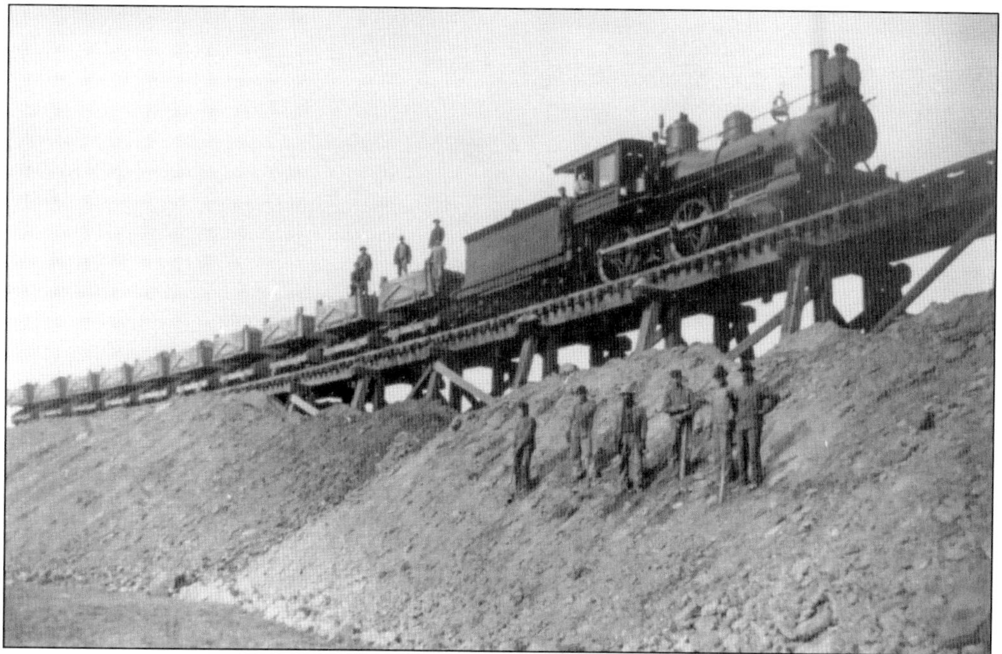

The large horseshoe curve at Swain, New York, was originally constructed by the Lackawanna & Pittsburgh Railroad as a wooden trestle. One of the first things the Shawmut did after its consolidation was to fill in the trestle, creating a berm. The locomotive shown here on this work train has yet to be re-lettered and still wears the initials for the Central New York & Western Railroad. (PS&NRRHS.)

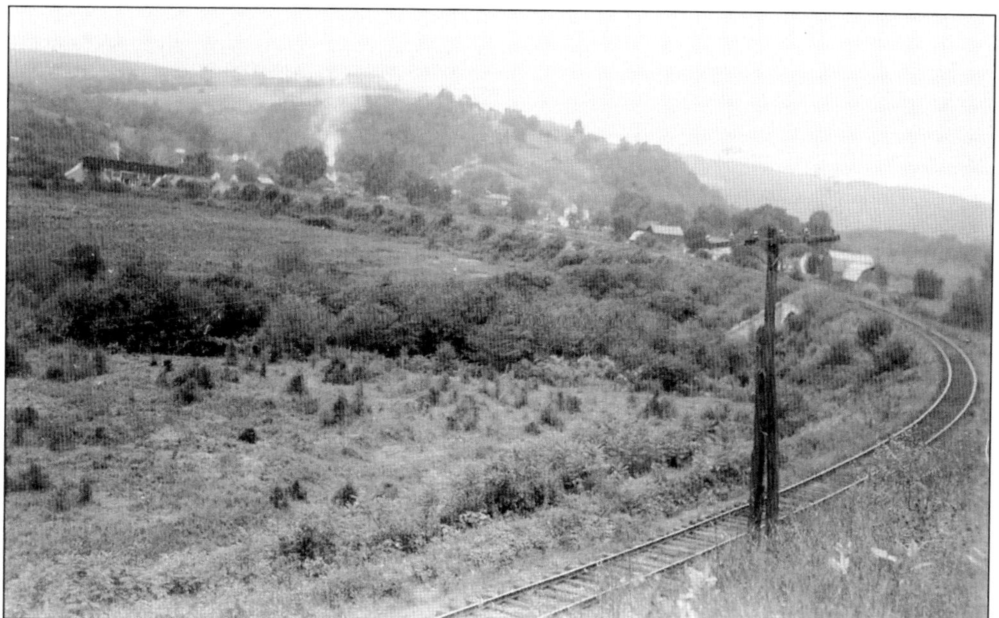

This 1945 photograph, with a view looking north, shows the horseshoe curve at Swain, New York, after it had been filled in for nearly 40 years. The steel bridge over the Erie Railroad is at upper left. On the right, directly behind the telephone pole, is the 30-foot concrete arch located at MP 17.6. This arch was added when the original trestle was filled in. (SMHS.)

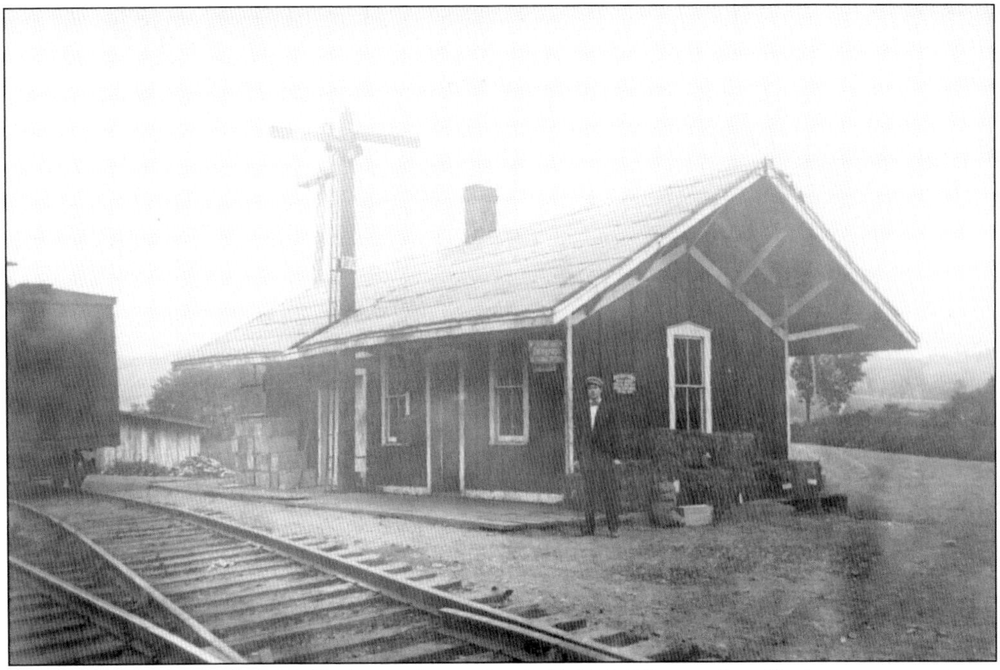

The hamlet of Birdsall, New York, was located at MP 26.0. The unidentified young man is, no doubt, the station agent. The telegraph call sign for this station was "BR." Located in the heart of an agricultural community, the station boasts bales of hay and wooden produce crates on the platform. The sign on the station advertises that it is also a Western Union Telegraph and Cable office. (PS&NRRHS.)

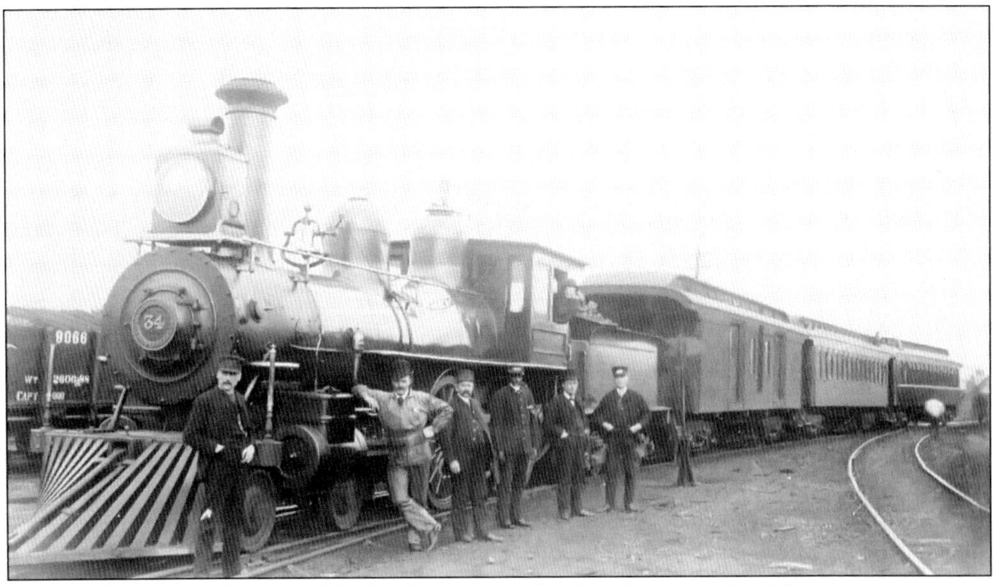

The standard-gauge division of the Lackawanna & Pittsburgh operated a deluxe passenger train between Wayland, New York, and Olean (via Belfast, New York) named the Cannonball. Service included a handsome parlor car. Up front is Engine No. 34 owned by the Rochester, Hornellsville & Lackawanna. It would later become No. 9 on the Shawmut. The location is believed to be Angelica, New York. (PS&NRRHS.)

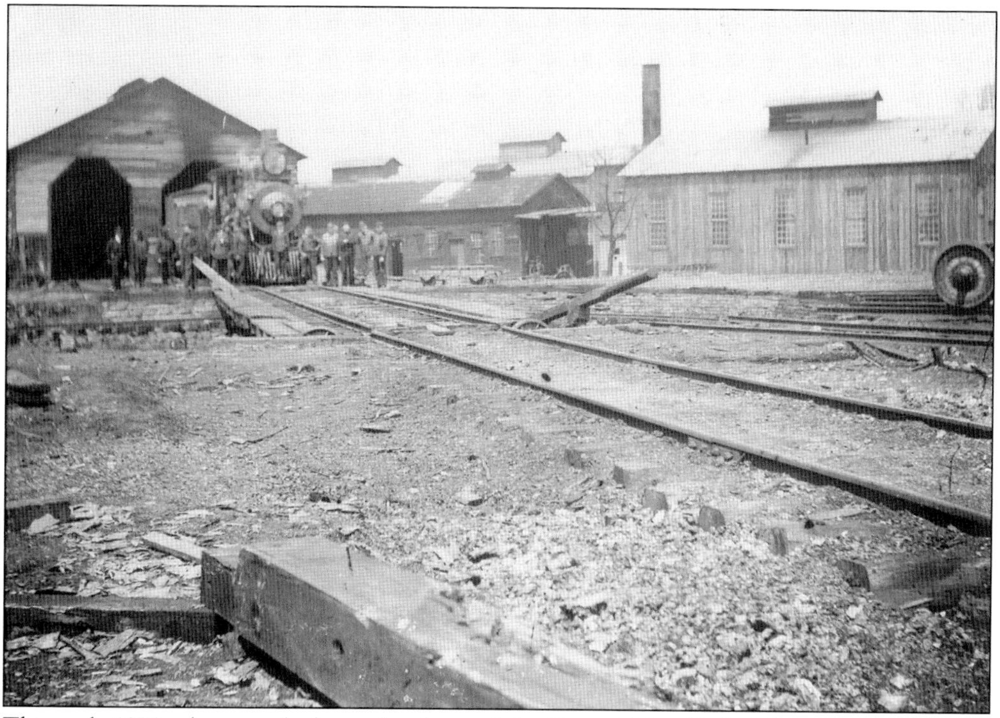

This early 1890s photograph shows the shops of the Central New York & Western in Angelica, New York. In the background (left) is the two-stall engine house. In front of the locomotive is an "Armstrong" turntable, so named because it was turned manually. To the right of the engine house are the machine shop, boiler house, and carpenters' shop, respectively. (PS&NRRHS.)

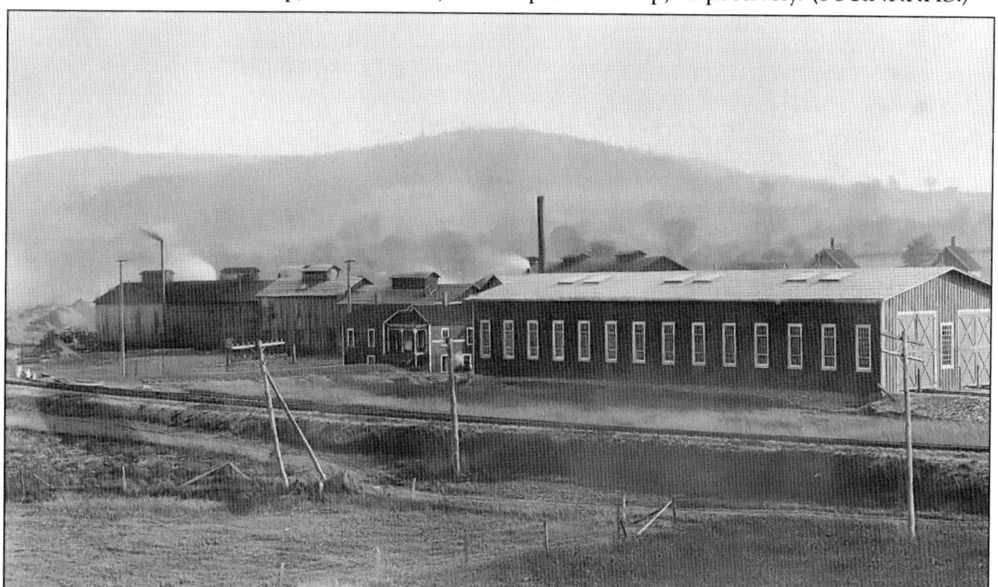

Shortly after the Shawmut came into being, it erected a new combined coach house and paint shop (right) as part of the Angelica, New York, shops. Behind the coach house (center) is the stores house, which also contained the superintendent's office. The Shawmut main line is seen in the foreground. (PS&NRRHS.)

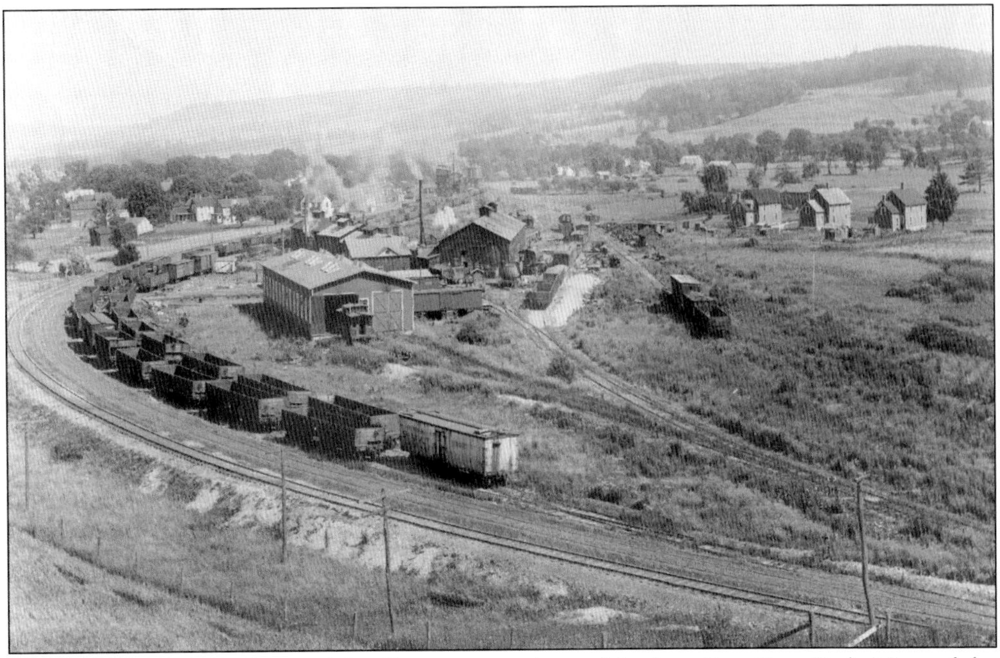

One of the two major shops of the Shawmut was located in Angelica, New York. Most of the shop buildings shown in the above photograph with a view looking east, taken about 1910, were originally built by the Central New York & Western Railroad. Note the white reefer car and the string of empty coal hoppers on the siding in the foreground. Today, the tracks curving through the photograph have been paved over as the appropriately named Railroad Avenue; Brookland Street crosses through the center from left to right, and Interstate 86 now crosses the hill on the right in the background. The shops seen below were consumed by fire in 1918. (Both, PS&NRRHS.)

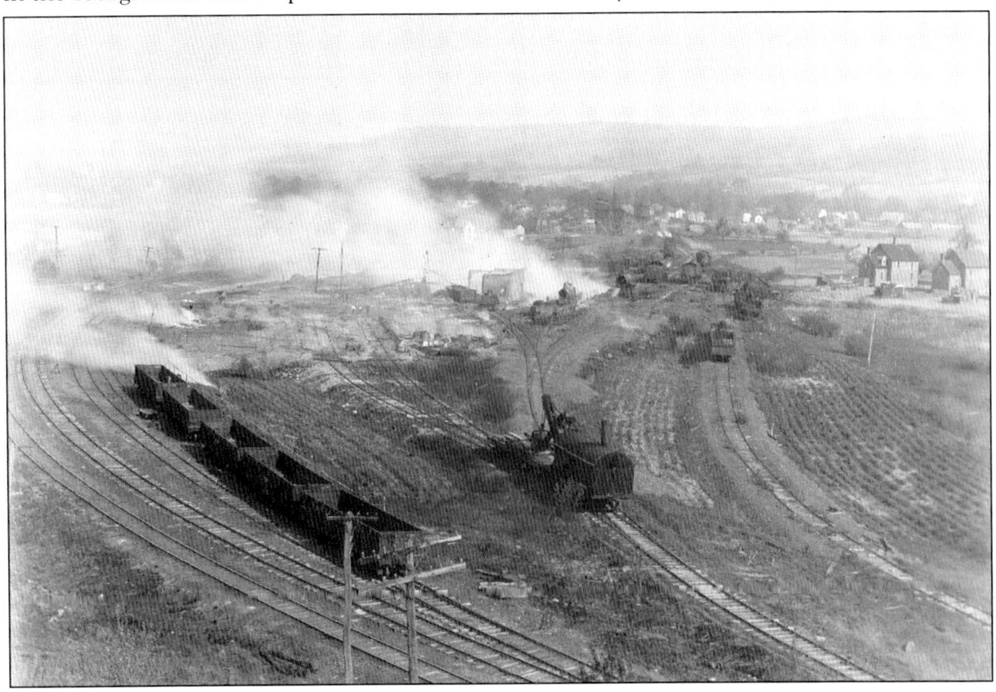

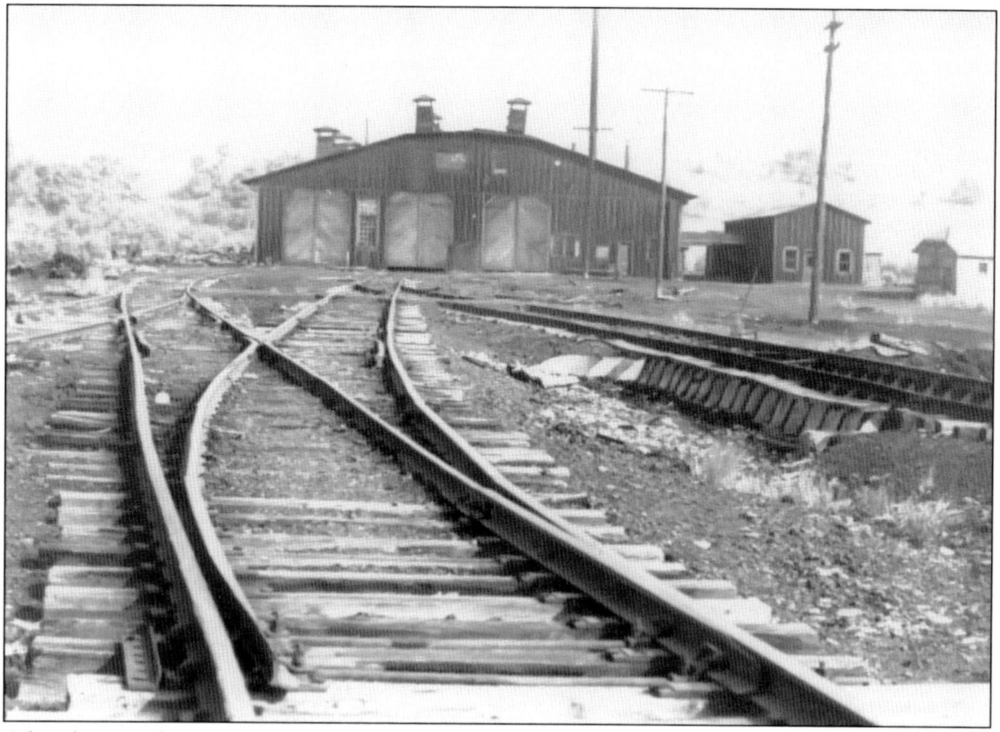

After the Angelica, New York, shops were destroyed in 1918, these more utilitarian shops replaced them. At the time of this photograph in 1946, the Shawmut Line was on borrowed time and most of the work had been transferred to the St. Marys, Pennsylvania, shops. Along the track at the right is the ash pit where locomotives would have their fires "dumped" before being moved inside the shop building. (PS&NRRHS.)

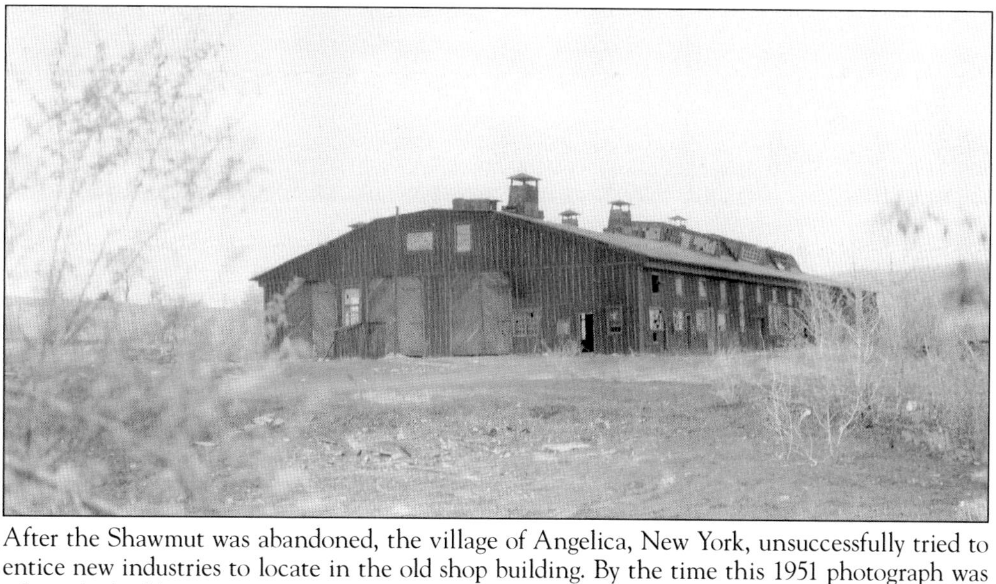

After the Shawmut was abandoned, the village of Angelica, New York, unsuccessfully tried to entice new industries to locate in the old shop building. By the time this 1951 photograph was taken, the building was stripped and broken and would shortly be torn down. Today, this scene is dotted with neat homes and well-groomed lawns. One would never know a railroad ever existed here. (SMHS.)

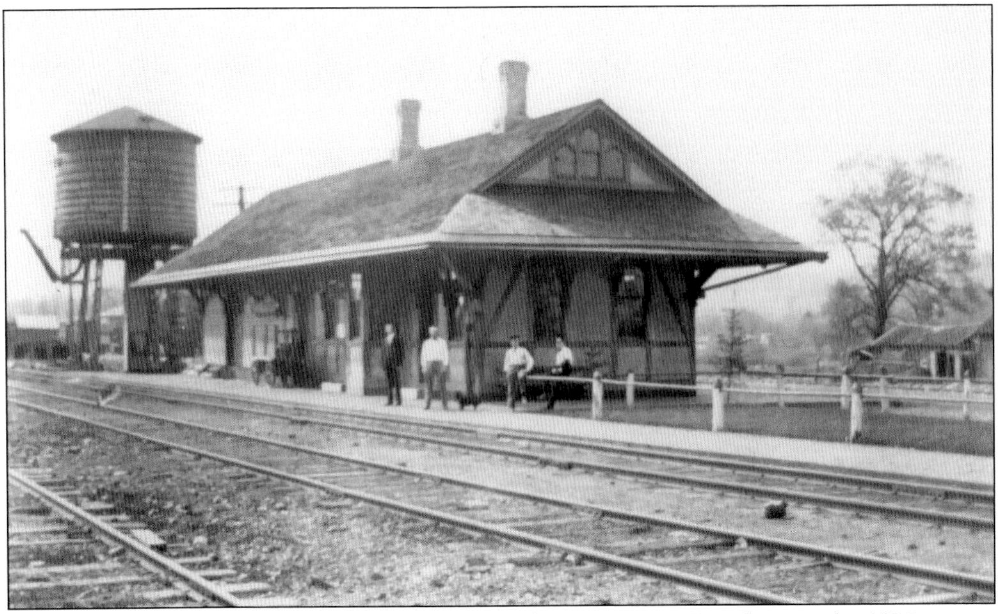

The first depot in Angelica, New York, was of wood construction. Seen here in the 1900s, it was located on South Street in the village. The passenger waiting room was closest to the photographer. The station agent's office (with its bay window) was in the middle of the building. The freight room was located at the far end. (PS&NRRHS.)

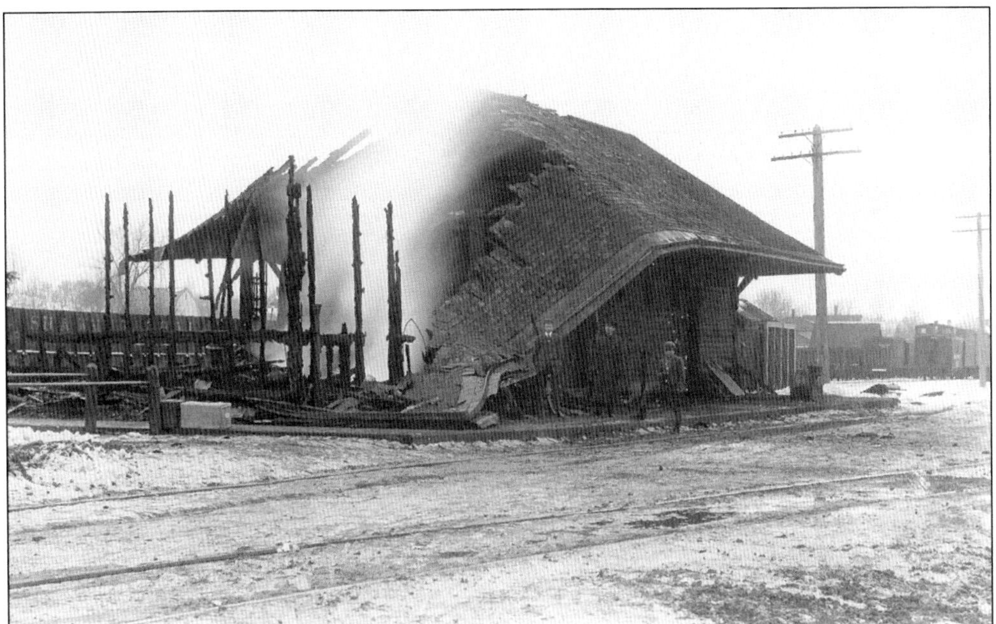

On Monday, January 24, 1910, fire destroyed the original wooden depot in Angelica, New York. Although there was no loss of life, the building was a total loss. This photograph with a view looking west was taken from South Street. Note that at some point prior to the fire, the water tower that was next to the depot had been removed. (PS&NRRHS.)

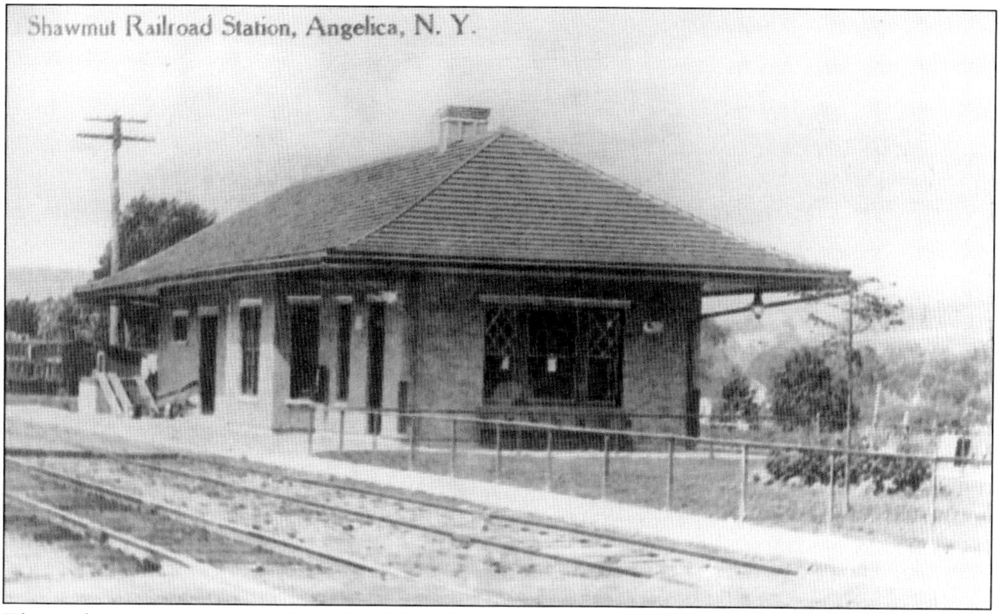

The replacement station in Angelica, New York, was built in 1910. Located on South Street in the village, it was constructed of yellow brick with a red tiled roof and included ornate leaded-glass windows. Erected to replace the original wooden depot that burned that same year, this building still stands today. (PS&NRRHS.)

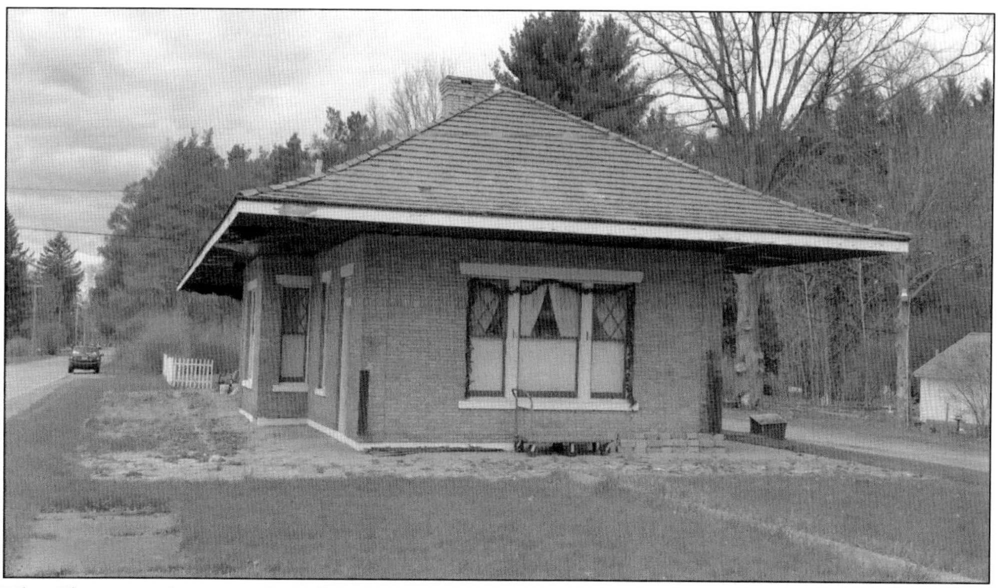

The Shawmut depot in Angelica, New York, now privately owned, has been preserved. The onetime main line (at left) has been replaced by the appropriately named Railroad Avenue. South Street originally connected directly with Park Circle in the center of the village, thus giving direct access to the Shawmut depot from town. Hurricane Agnes washed out the South Street bridge over Angelica Creek in 1972. (Author's collection.)

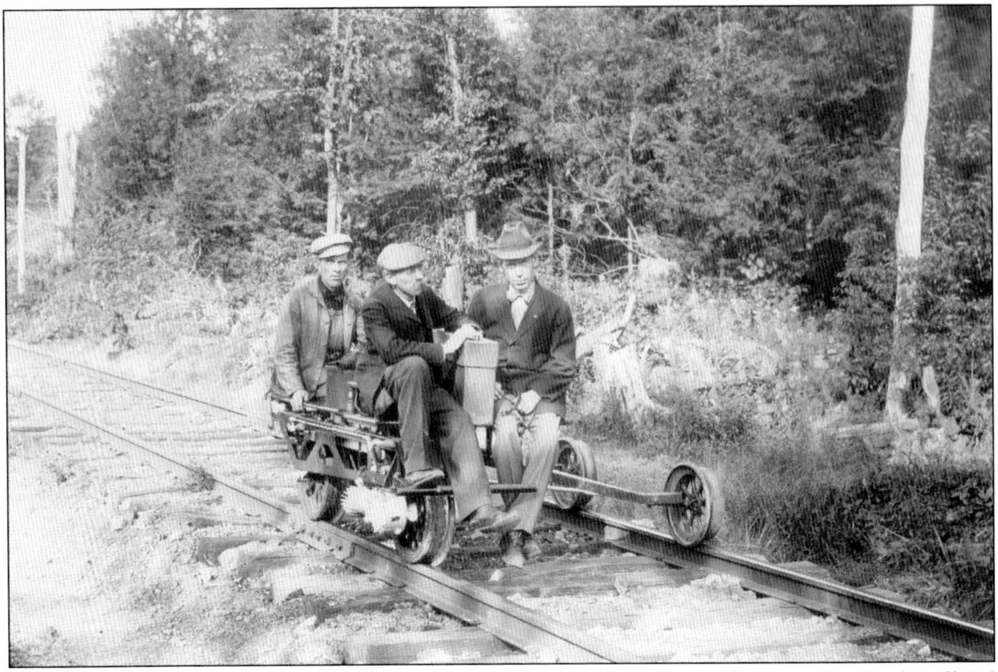

Many of the early photographs of the Shawmut, including many in this book, were taken by the official company photographer, George E. Mott (center), of Angelica, New York. In this image, Mott is seen riding a track "speeder" in the company of J.N. Thompson (right), superintendent of maintenance of way. The speeder is being operated by machinist Frank Common (left). (SMHS.)

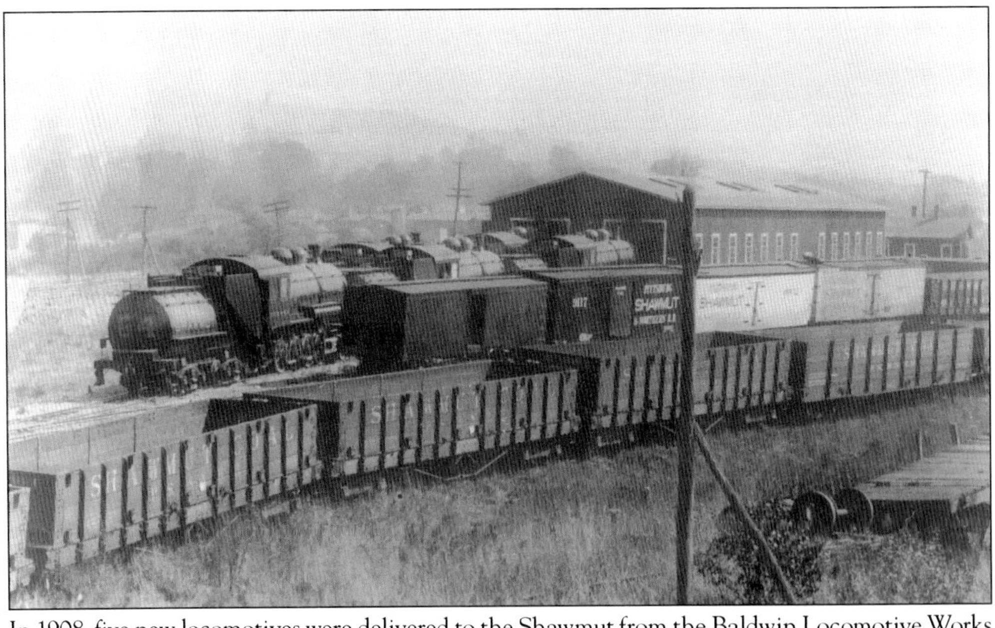

In 1908, five new locomotives were delivered to the Shawmut from the Baldwin Locomotive Works of Philadelphia, Pennsylvania. The locomotives were inspected in the Angelica, New York, shops before being turned over for general operation by the railroad. Baldwin would produce a majority of the locomotives operated by the Shawmut. (PS&NRRHS.)

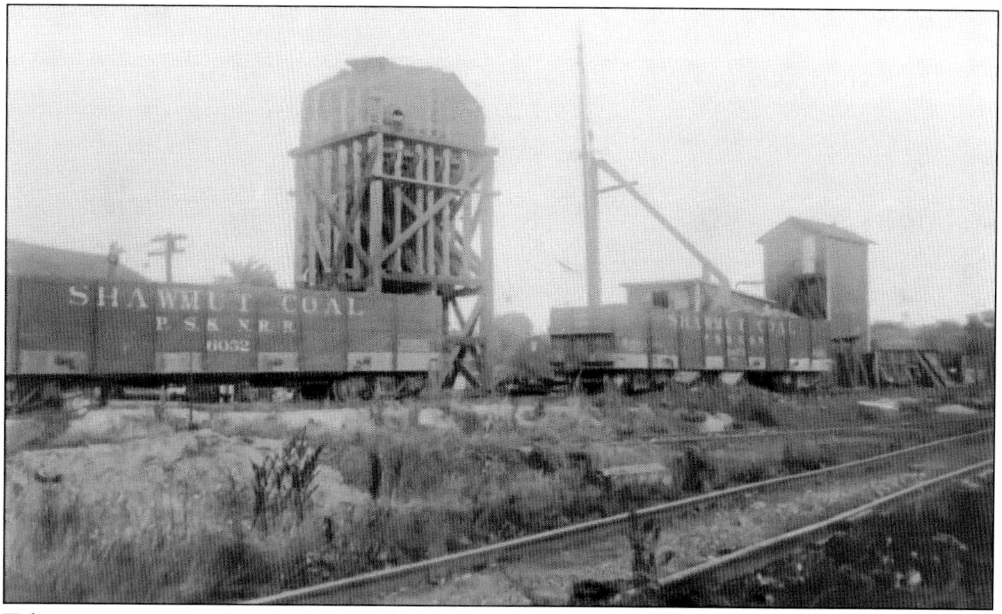

Taken sometime in the 1900s, this photograph shows the coaling tower (left) and sand house (right) in the Angelica, New York, yards. Soft coal fueled all of the Shawmut's locomotives. This coal was produced in mines owned by the Shawmut Mining Company and delivered to the coal dock in Shawmut-owned hopper cars. (PS&NRRHS.)

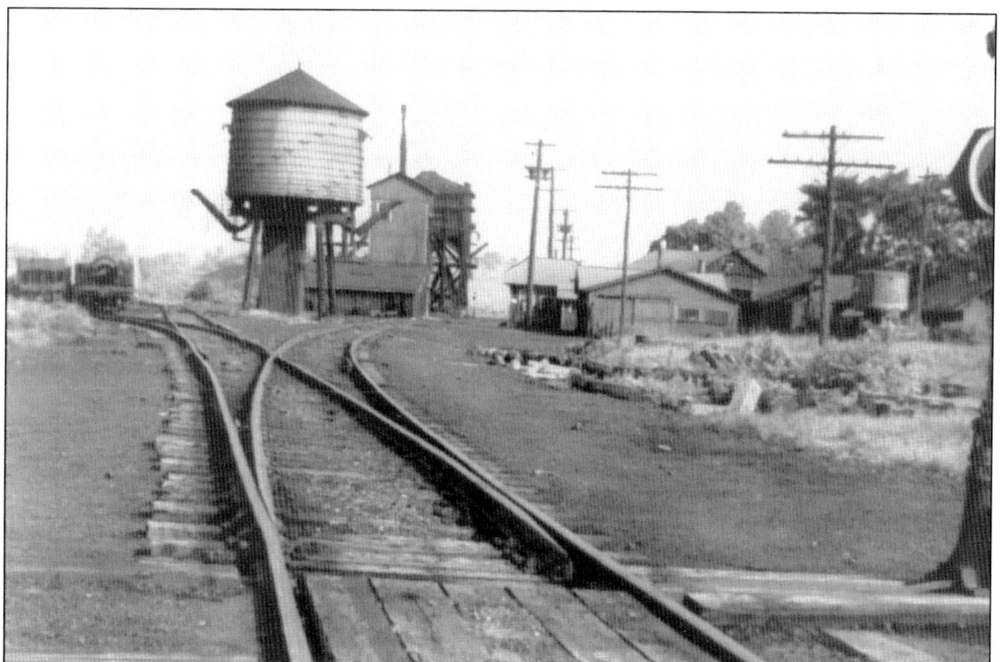
In the 1940s, the most prominent feature of the Angelica, New York, engine servicing facilities is the 50,000-gallon double-spout water tank. Behind it stands the sand tower. Sand was used by the locomotives to improve traction. Behind that is the hoist-operated coaling tower. To the right of these stand the blacksmith and carpenters' shops. (PS&NRRHS.)

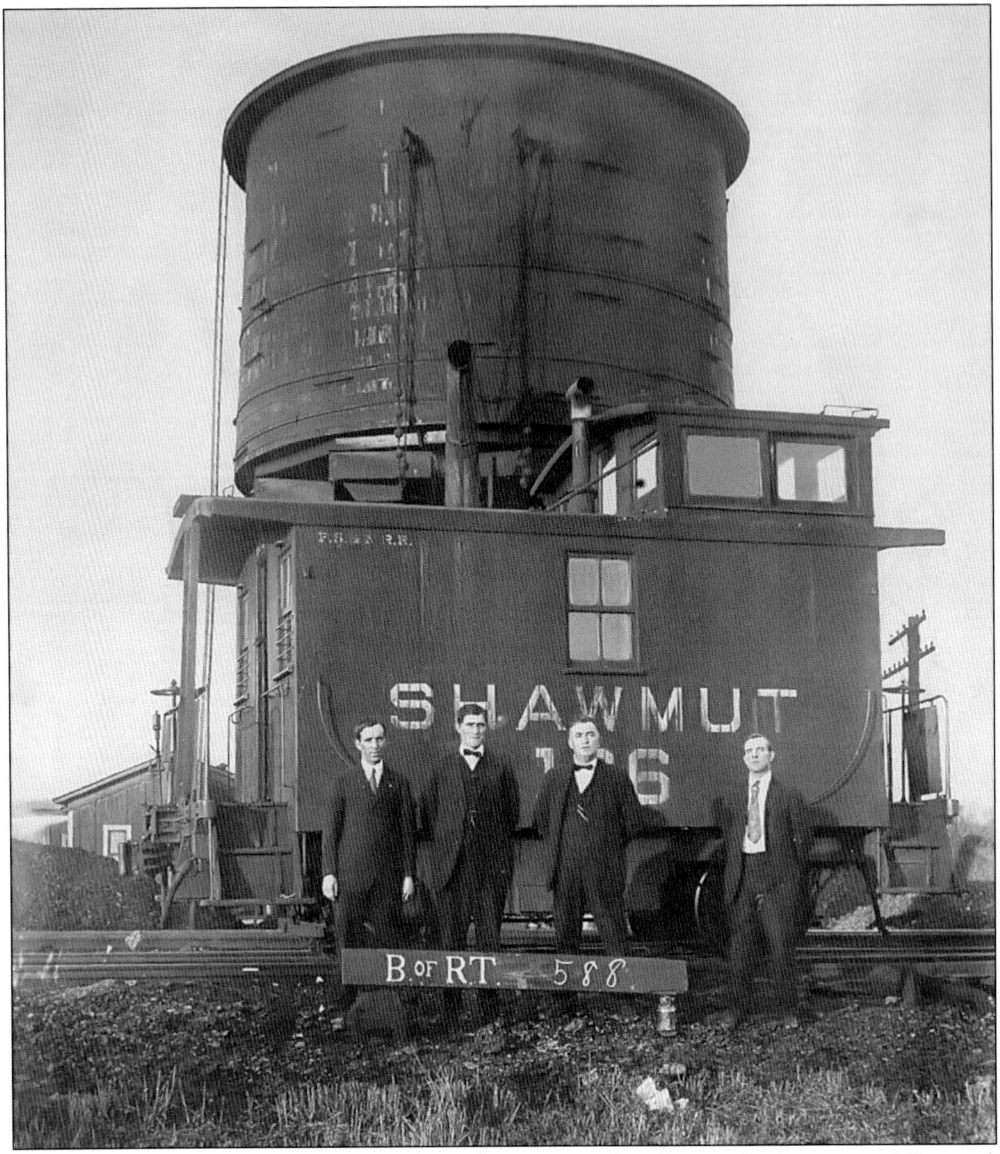

The trade union that represented members of train crews (conductors, brakemen, and flagmen) on the Pittsburg, Shawmut & Northern was the Brotherhood of Railroad Trainmen. Here in 1914, members of Lodge 588 pose in front of a bobber (four-wheel) caboose positioned in front of the Angelica, New York, water tower. From left to right are E. Ford, P. Ford, Tom Rochford, and H. Barnett. Each craft on the railroad was represented by its own union: engineers by the Brotherhood of Locomotive Engineers, firemen by the Brotherhood of Locomotive Firemen, station agents by the Brotherhood of Railway Clerks, and car inspectors and repairmen by the Brotherhood of Railway Carmen. The selection of a caboose as the background for their portrait is an appropriate one, as cabooses served as the trainmen's rolling office and home while at work on the railroad. (SMHS.)

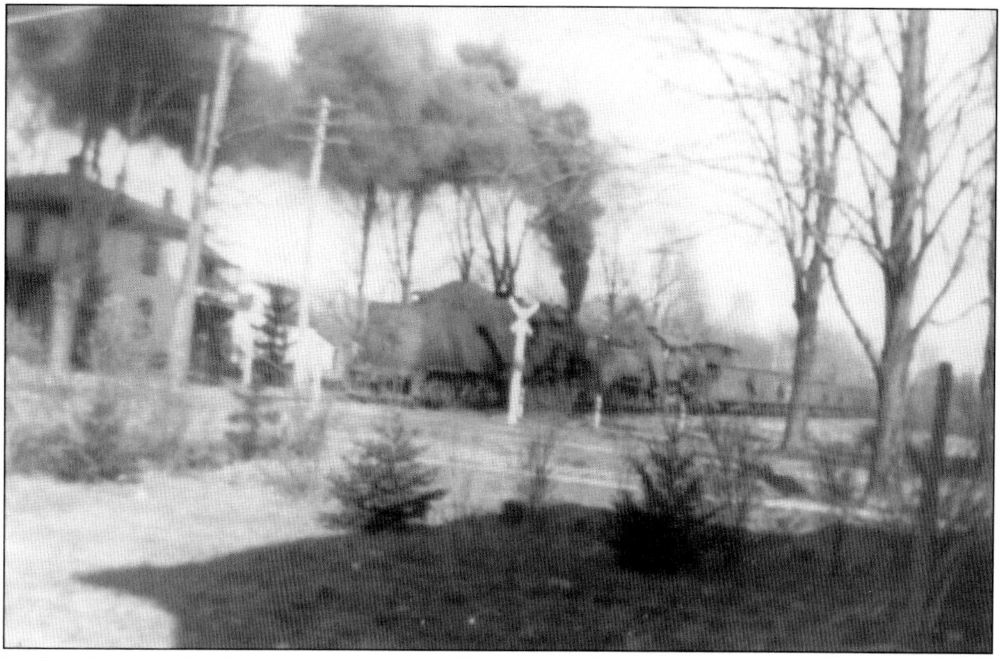

In this photograph, taken sometime in the 1930s, two pusher engines have just cleared the Olean Street crossing in the village of Angelica, New York. Grades on the Shawmut were severe and it was common to see five locomotives working the heavy northbound coal trains—two on the front, a third cut in 10 cars back, and two pushing on the rear. (PS&NRRHS.)

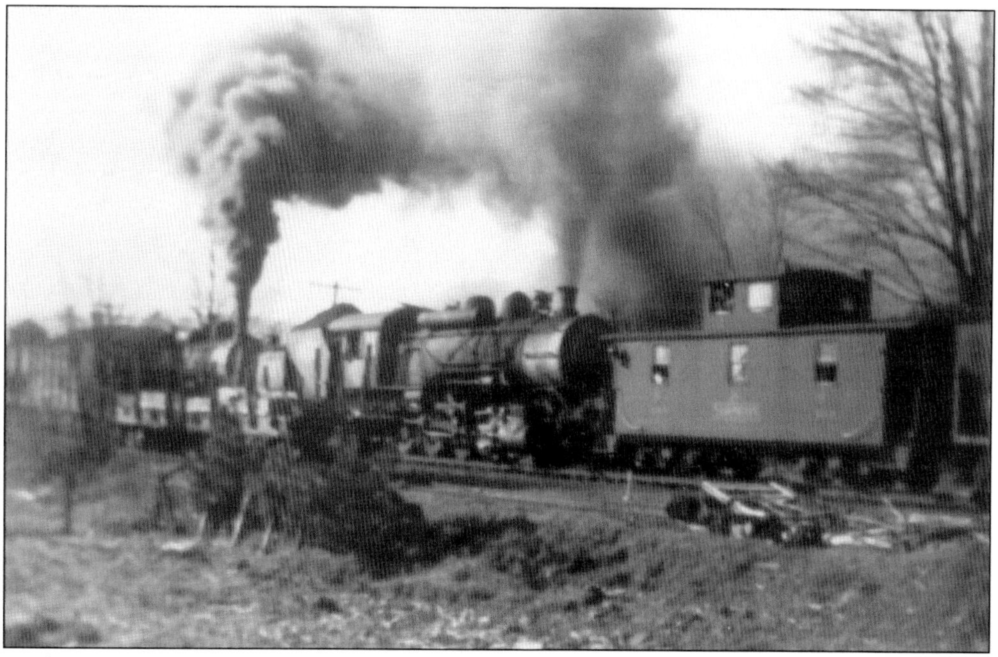

In about 1940, another pair of pusher engines is seen working hard on a northbound coal train at the Olean Street crossing in Angelica, New York. The train is just getting under way again, after having stopped to take on coal and water. The plumes of black smoke indicate just how hard these engines are working. (PS&NRRHS.)

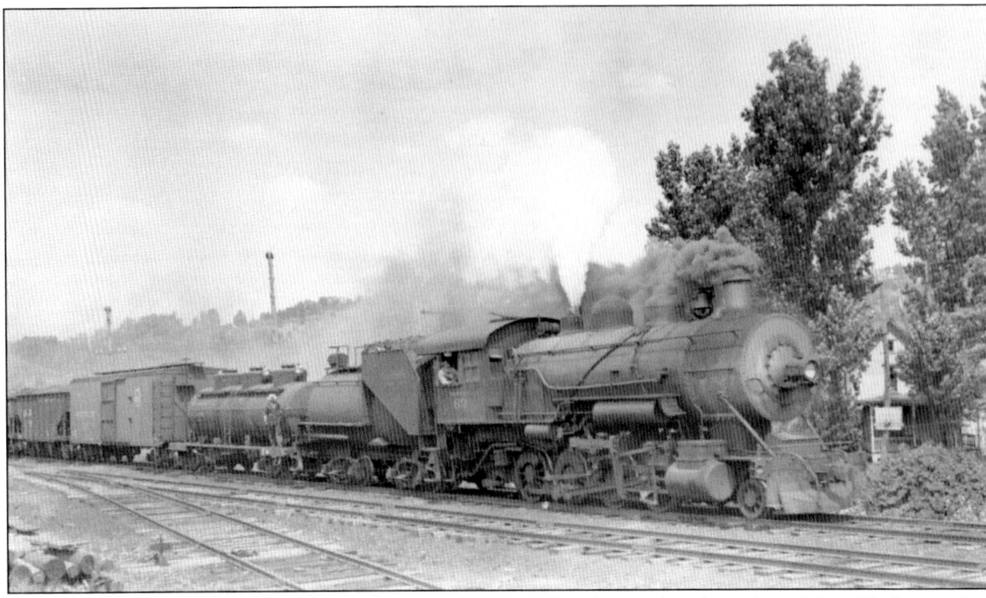

Engine No. 69 is seen switching cars on a through freight at the Angelica, New York, yard in 1940. The tank car immediately behind the tender has three expansion domes, indicating that it was comprised of three separate compartments, each one capable of carrying different grades of petroleum products. (PS&NRRHS.)

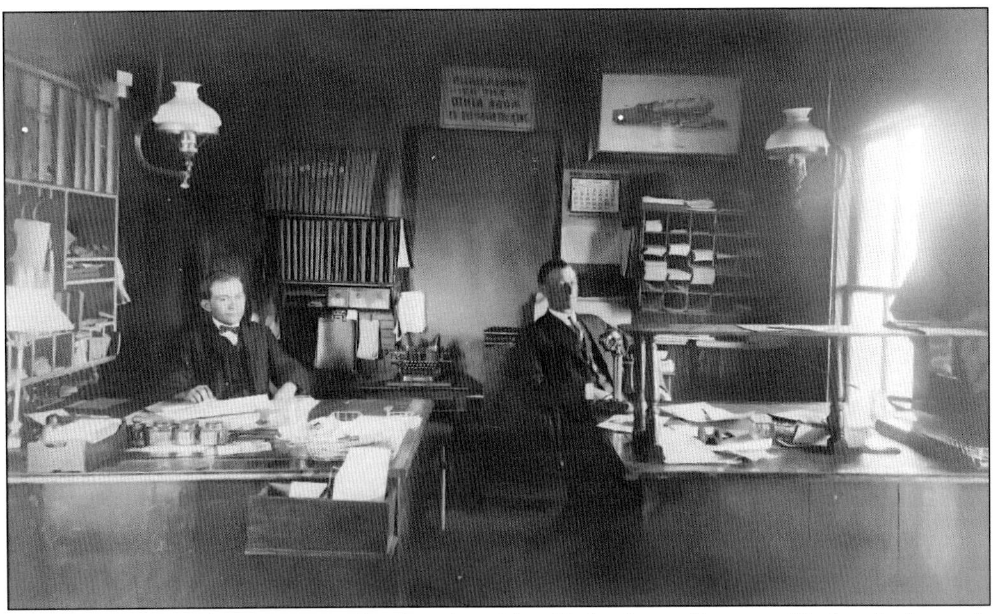

In the days before the computer, the Angelica, New York, shop office was filled with the tools of the bookkeeping trade: ink wells, rubber stamps, ledgers, a manual typewriter, and plenty of paper. This October 1907 photograph shows Lewis L. Storms (storehouse foreman) and Isaac "Ike" Irvin (general foreman); it is unknown which man is which. (SMHS.)

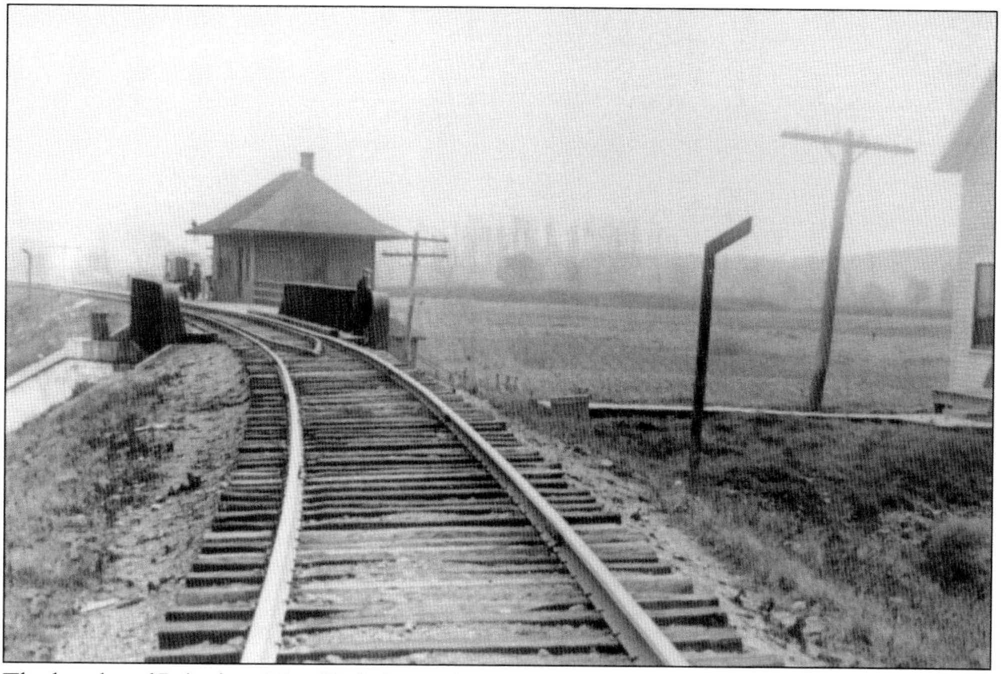

The hamlet of Belvidere, New York, located at MP 41.1, was where the Buffalo & Susquehanna (B&S) Railway's main line from Wellsville, New York, to Buffalo crossed over the Shawmut main line. The view in this photograph from about 1910 is looking south from the B&S main line and shows the B&S depot. (PS&NRRHS.)

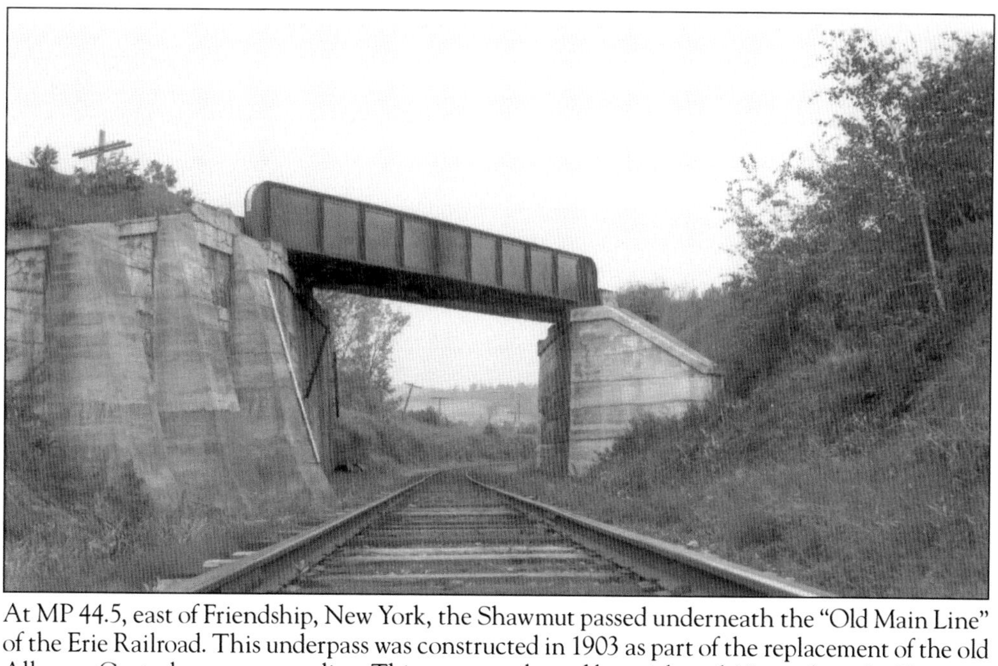

At MP 44.5, east of Friendship, New York, the Shawmut passed underneath the "Old Main Line" of the Erie Railroad. This underpass was constructed in 1903 as part of the replacement of the old Allegany Central narrow-gauge line. This area was plagued by quicksand. Notice how the Shawmut added buttresses to the abutment at left to prevent it from collapsing. (PS&NRRHS.)

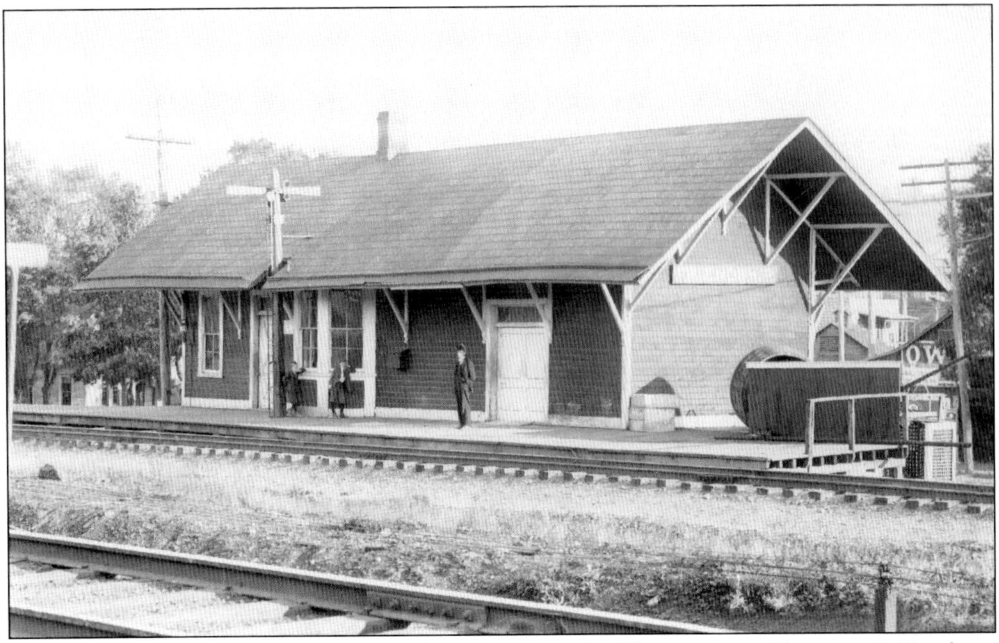

The village of Friendship, New York, was located at MP 46.1. The Pittsburg, Shawmut & Northern grade through the village was south of and parallel to the Erie Railroad. The Friendship depot, shown here about 1910, was located at the corner or Depot Street and Maple (also known as Erie) Avenue. (PS&NRRHS.)

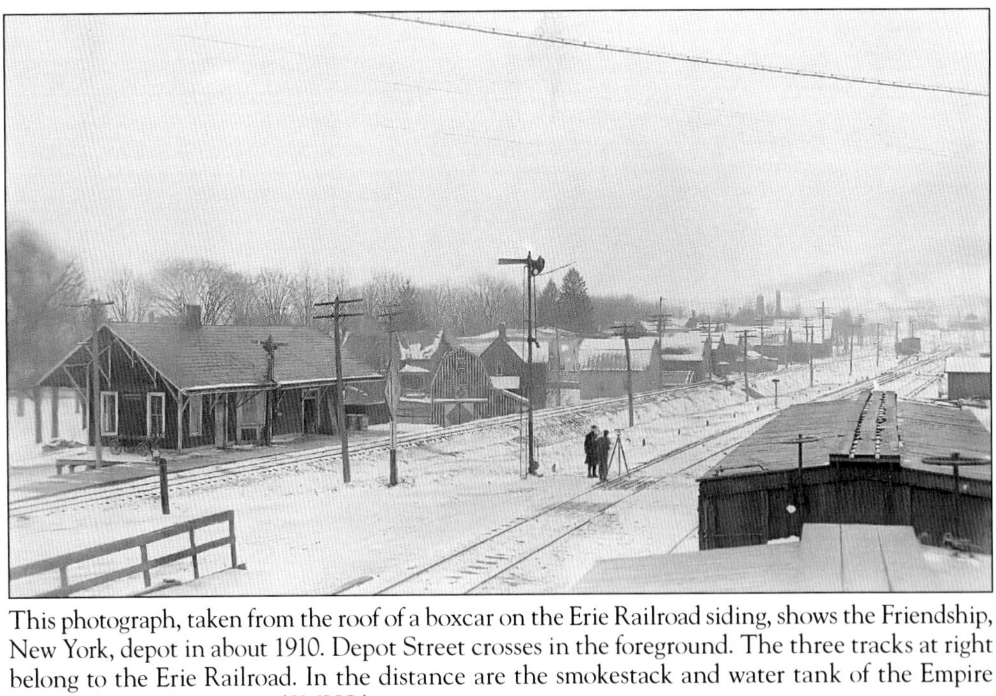

This photograph, taken from the roof of a boxcar on the Erie Railroad siding, shows the Friendship, New York, depot in about 1910. Depot Street crosses in the foreground. The three tracks at right belong to the Erie Railroad. In the distance are the smokestack and water tank of the Empire Sash and Door Company. (SMHS.)

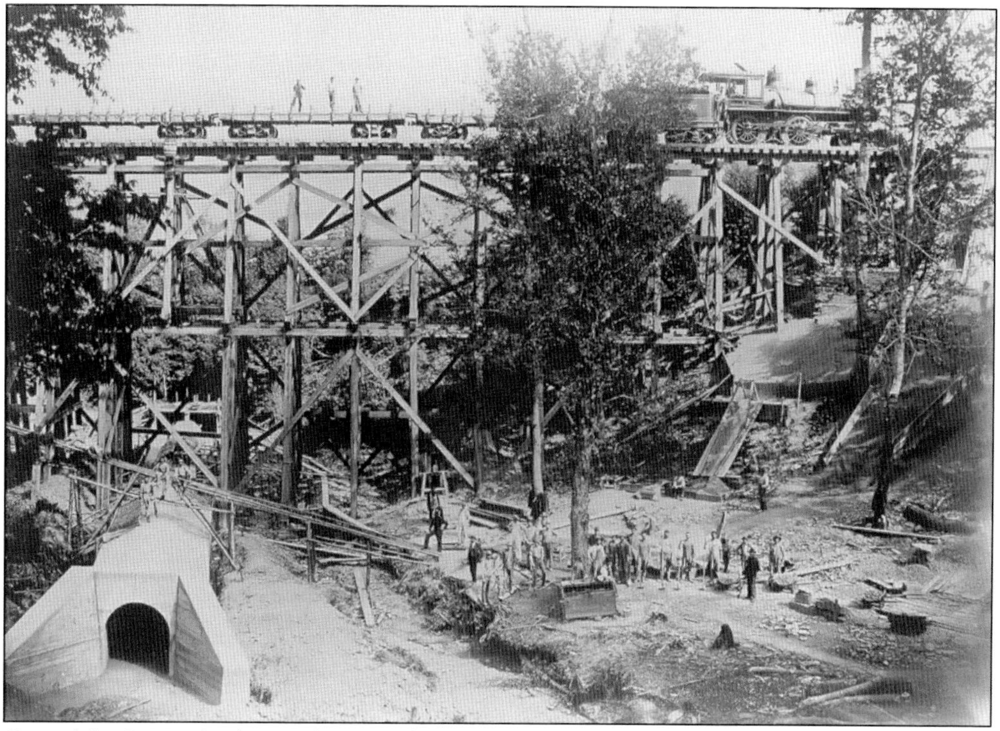

One of the first tasks the newly created Shawmut was faced with was the reconstruction of the old Allegany Central line between Angelica, New York, and Bolivar. This photograph, taken around 1902, shows one of the old narrow-gauge trestles being replaced by a fill. The location was MP 49.0, just south of Nile, New York. (SMHS.)

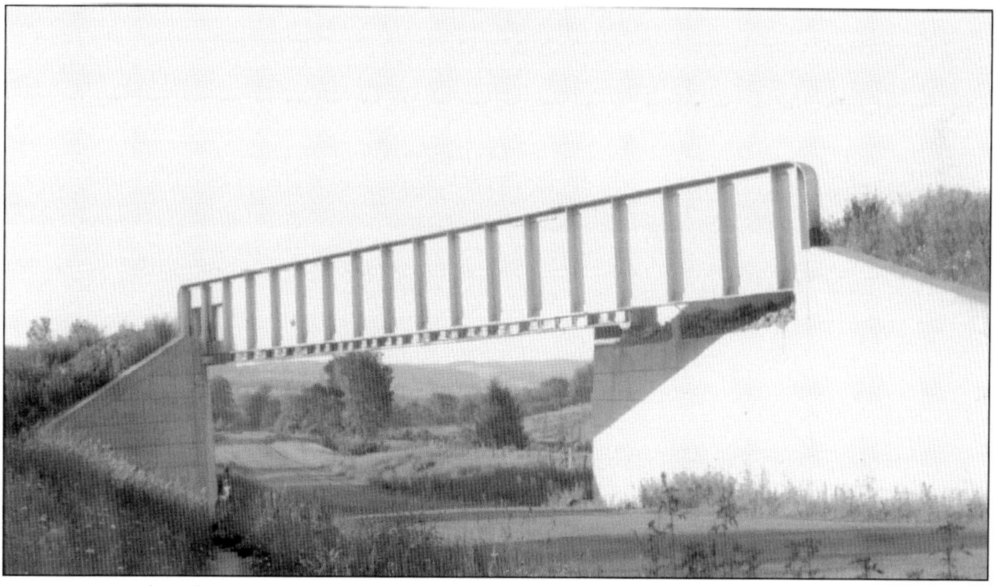

At MP 50.0, the Shawmut crossed over the West Notch highway, near Nile, New York. In the summer of 1940, the Shawmut installed this new replacement bridge. The view in this photograph looks south. Although the road appears to be going downgrade, the Shawmut was still climbing upgrade to the West Notch. (PS&NRRHS.)

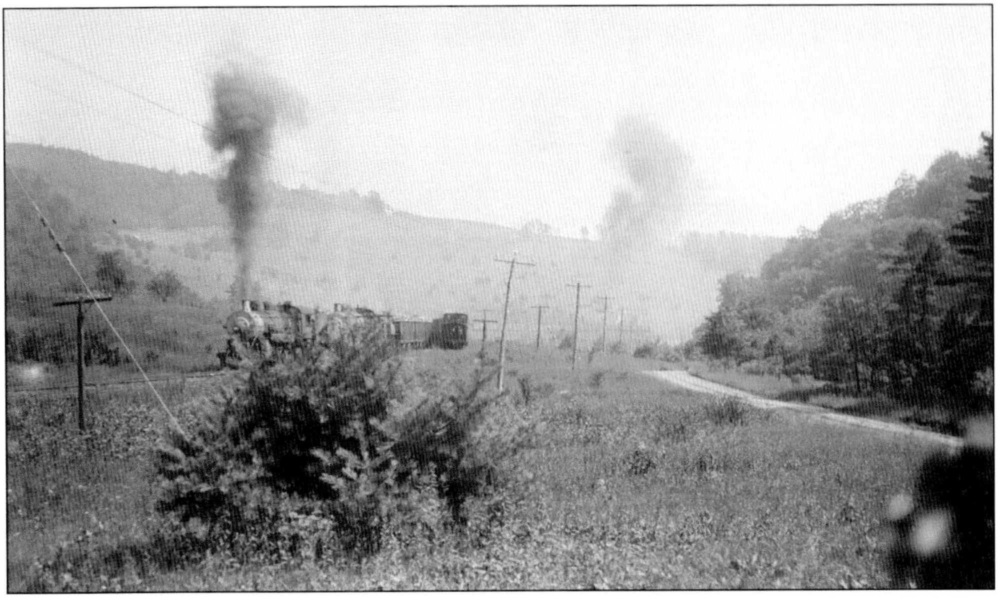

The summit of the grade between Richburg and Friendship, New York, was at a place called West Notch. Located at MP 53.3, it included a passing siding that permitted meets between opposing trains before they descended down either side of the hill. Seen here is a northbound train led by engine No. 75 with two pushers on the rear in the distance. (SMHS.)

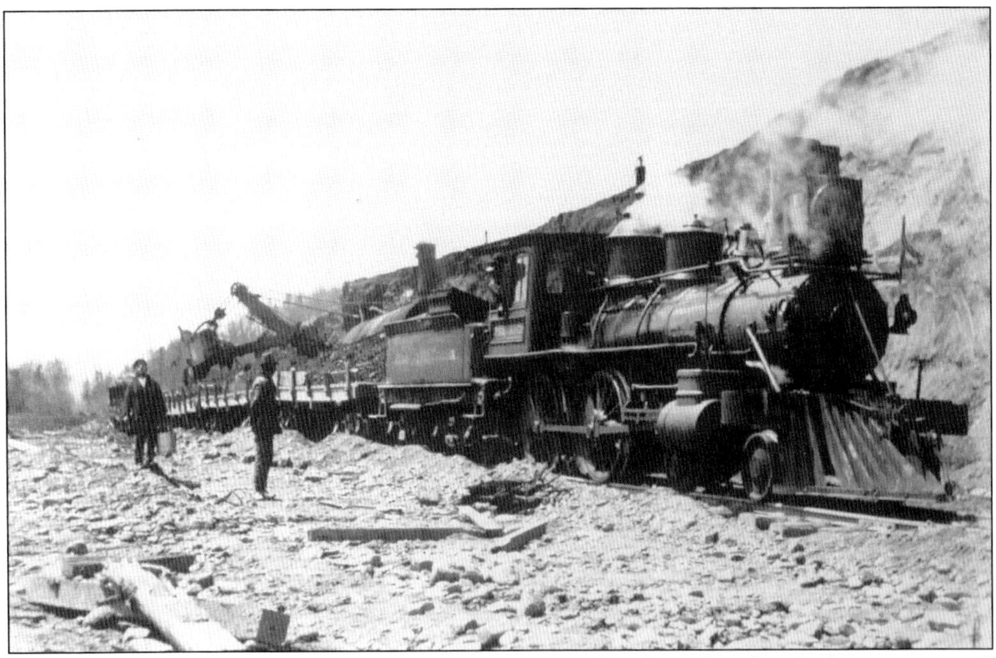

Between 1899 and 1910, the newly created Shawmut Railroad was faced with the monumental task of connecting its various predecessor lines into a unified railroad. This scene, taken about 1903, shows engine No. 1 on a construction train north of Richburg, New York. Notice the steam shovel digging the cut behind the workmen and the train. (PS&NRRHS.)

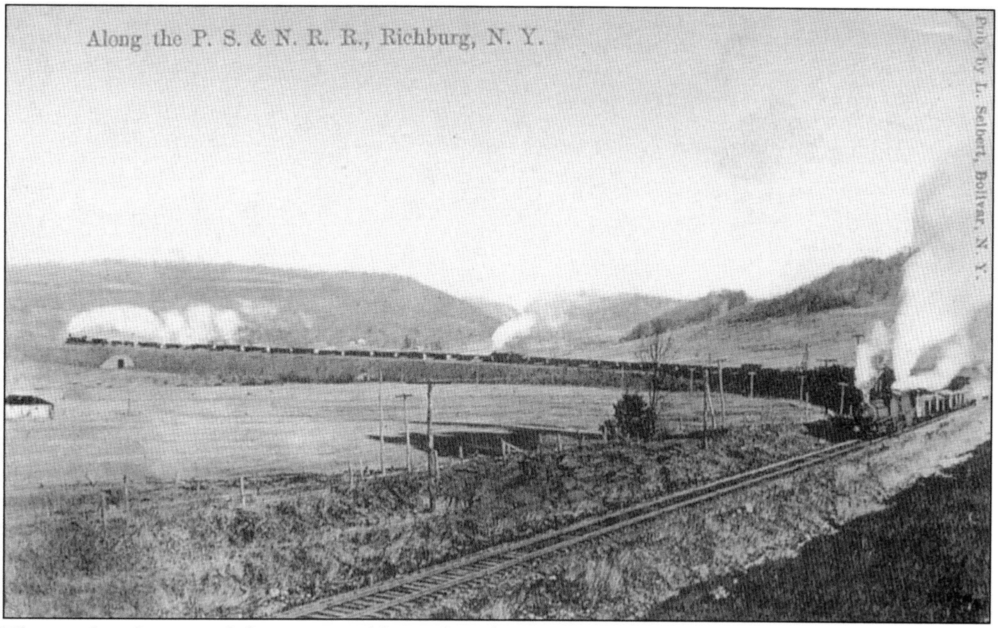

This undated postcard shows a northbound coal train swinging around the curve at MP 56.2. To gain elevation for the climb up the West Notch grade, the Shawmut looped around the village of Richburg, New York, on three sides, crossing the valley on a huge fill at a location named Cadytown. It was named for the Cady family farm, which occupies the center of this view. (PS&NRRHS.)

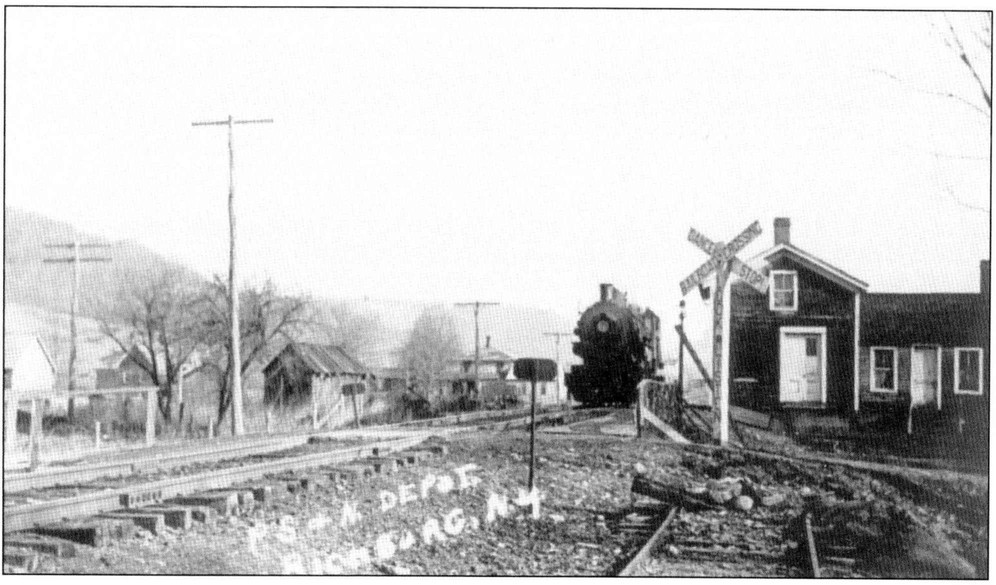

The Shawmut station (at right) in Richburg, New York, was located at MP 57.2. In 1914, an overheated stove in the waiting room caused considerable fire damage. This undated photograph, with a view looking north toward Cadytown, shows a helper engine returning "light" back to Bolivar. The crossing in the foreground is Richburg Hill Road, also known as Depot Street. (PS&NRRHS.)

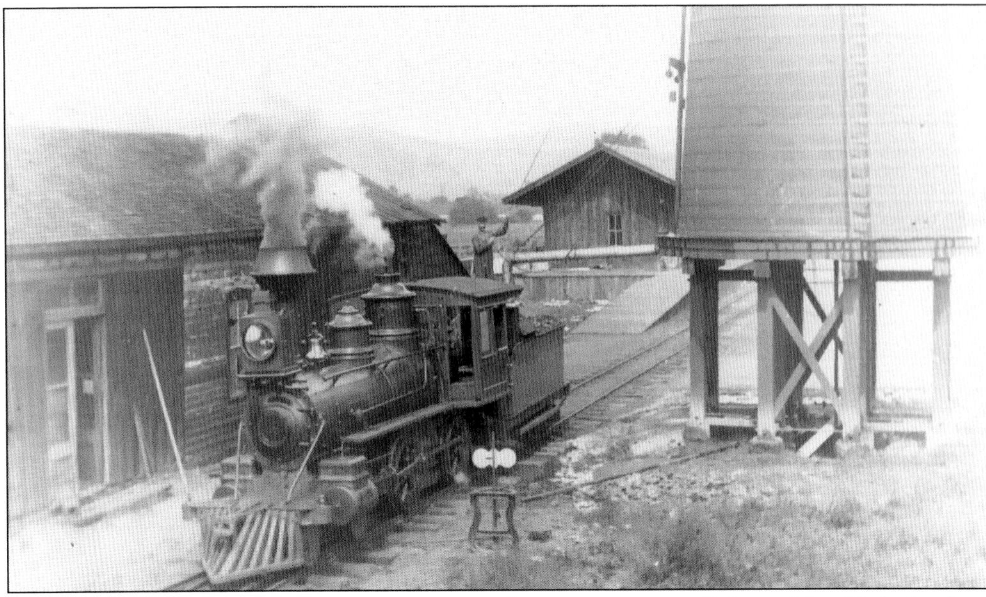

Allegany Central engine No. 4 is seen next to the water tower in Bolivar, New York, in about 1882. This section of the line would remain narrow gauge until about 1902, when the PS&N would convert it to standard gauge. In doing so, the Shawmut realigned much of the old track to eliminate curves. (PS&NRRHS.)

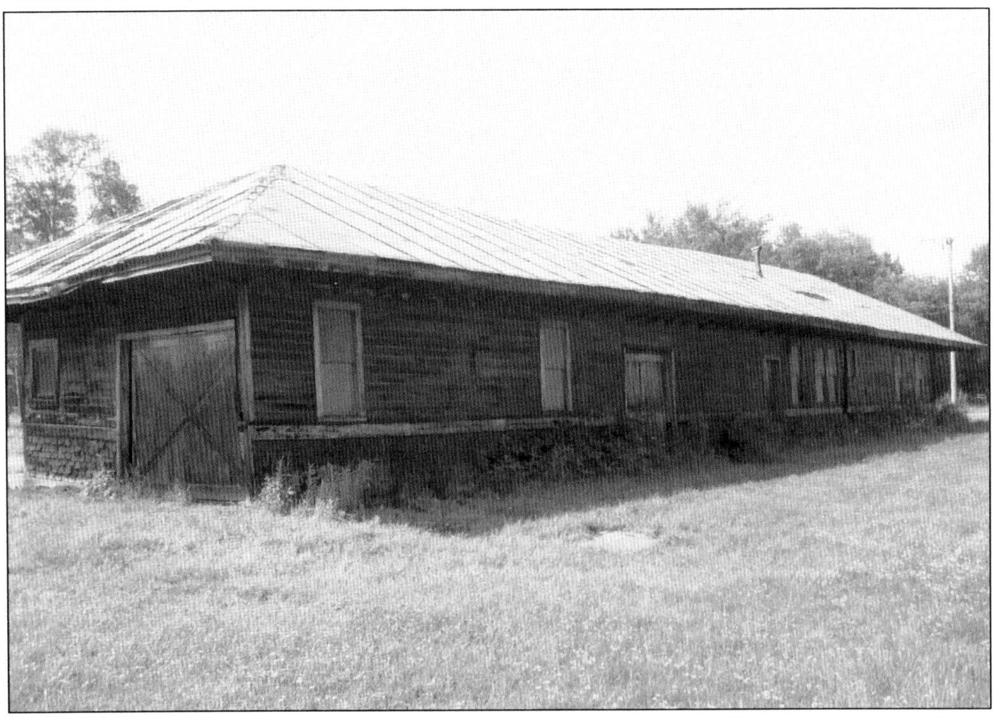

The Bolivar, New York, station was located at MP 59.1. Constructed in 1902 as part of the rebuilding and realignment of the line from narrow to standard gauge, it was located in the middle of the old Allegany Central roadbed. This building is presently undergoing preservation by the Pioneer Oil Museum of New York. (Tom Manning.)

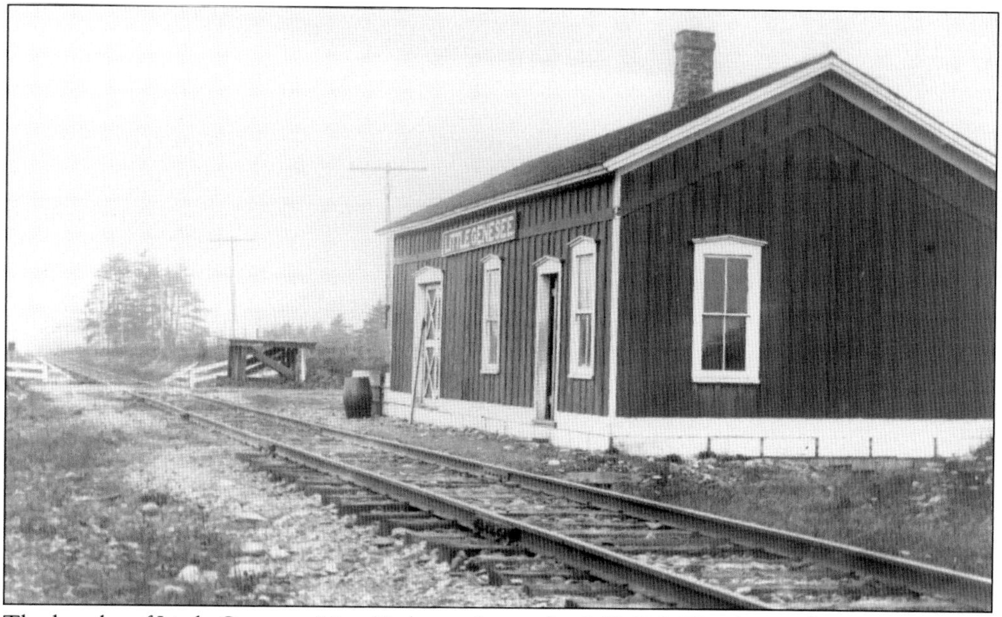

The hamlet of Little Genesee, New York, was located at MP 62.1. The depot, shown in this view looking south about 1910, was located on Salt Rising Road. The platform located on the far side of the road was where local farmers would bring fresh milk in galvanized milk cans for loading onto the trains. (PS&NRRHS.)

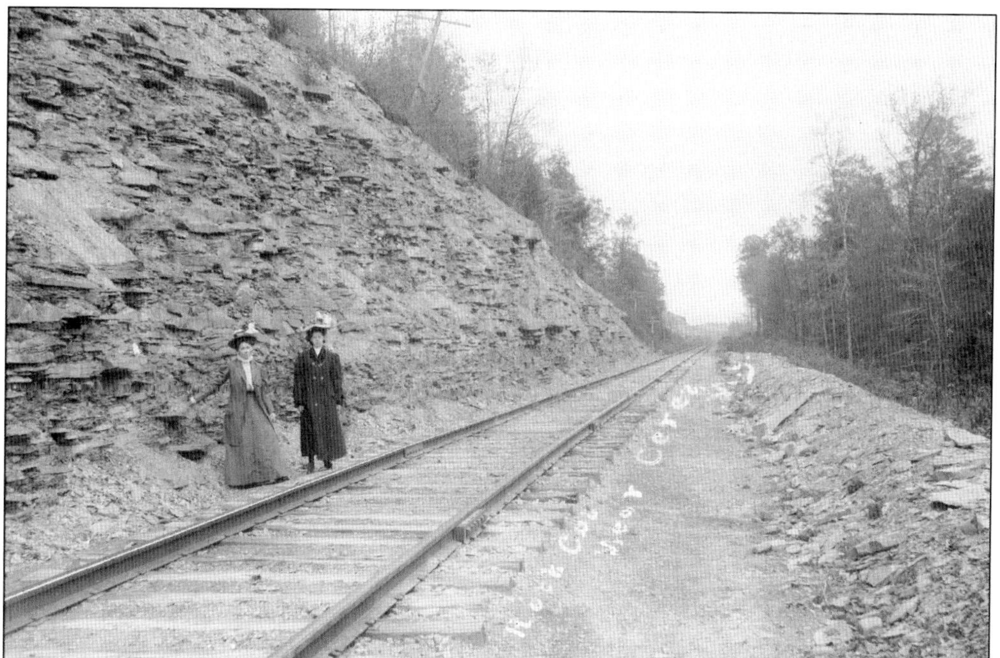

This rock cut, located near the Sanford Hollow Road crossing at MP 63.9, was constructed in 1902 when the Shawmut converted the line to standard gauge. The early narrow-gauge line followed the many curves of the Little Genesee Creek up the valley. The reconstruction effort included the elimination of many of the curves. The resulting tangent track seen here was nearly a mile long. (SMHS.)

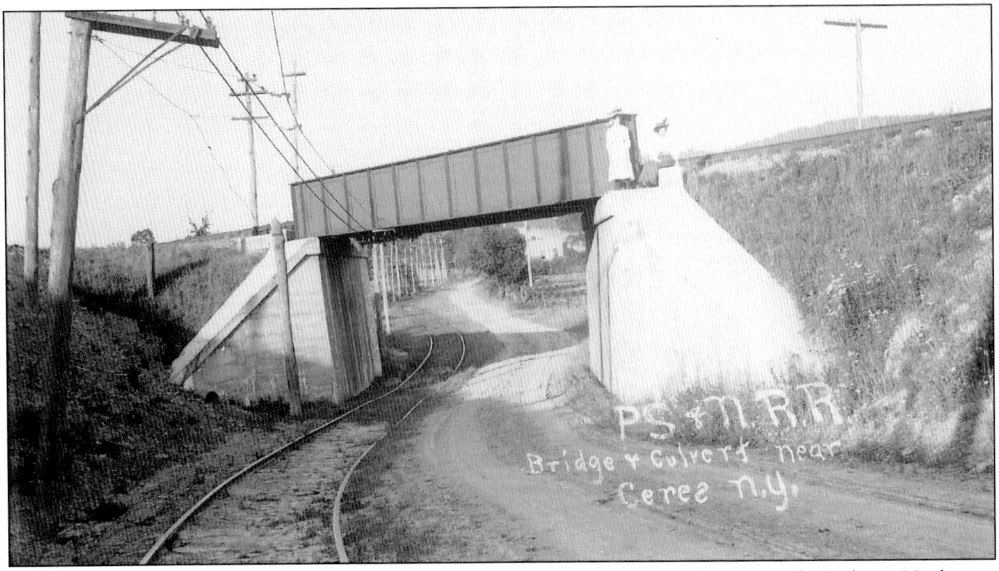

Just east of Ceres, New York, at MP 65.2, the Shawmut crossed over the Portville-Bolivar Highway, what would later become NY 17. In addition to the highway, the bridge also crossed over the tracks of the Western New York & Pennsylvania Traction (WNY&PT) Company. In the background above, through the bridge span, one can see the electric generating plant for the traction company. With the demise of the WNY&PT in 1927, the generating station would become a dance hall hosting big bands in the 1940s and later become the Coliseum roller-skating rink. In the view looking west below, one can see a Bolivar-bound trolley passing a horse-drawn wagon. (Above, SMHS; below, PS&NRRHS.)

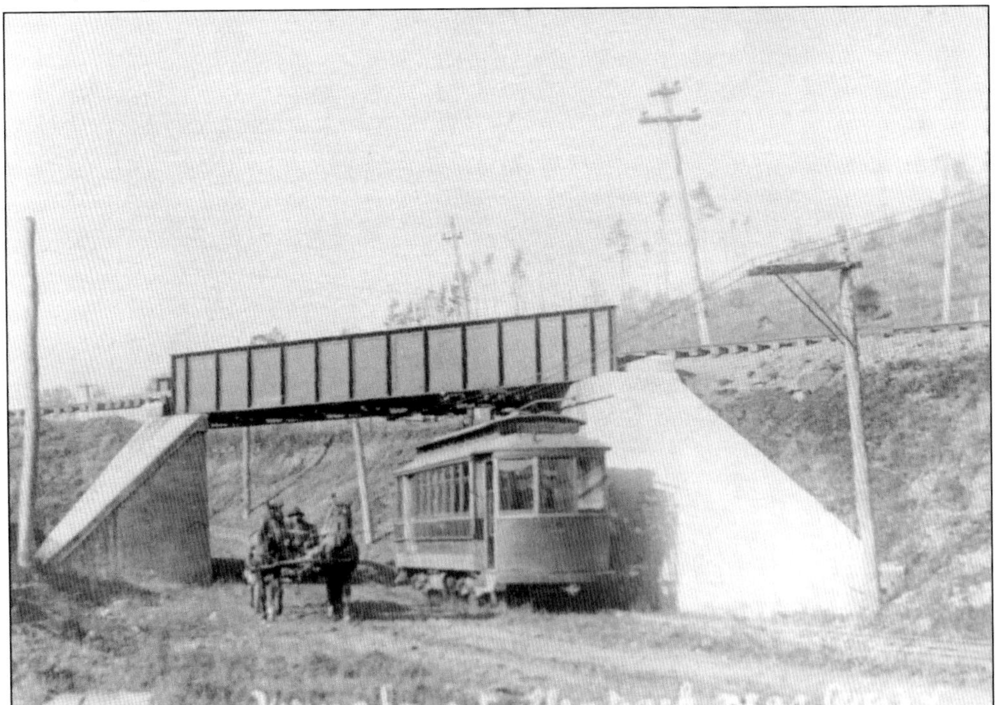

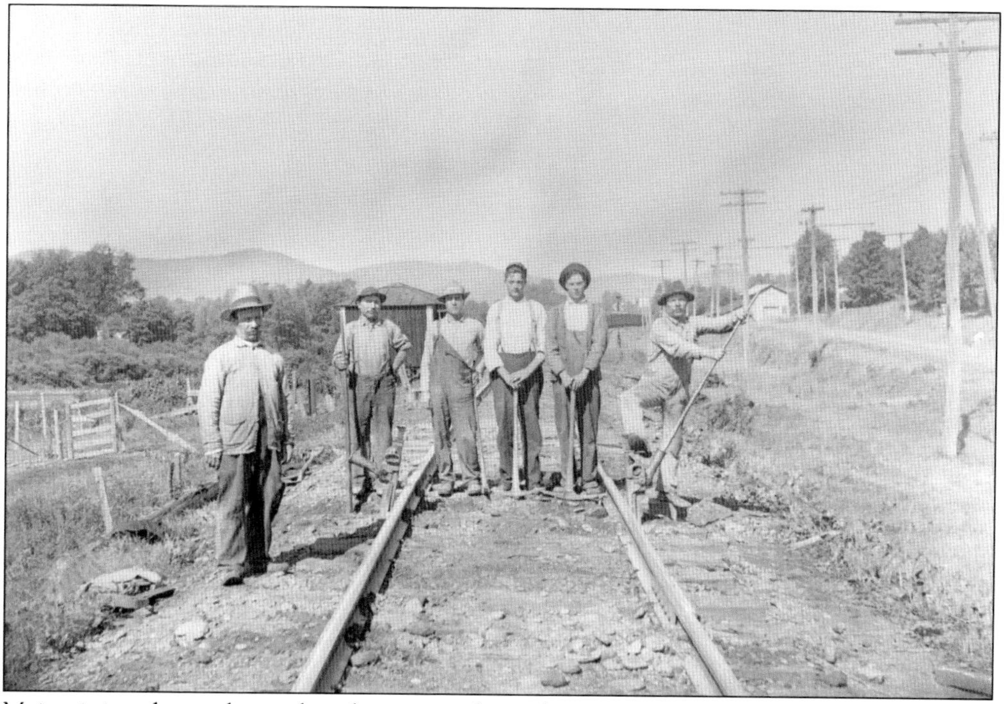

Maintaining the track was done by groups of men know as section gangs. One such gang was "tamping" the track in Ceres, New York, about 1905. The two men with the jacks would raise the rails up to level while the other three men would use their picks to work the ballast stone around the ties to maintain a level track. The man standing at left was their foreman. (PS&NRRHS.)

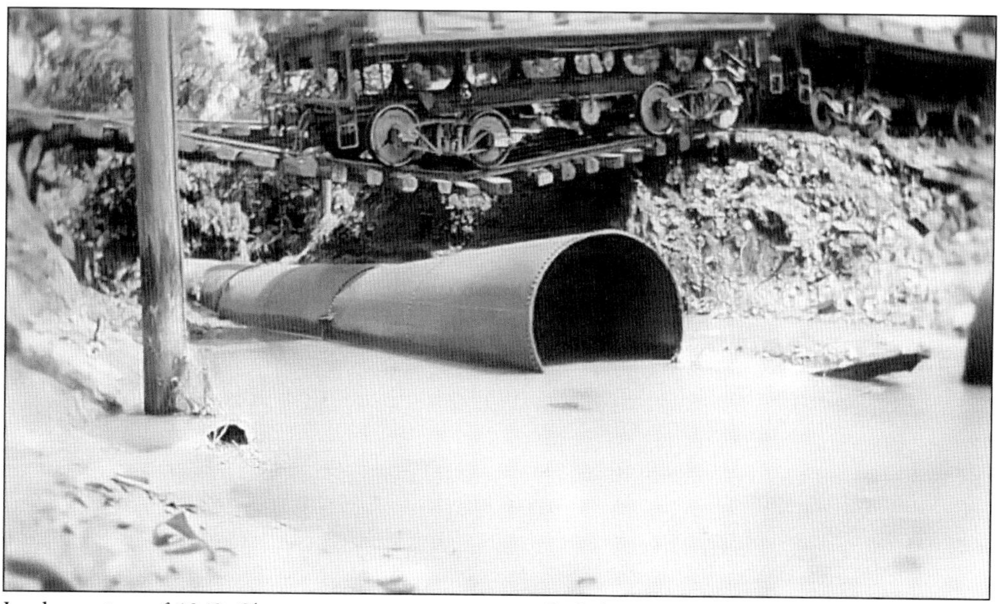

In the spring of 1942, Shawmut section gangs installed this new 72-inch culvert made of steel boiler shell at MP 65.97. On July 18, 1942, severe flooding in the region caused this washout. Seen here is a construction train gently backing gravel cars over the washout in the process of restoring the track grade. (SMHS.)

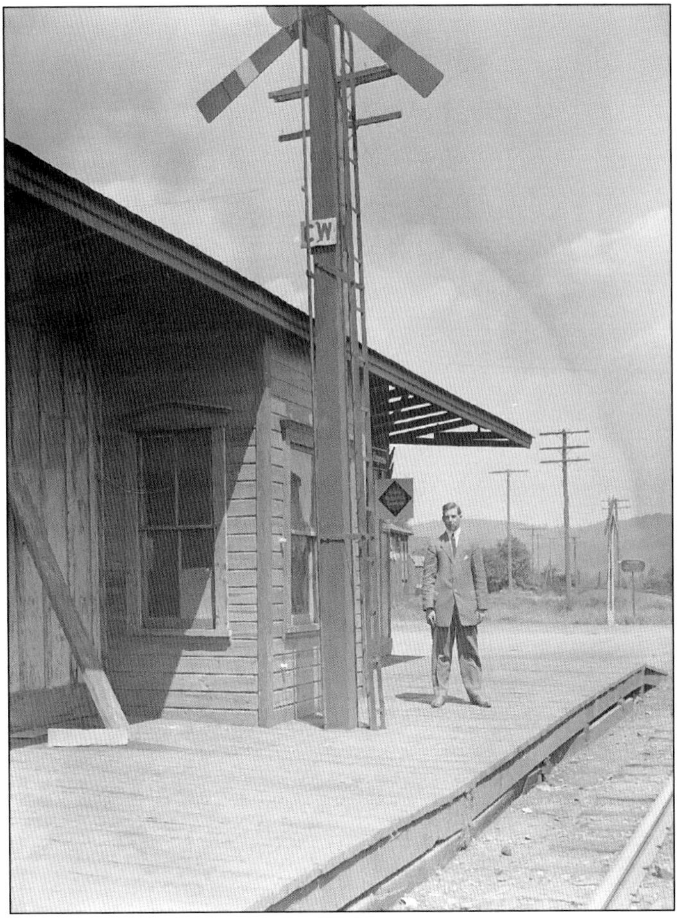

The Shawmut depot at Ceres, New York, was located in the center of the hamlet at MP 62.3. Seen here in about 1905 is a well-dressed station agent. The sign next to the agent is for the Western Union Express Company. The letters "CW" on the signal mast are the telegraph call letters for this station. (SMHS.)

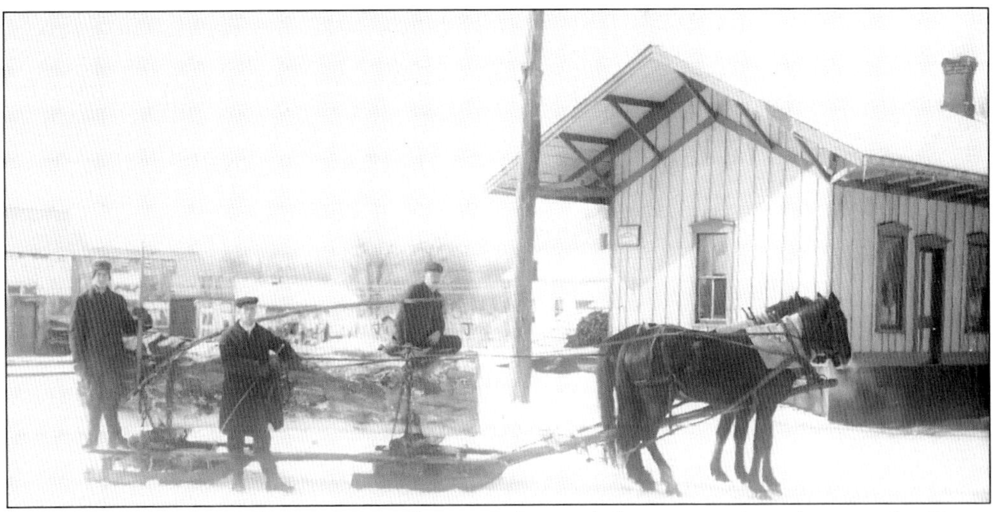

This winter 1903 scene shows a team of horses pulling a sled carrying a large log near the Ceres, New York, station of the Shawmut. Several lumber mills were once located south of the Shawmut tracks and along the banks of Oswayo Creek. These men obviously paused for a portrait while on their way to one of the mills. (SMHS.)

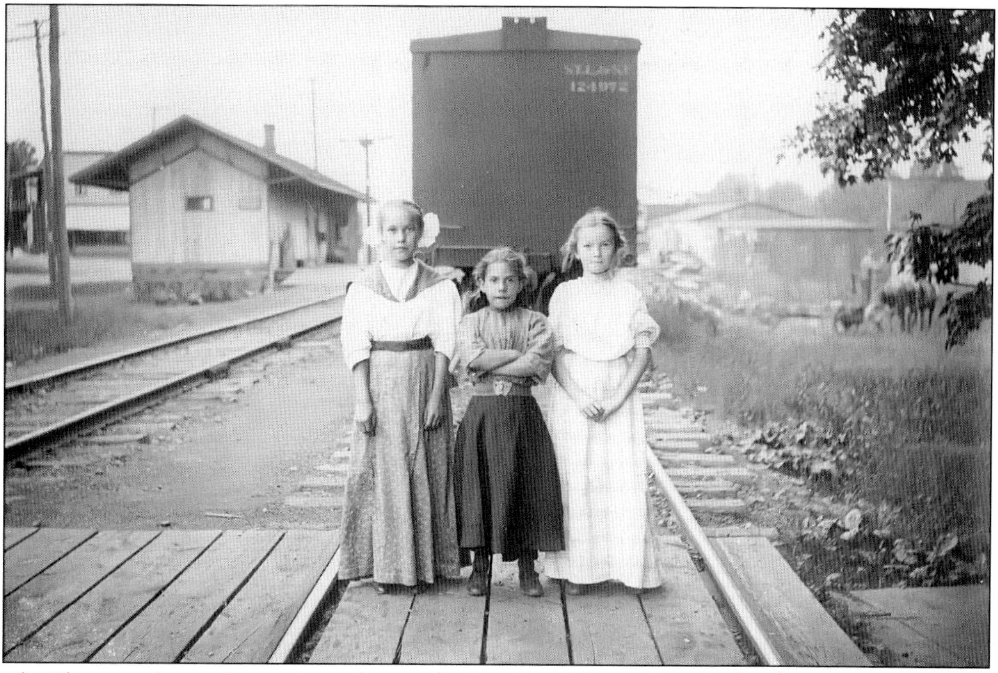

The Shawmut located a passing siding in the hamlet of Ceres, New York. The main line (at left) passed closest to the station. Just west of the station was the Ceres Methodist Church. The wooden pedestrian crossing in the foreground served the church. These young girls, wearing their Sunday best dresses, pause for a picture in about 1915. (SMHS.)

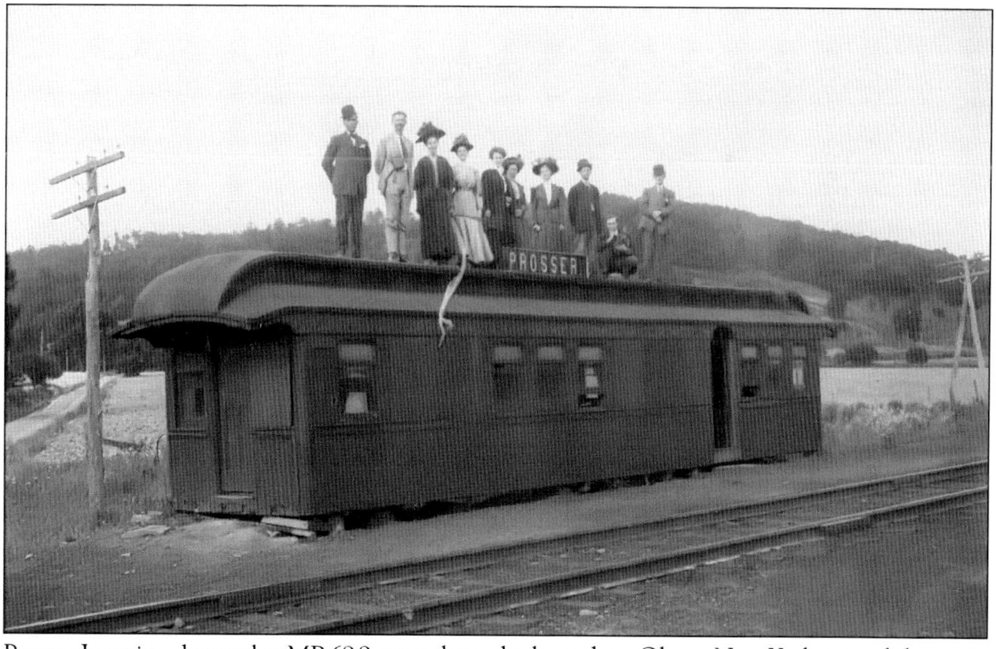

Prosser Junction, located at MP 69.9, was where the branch to Olean, New York, joined the main line. This 1907 photograph demonstrates that the amount of passenger traffic at the junction did not justify the outright construction of a station building. Instead, the Shawmut reused one of the old Lackawanna & Pittsburgh narrow-gauge combination cars. (PS&NRRHS.)

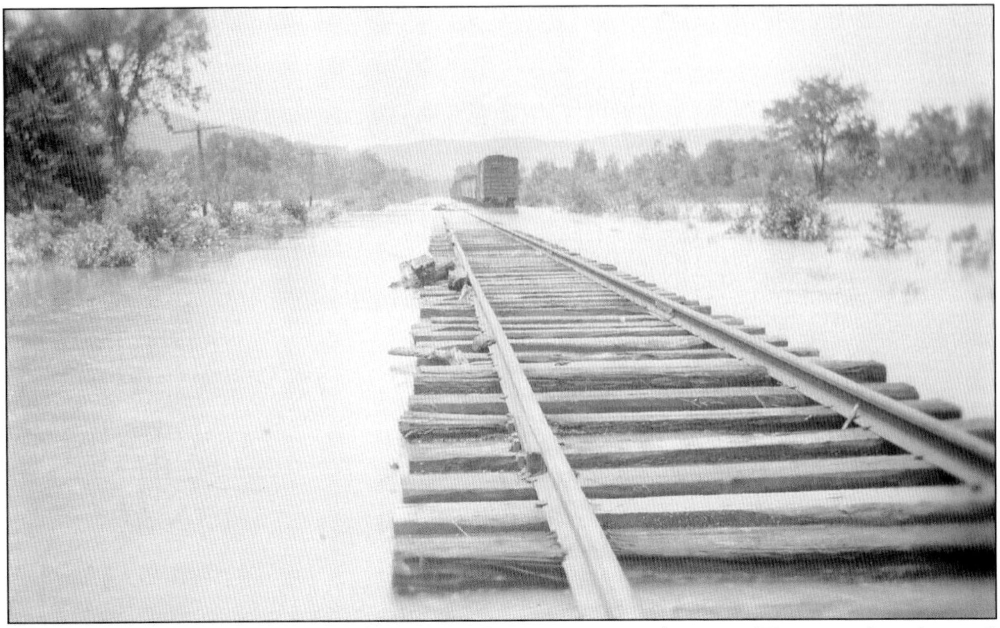

On July 18, 1942, much of the yard at Prosser Junction was underwater. The main line (center) stayed visible, but the passing siding (left) is completely inundated. The storage track, with cars on it in the distance, is also underwater. Ahead of the cars and also hidden by the flood is the south leg of the wye leading to the Olean Branch. (SMHS.)

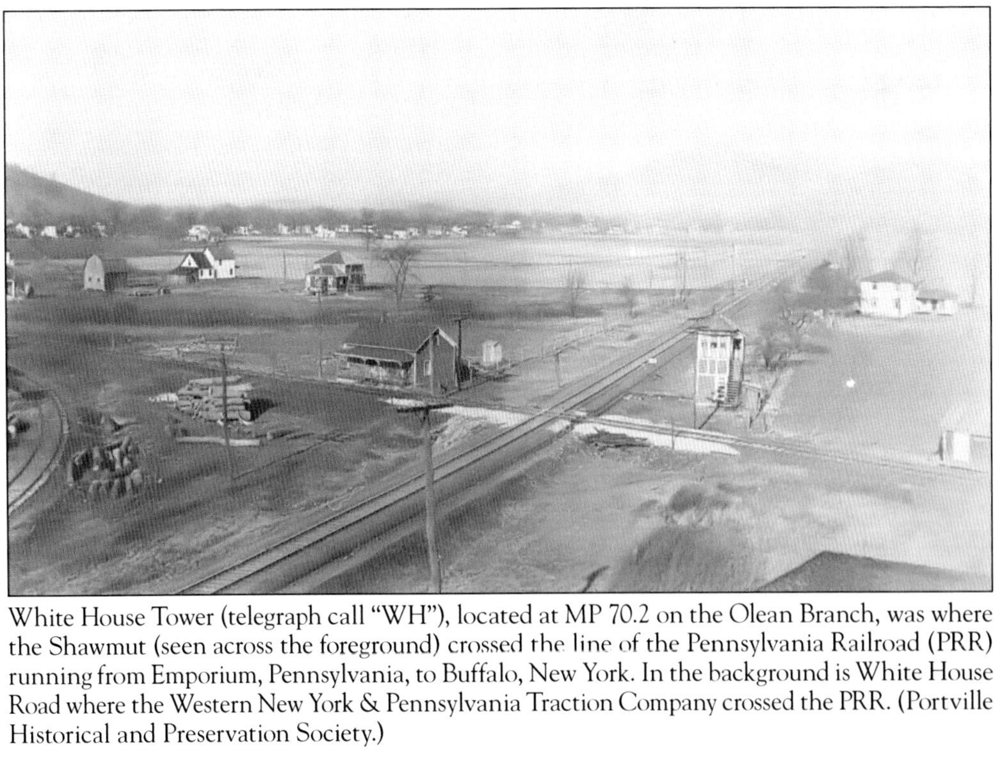

White House Tower (telegraph call "WH"), located at MP 70.2 on the Olean Branch, was where the Shawmut (seen across the foreground) crossed the line of the Pennsylvania Railroad (PRR) running from Emporium, Pennsylvania, to Buffalo, New York. In the background is White House Road where the Western New York & Pennsylvania Traction Company crossed the PRR. (Portville Historical and Preservation Society.)

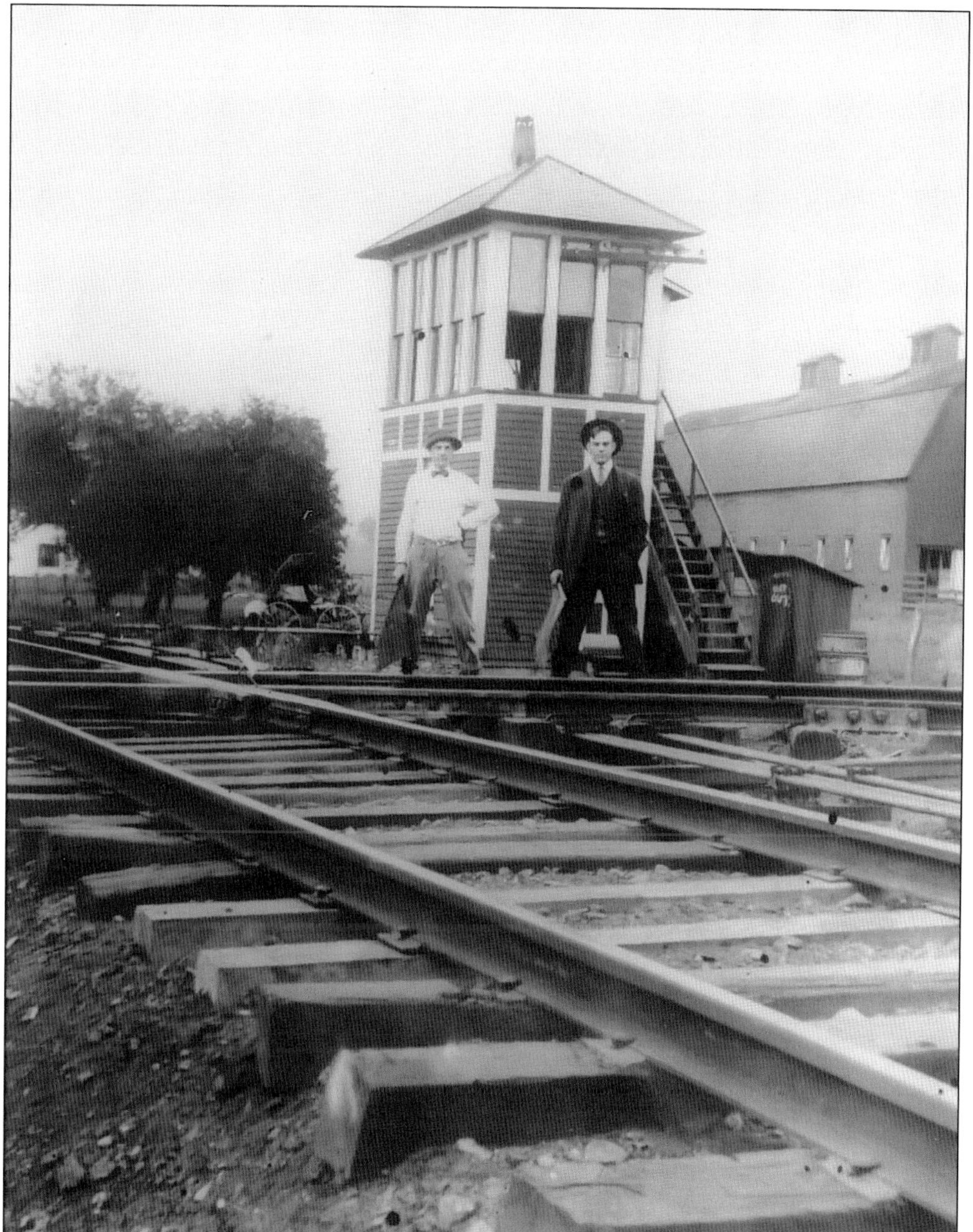

White House Tower in seen sometime in the 1900s. The Pennsylvania Railroad's track is in the foreground. The Shawmut's Olean Branch crosses from left to right—Olean to the left and Prosser Junction to the right. Both men hold flags, standing ready to flag down a presently arriving train. The train order(s) are tied up on the end of the stick lying on the Shawmut's rail, ready to be handed up on the fly. In the left background are two young lads (one standing, one sitting under the shade of the tree) ready to observe the pending action. To the right of the PRR's track and ducking under the Shawmut's rails are the connecting rods that control the home signals and derails of the interlocking plant. Called an "Armstrong" tower, these mechanical machines relied entirely on the strength of the operators who manned them. (SMHS.)

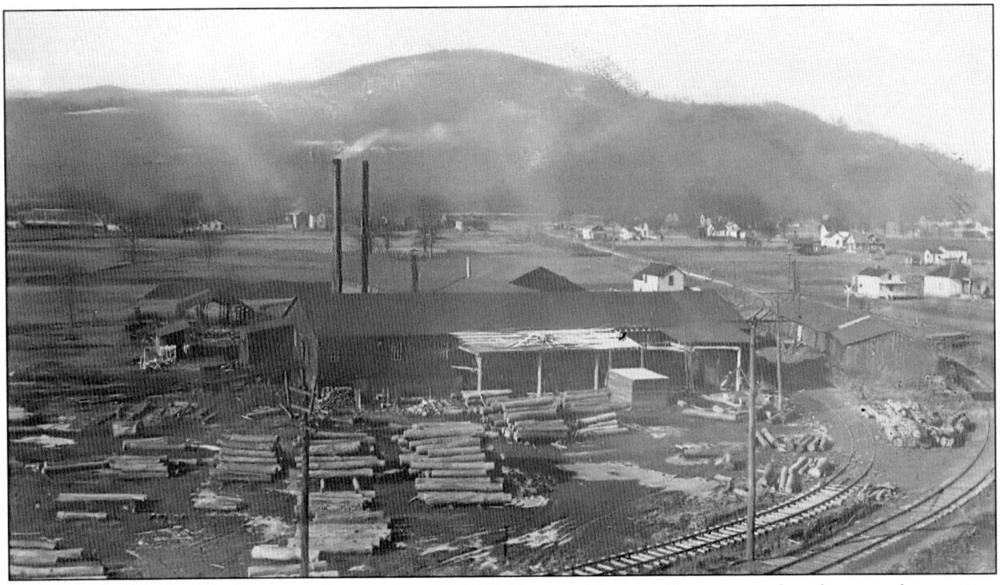

The Portville Basket Factory, located at MP 70.3, was diagonally across the diamond crossing from White House Tower. It was served by both the PS&N and the PRR, but the sidings did not connect as this was not a permitted interchange point. The view in this photograph looks west, with the village of Portville in the distance. (Portville Historical and Preservation Society.)

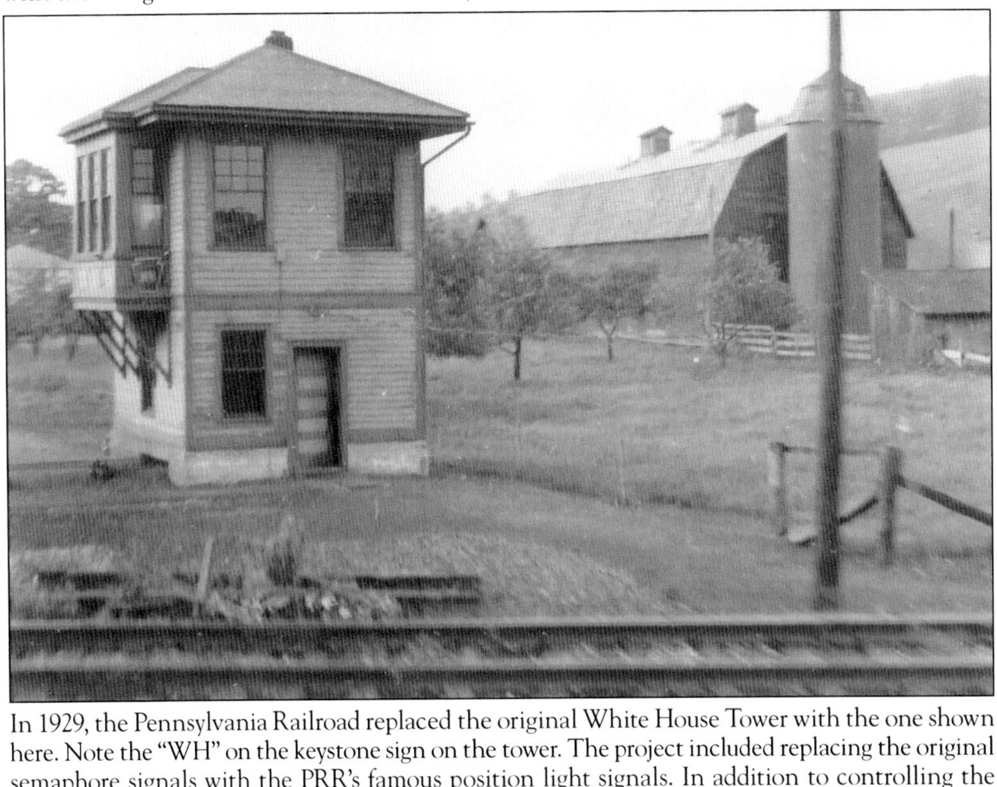

In 1929, the Pennsylvania Railroad replaced the original White House Tower with the one shown here. Note the "WH" on the keystone sign on the tower. The project included replacing the original semaphore signals with the PRR's famous position light signals. In addition to controlling the Shawmut crossing, WH also remotely controlled the track switches and signals at Haskell Road to the north and State Line to the south. (Portville Historical and Preservation Society.)

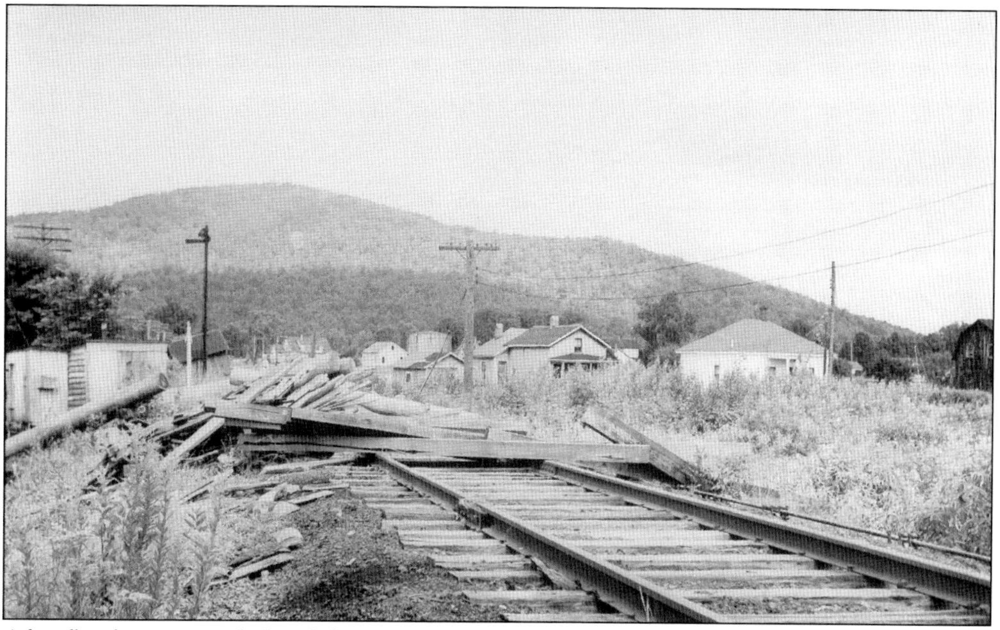

After floodwaters receded on July 19, 1942, debris was strewn cross the Shawmut tracks just west of White House Tower. The houses at right are on Anderson Road. The houses in the distance are on South Main Street. The eastbound home signal protecting the interlocking plant is along the tracks at left. (PS&NRRHS.)

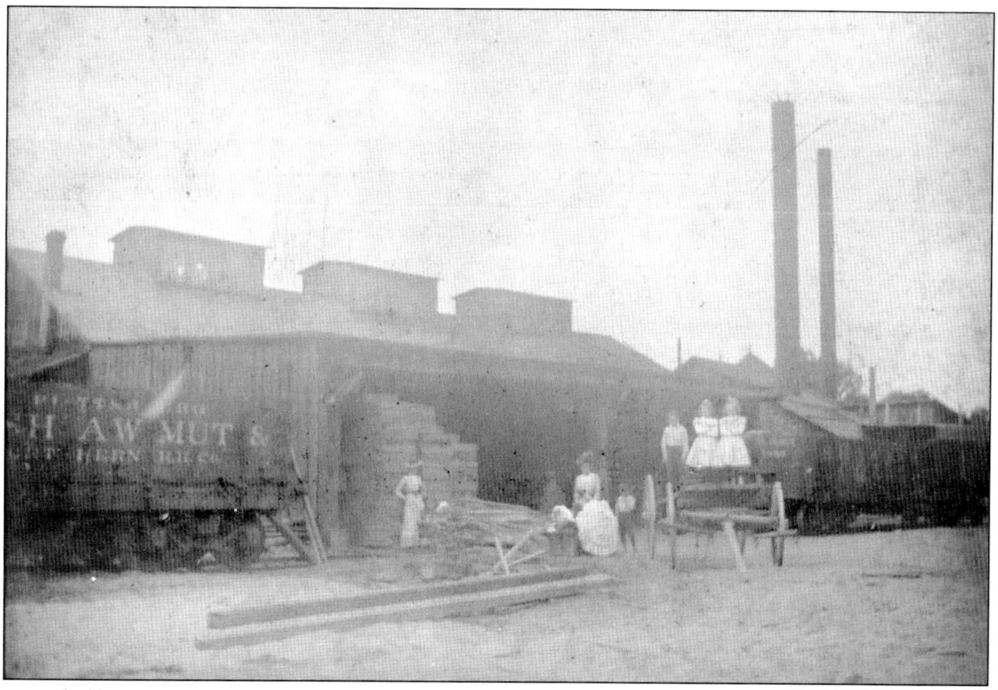

Founded by brothers Orren and William Wallace Weston in the 1850s, Westons Mills, New York, was located at MP 73.8 on the Shawmut's Olean Branch. Seen here, in this view looking east in the 1900s, is their mill. It received inbound Shawmut coal and shipped out finished lumber. (Portville Historical and Preservation Society.)

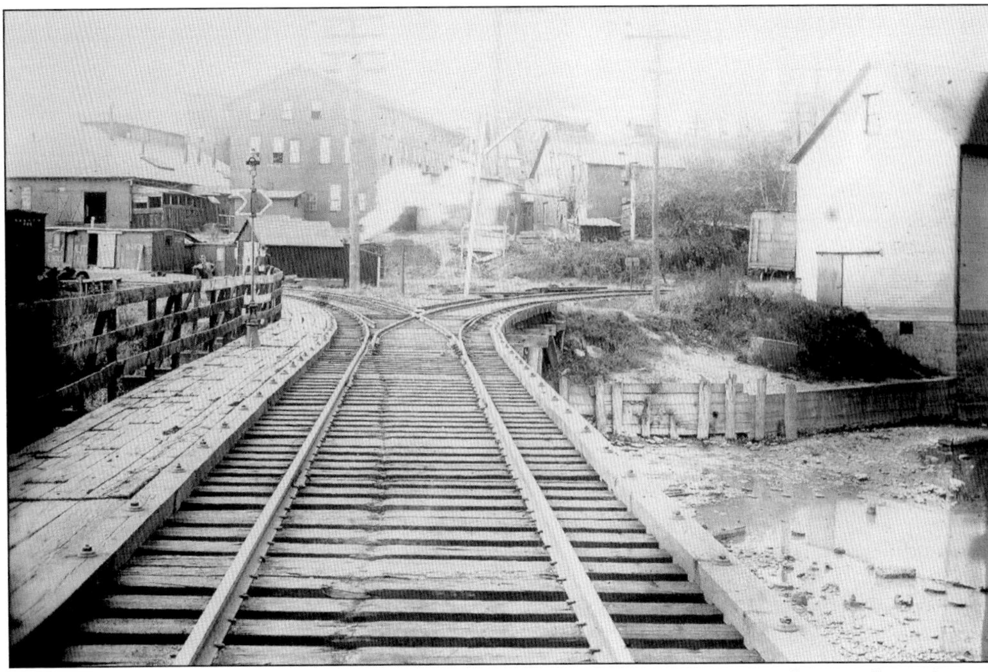

The Shawmut's bridge over Olean Creek, located at MP 76.4, was constructed as two legs of a wye with the track switch in the middle of the bridge. The original bridge, seen above, was constructed by the narrow-gauge Olean Railroad on top of the pilings that supported the aqueduct of the old Genesee Valley Canal. The bridge was simply widened to standard gauge by the Shawmut in 1902. Shown below in the 1940s is the replacement bridge that was constructed in 1918. It stood until the late 1980s, having served the Shawmut, the Pennsylvania, Penn Central, and Conrail. (Both, PS&NRRHS.)

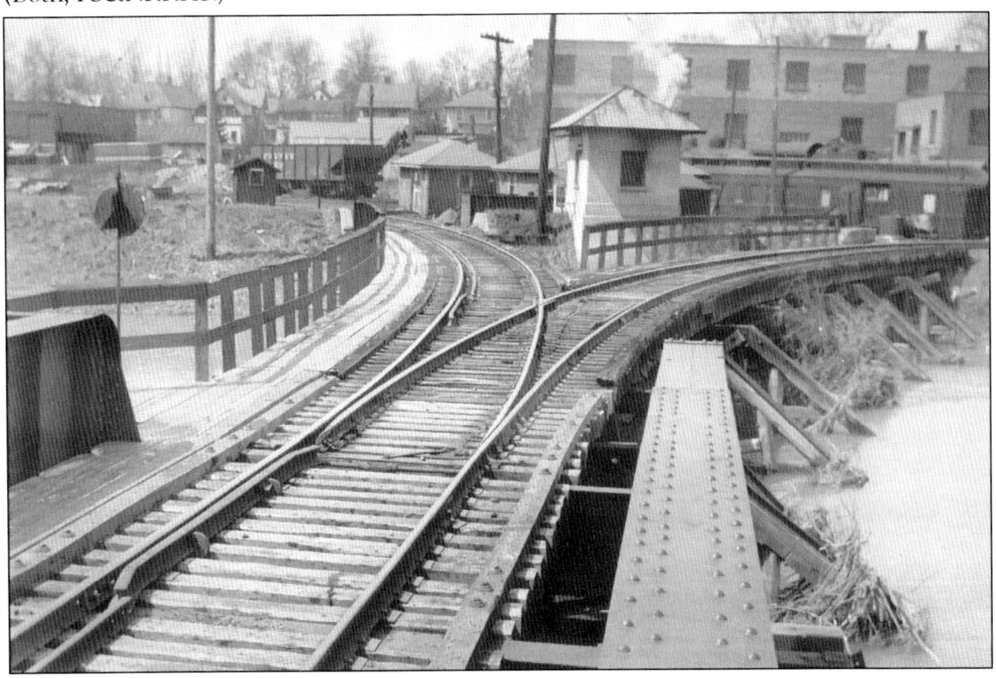

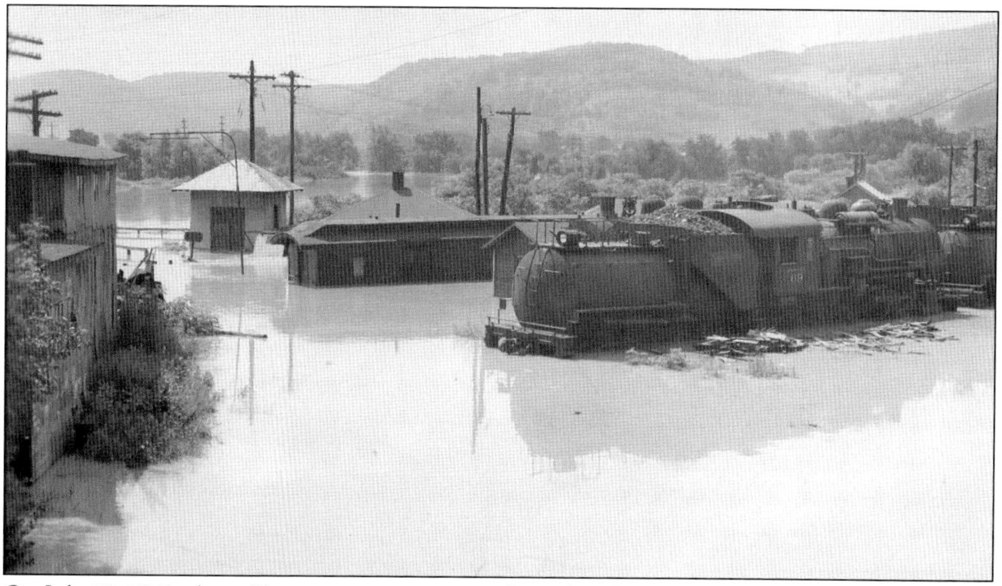

On July 18, 1942, three Shawmut engines sit in about four feet of water in the Olean, New York, yard. This photograph, with a view looking south, was taken from the East State Street bridge that passed over the interchange track that was jointly used by the Shawmut and the Pennsylvania Railroad. (SMHS.)

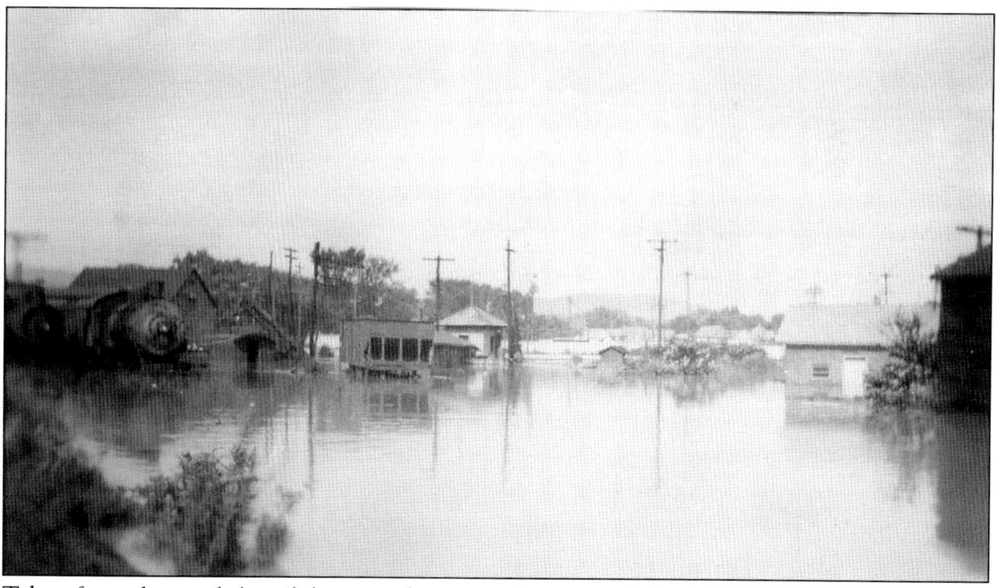

Taken from the south leg of the wye, this is another view of the July 18, 1942, flood in Olean, New York. This photograph, with a view looking east across the Olean Creek, was taken from the elevated siding that served the Market Basket warehouse. Bradner Stadium is in the background. (SMHS.)

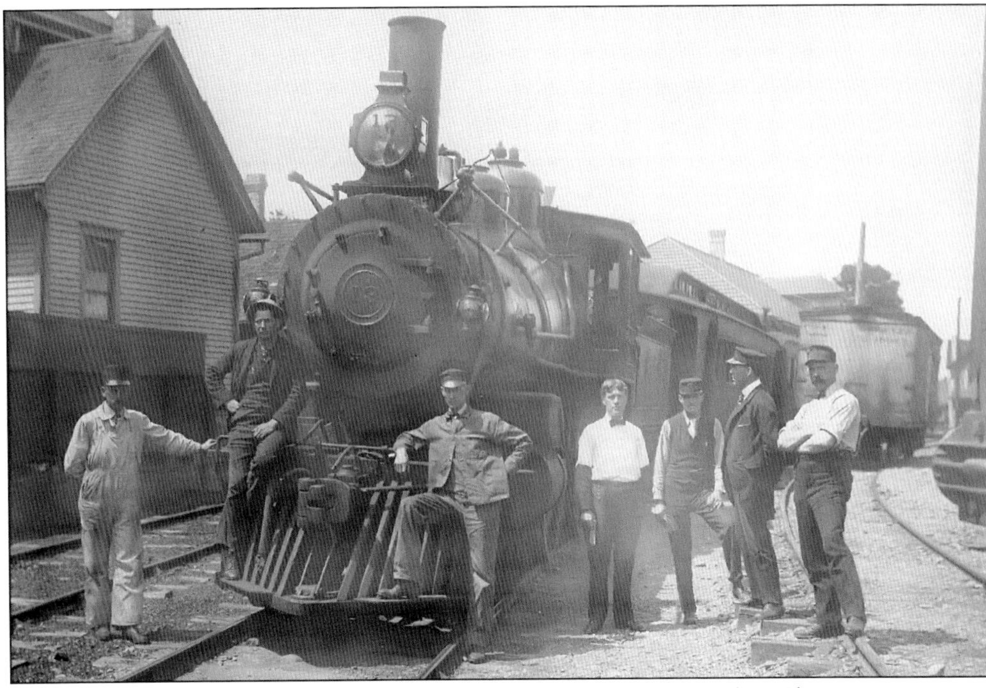

In this photograph taken sometime in the 1910s in Olean, New York, a Shawmut train crew poses with engine No. 13. Notice the headlight is from engine No. 12. In the background, above the passenger cars, is the roof of the Olean depot. The houses at left are on East Green Street. (SMHS.)

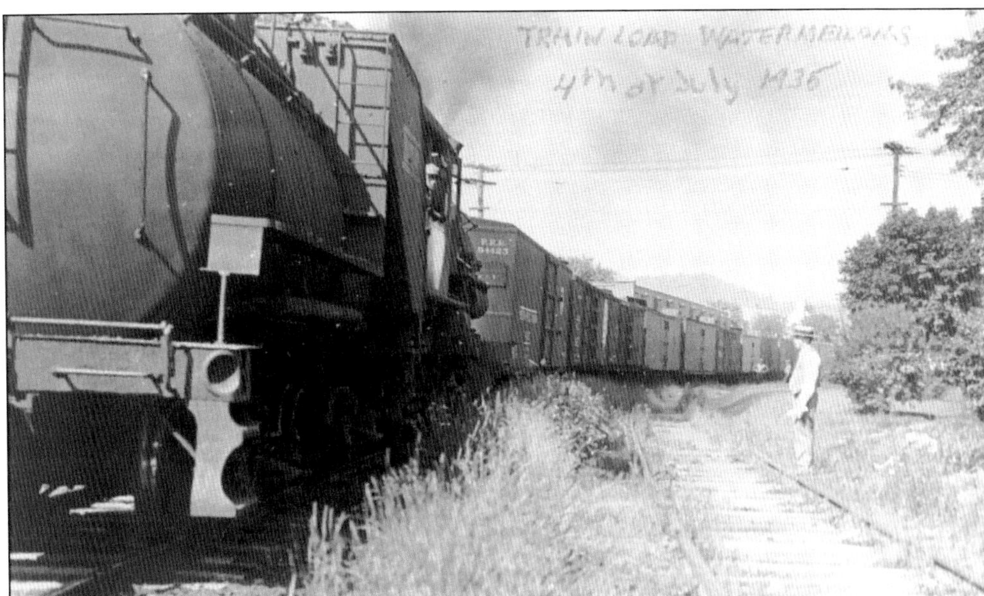

In the days before home refrigerators were common, a major community event was the delivery of the watermelon train. In this view looking west and from Adams Street in Olean, New York, a train of watermelons is being delivered to the Olean Wholesale Grocery warehouse that was located on South Barry Street. (PS&NRRHS.)

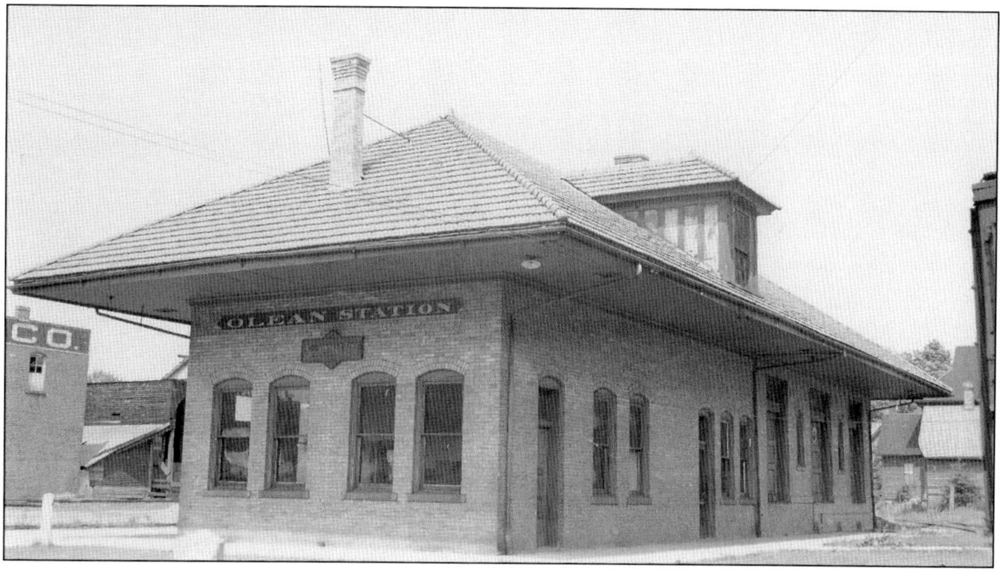

The Shawmut depot in Olean, New York, was a handsome yellow brick building with a red tiled roof. It was located at the corner of South Union and East Green Streets. The view in the June 16, 1946, photograph above looks east from South Union Street. The photograph below was taken in 1950. In the background was the Bissett Brothers Storage and Coal Company. In later years, that building housed Leo's Grocery Store. The station was torn down in 1965 to provide additional parking space for Leo's. Leo's was consumed by fire in 1975, and this space is today the parking lot for Ried's Food Barn. (Both, SMHS.)

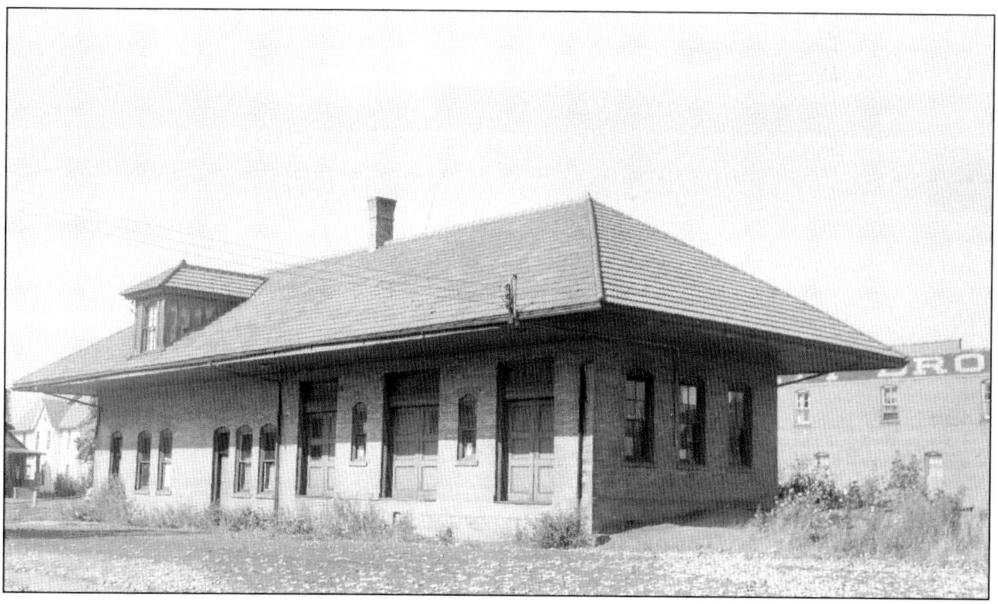

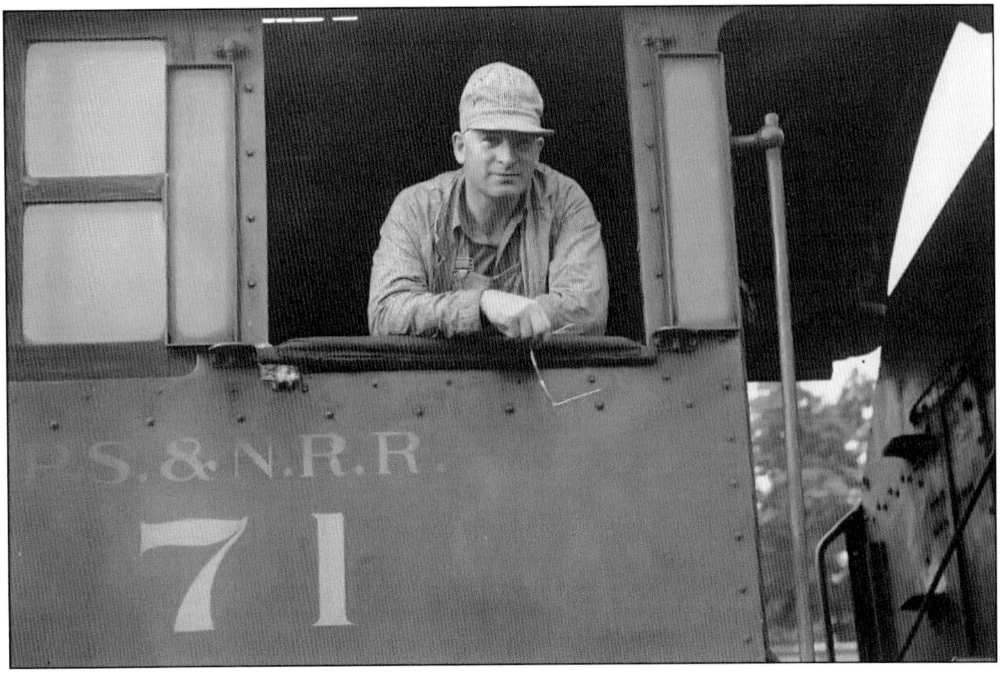

Due to damage north of Angelica, New York, from the July 1942 flood, the Shawmut was forced to detour operations onto the Erie Railroad between Hornell, New York, and Friendship. Engineer ? Geoner (above) pauses for his photograph on the fireman's side of the cab of engine No. 71 in Wellsville during a detour run. Engine No. 75 (below) leads a detour move west through Wellsville. All detour moves required an Erie employee as a "pilot" observer in the cab of the Shawmut locomotive. One such pilot was amazed at the pulling power of those little Shawmut engines, compared to the big S-class engines of the Erie. (Above, SMHR; below, PS&NRRHS.)

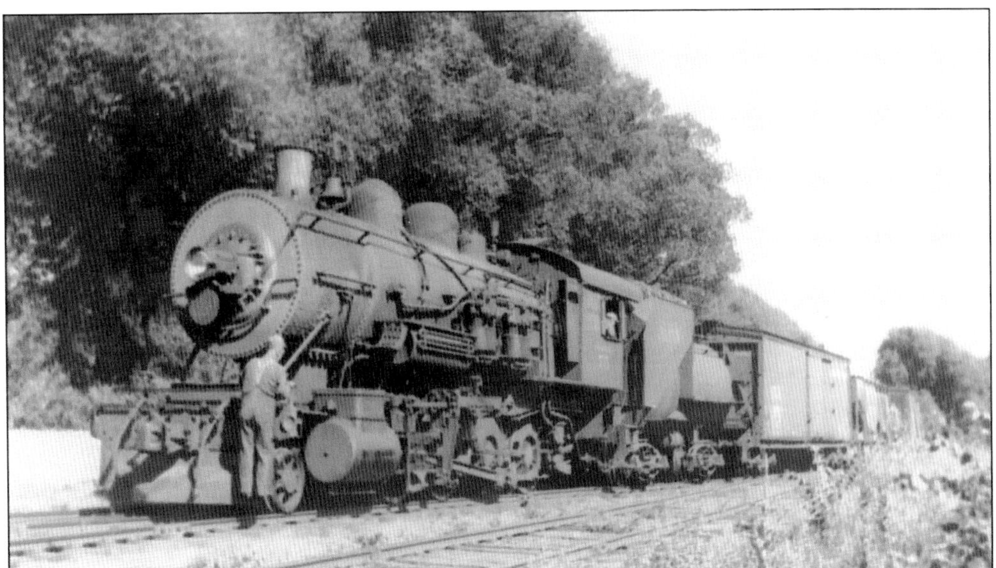

Two

THE SHAWMUT IN PENNSYLVANIA

After crossing the New York State line (see chapter 1) at MP 70.5, the Pittsburg, Shawmut & Northern Railroad entered the commonwealth of Pennsylvania in Ceres Township. The main line extended to Hyde, Pennsylvania, at MP 145.6, just north of Brockport. A majority of this trackage was constructed after the Shawmut had been consolidated: the trackage near the state line, the trackage north of Smethport, Pennsylvania, and the large double loop on the grade between Kasson and Clermont, Pennsylvania.

The headquarters of the railroad, its largest classification yard, and the motive-power shops of the Shawmut were located in St. Marys, Pennsylvania, at MP 125.2. These shops were staffed by German immigrants who were masters of their trade. In spite of the fact that the Shawmut was perpetually starved for cash, these German laborers lovingly maintained the locomotive fleet in excellent condition—locomotives that would have been considered ready for scrapping by other railroads.

St. Marys was also where the Office of the Chief Dispatcher and his staff of dispatchers were located. They controlled all movements along the entire railroad from this central location.

Paine Junction, located south of St. Marys at MP 132.4, was where the wholly owned Kersey Railroad branched off the main line. The Kersey provided access to the many mines owned and operated by the Shawmut Mining Company (a railroad subsidiary) in the mining villages of Byrnedale, Force, and Tyler, all located in Elk County, Pennsylvania.

Most of the operating crews in Pennsylvania were based out of the St. Marys yard. Crews would operate "mine runs," taking empty coal hoppers south and spotting them at the many coal tipples along the way. On the return trip north, they would bring strings of loaded hoppers back up to St. Marys where the yard crews would assemble them into full trains to be sent north. Still other crews would then drag these completed trains up the long climb to North Fork and Clermont, Pennsylvania, and on into New York State.

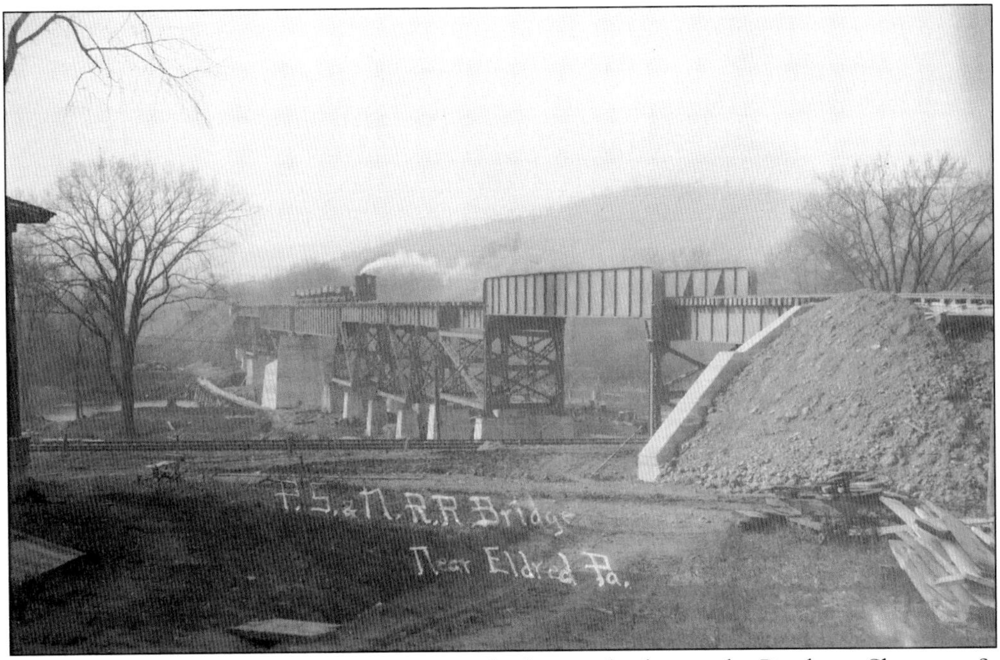

State Line Viaduct, located at MP 71.0, was the longest bridge on the Pittsburg, Shawmut & Northern: 612 feet. The bridge crossed the Allegheny River, the Pennsylvania Railroad, and the Portville to Eldred highway. This 1909 photograph shows the bridge under construction. Note the tank engine pushing a string of dump cars. (PS&NRRHS.)

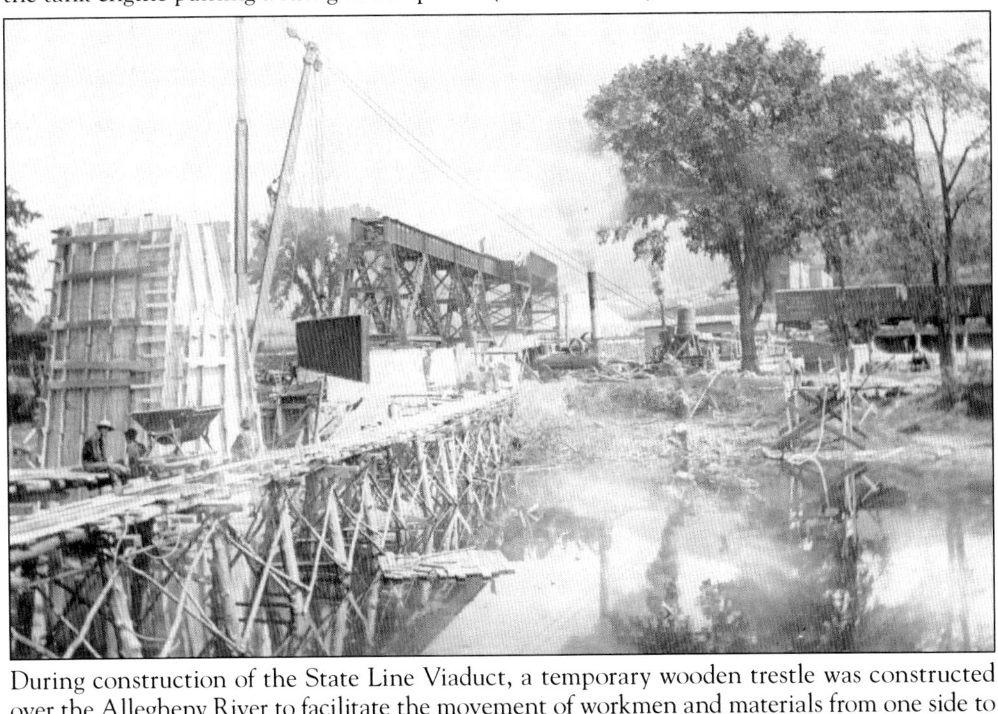

During construction of the State Line Viaduct, a temporary wooden trestle was constructed over the Allegheny River to facilitate the movement of workmen and materials from one side to another. This 1908 photograph shows the first of the four long girders that will span the river being hoisted into place. (PS&NRRHS.)

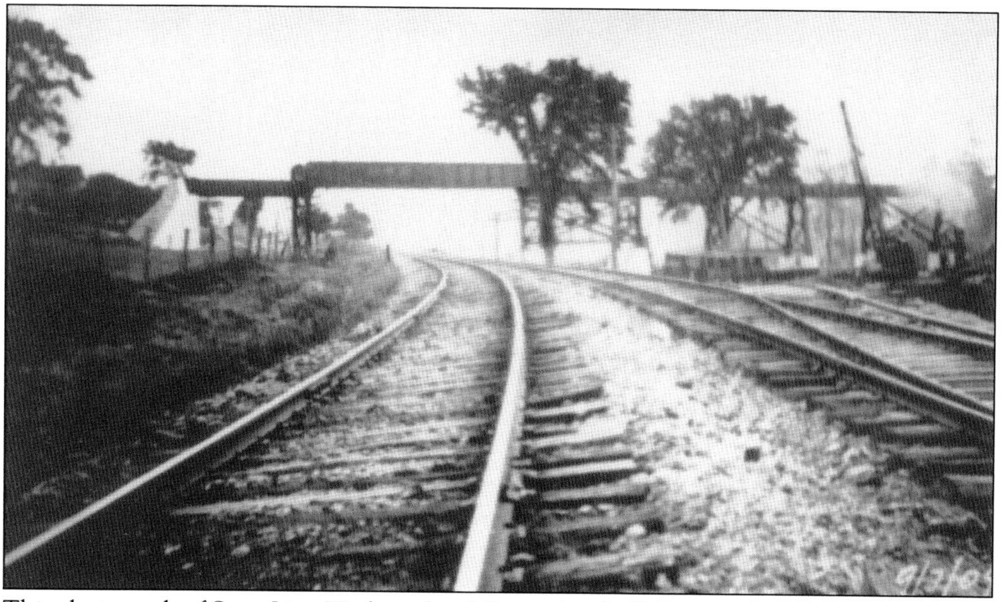

This photograph of State Line Viaduct, dated September 3, 1909, was taken looking south from the Pennsylvania Railroad tracks. The concrete abutment (left) is in place, but the earthen grade behind it has yet to be filled in. The temporary siding (right) was installed for the delivery of construction materials. (PS&NRRHS.)

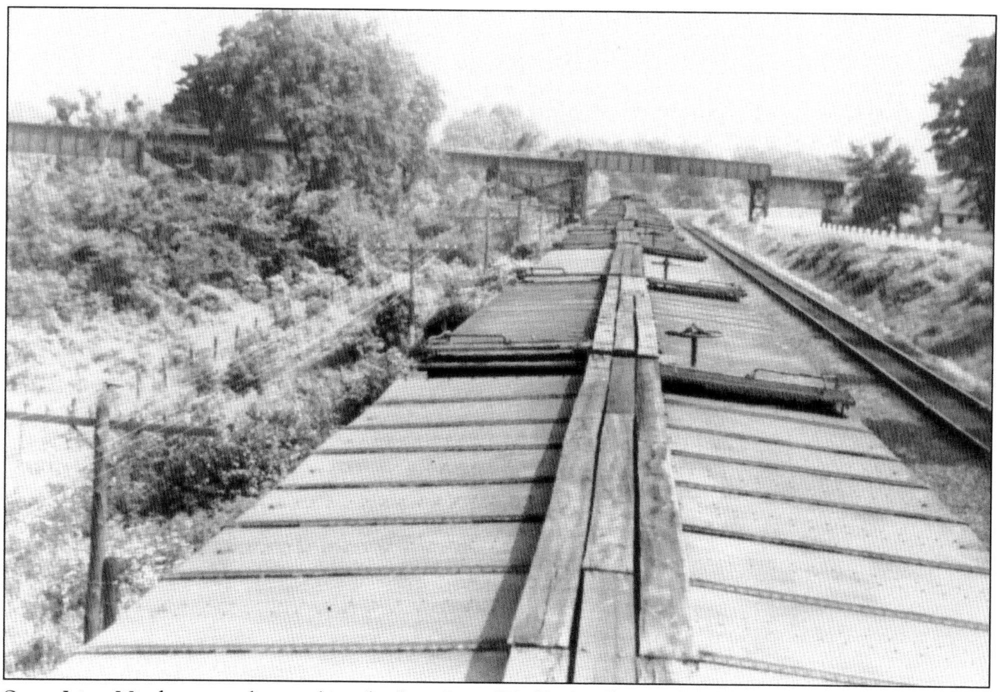

State Line Viaduct was located in the hamlet of Bullis Mills in Eldred Township, Pennsylvania. The hamlet was named after the lumber mill that had been erected along the Allegheny River by brothers Charles A. and Spencer S. Bullis. The view in this photograph, taken in the 1930s, looks north from the top of a string of boxcars standing on the Pennsylvania Railroad main line. (PS&NRRHS.)

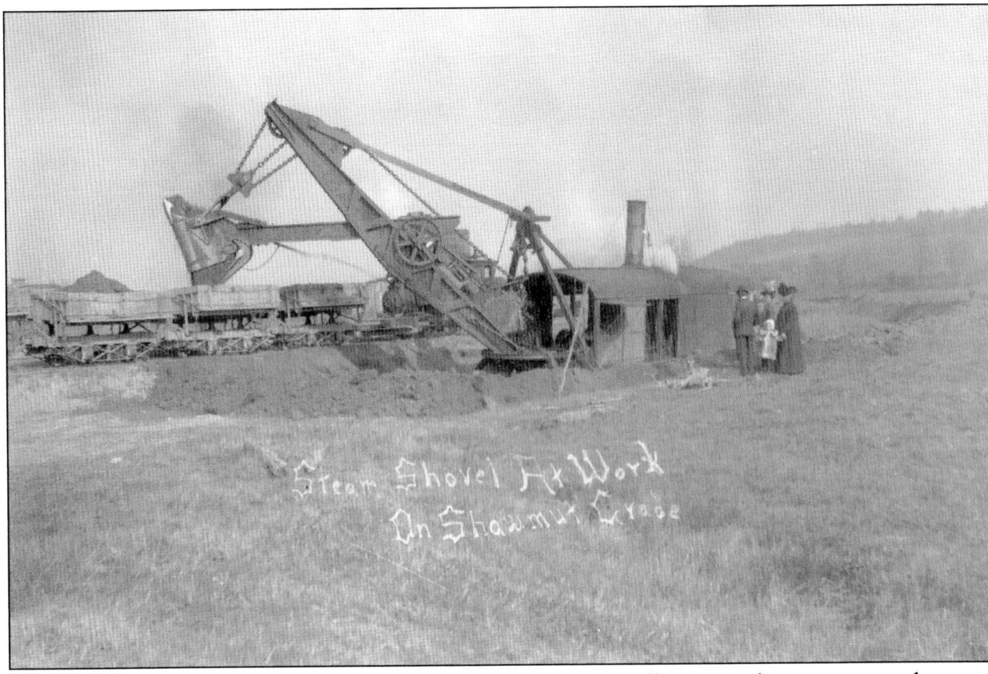

The western approach to the State Line Viaduct in Bullis Mills, Pennsylvania, required a great deal of fill in order to elevate the track well above the floodplain of the Allegheny River. A large steam shovel, seen above, was employed to dig the fill and then load it into dump cars. Note how the shovel is digging along in its own self-made trench while the dump cars are positioned at the perfect height for filling. The dump cars, pictured below, were then moved along temporary construction tracks by steam-powered dinkies (small engines). This 1909 construction scene obviously drew some onlookers. (Both, PS&NRRHS.)

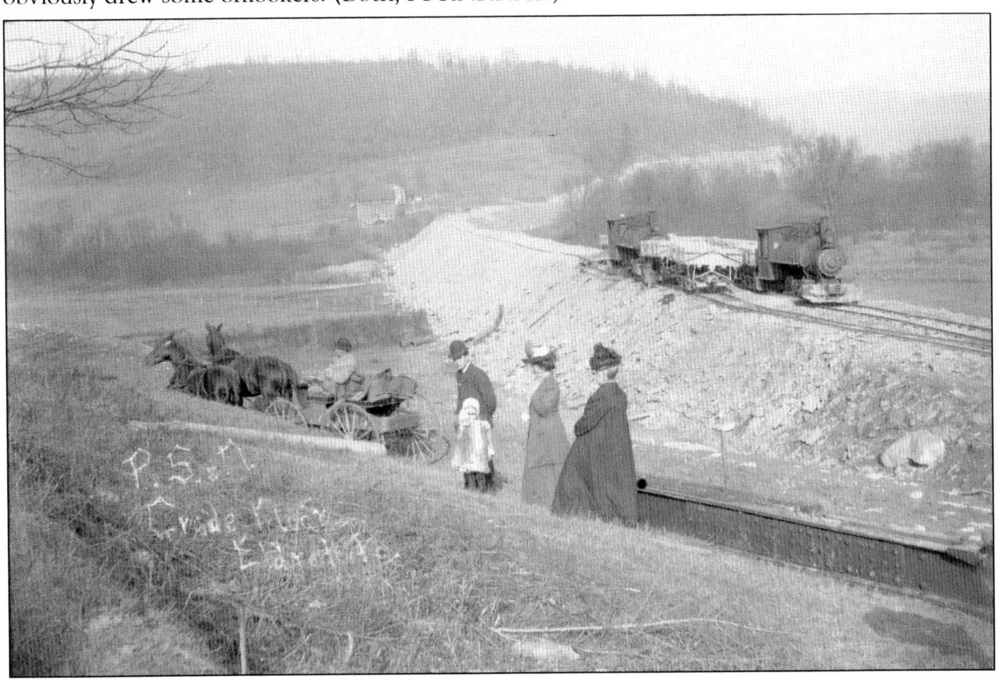

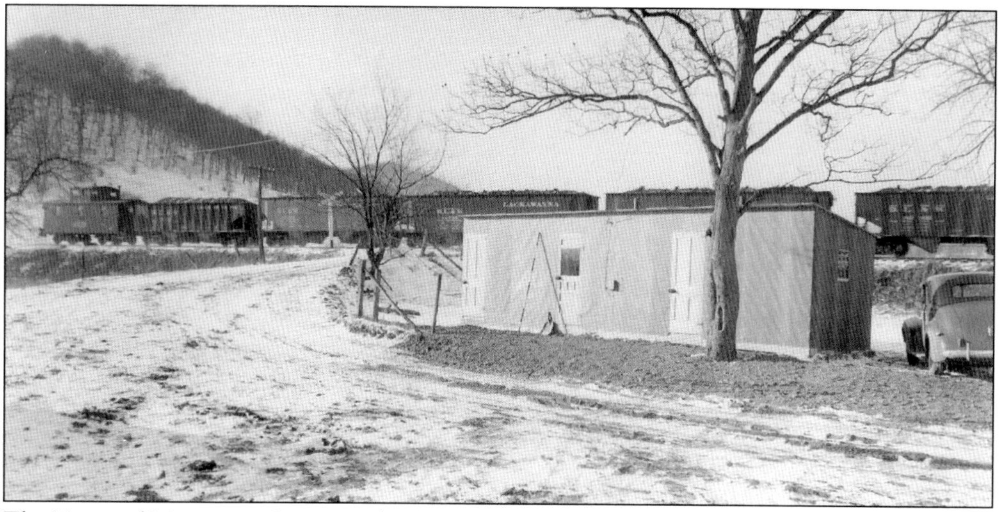

The National Munitions Company, located at MP 74.2 along Artline Road in Eldred Township, Pennsylvania, was the largest wartime production facility in McKean County. It was incorporated in January 1941. This March 4, 1941, photograph shows the temporary office, road location, and railroad crossing. The Shawmut train is northbound. (Eldred World War II Museum.)

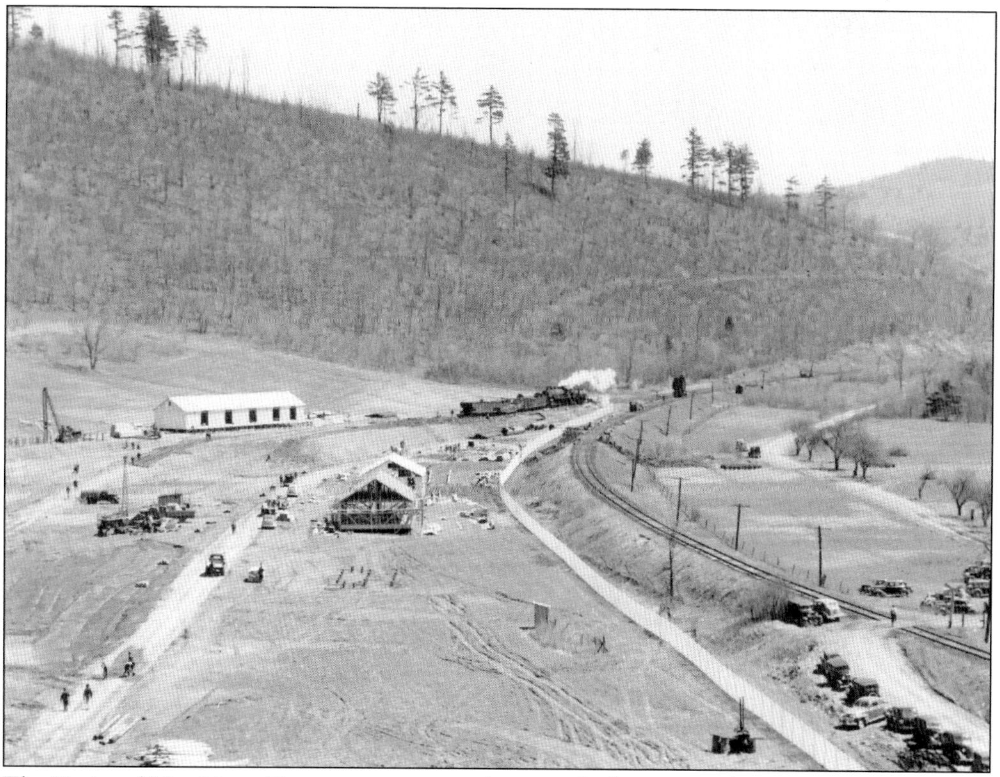

The National Munitions Company constructed its new facility on nearly 2,000 acres in Big Loop and Little Loop Hollows in Eldred Township, Pennsylvania. This spring 1941 photograph with a view looking north shows a Shawmut locomotive with hoppers cars dumping fill dirt to bring the sidings up to grade. The PS&N main line arcs across the scene in the right side of the picture. (Eldred World War II Museum.)

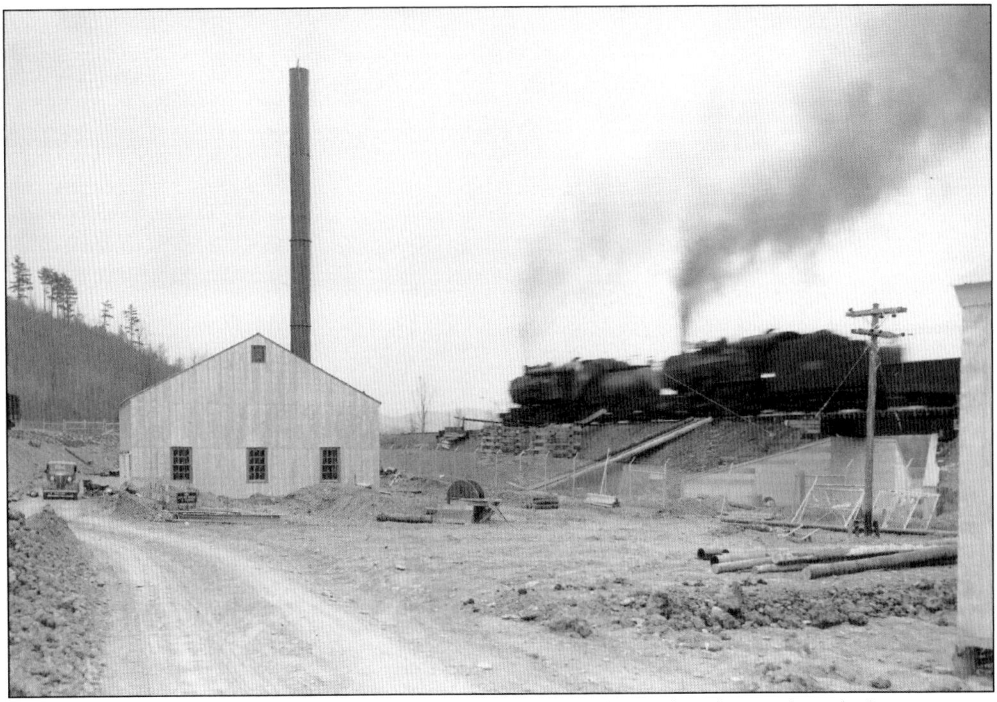

The powerhouse for the National Munitions Company was located at the north end of its property. It provided steam to all of the buildings within the facility. This photograph, taken spring 1941, shows a double-headed northbound Shawmut train. The bridge at right is also newly constructed and will serve as the main entrance to the facility. (Eldred World War II Museum.)

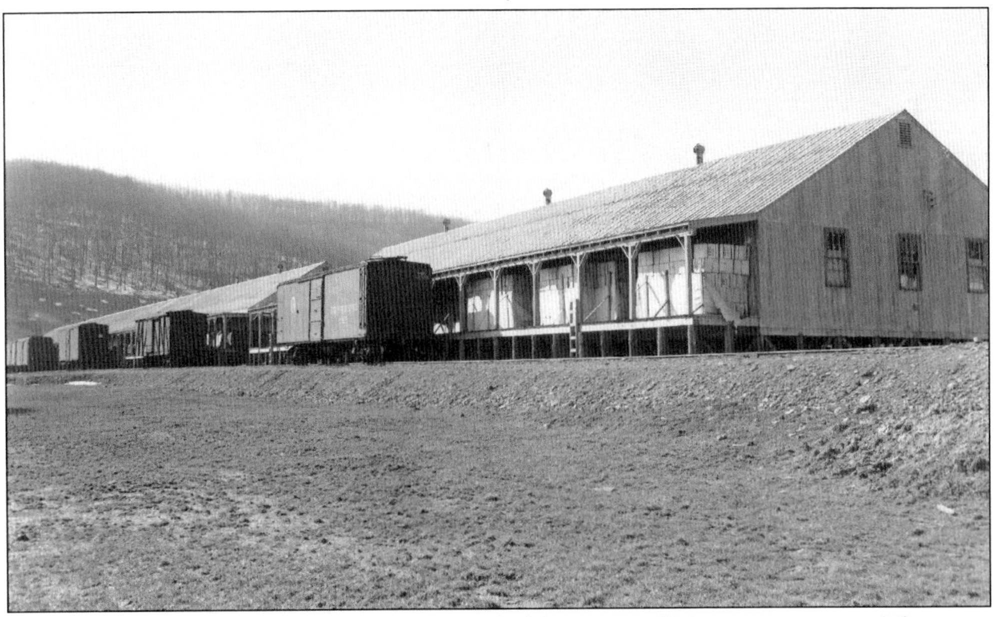

Warehouses No. 1–3 were located at the east end of the National Munitions property. They were served by the standard-gauge Shawmut sidings on their east sides and the facility's internal narrow-gauge tracks on the west sides. The warehouses provided storage and transloading facilities for both inbound materials and outbound finished munitions. (Eldred World War II Museum.)

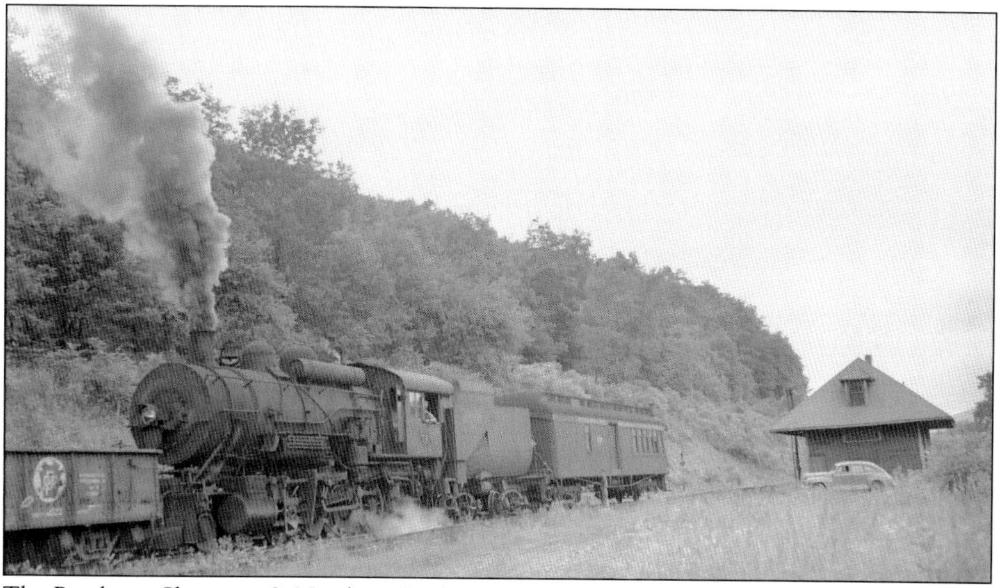

The Pittsburg, Shawmut & Northern Railroad was abandoned on April 1, 1947. It was sold to Harry W. Findley, a scrap dealer from Carnegie, Pennsylvania. Findley created the Shawmut Railroad Supply Corporation to do the actual scrapping. In August 1947, engine No. 71 lifts the rails at West Eldred, Pennsylvania. (SMHS.)

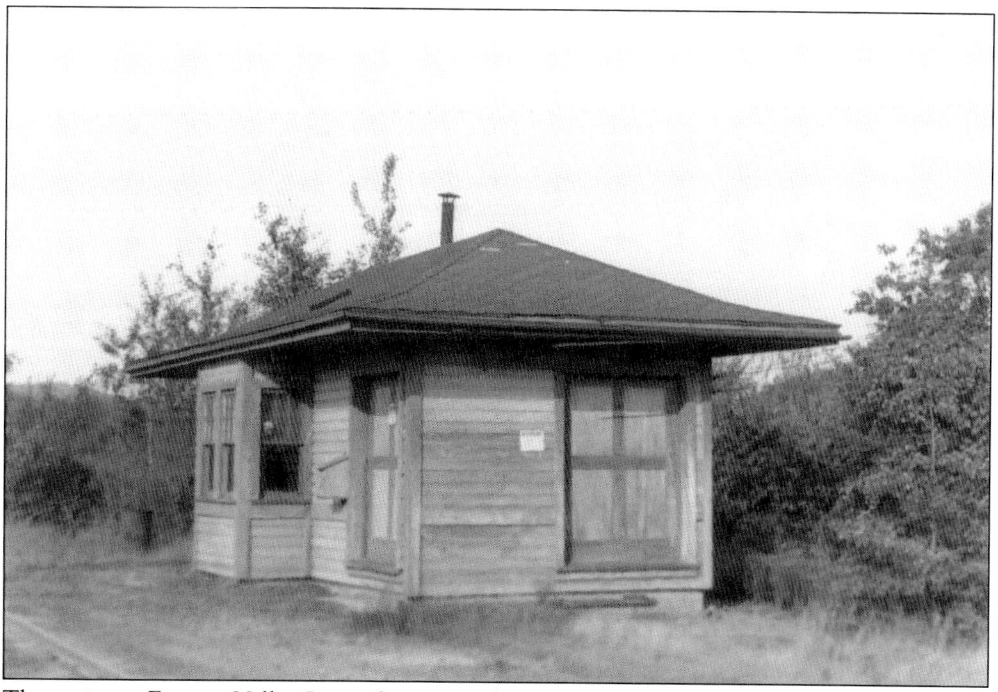

The station at Farmers Valley, Pennsylvania, was located at MP 84.1. This building was constructed in the summer of 1930 due to increased traffic levels being generated by the nearby Quaker State oil refinery. A full-scale replica of this station now houses the PS&NRRHS archives in Angelica, New York (see page 127). (PS&NRRHS.)

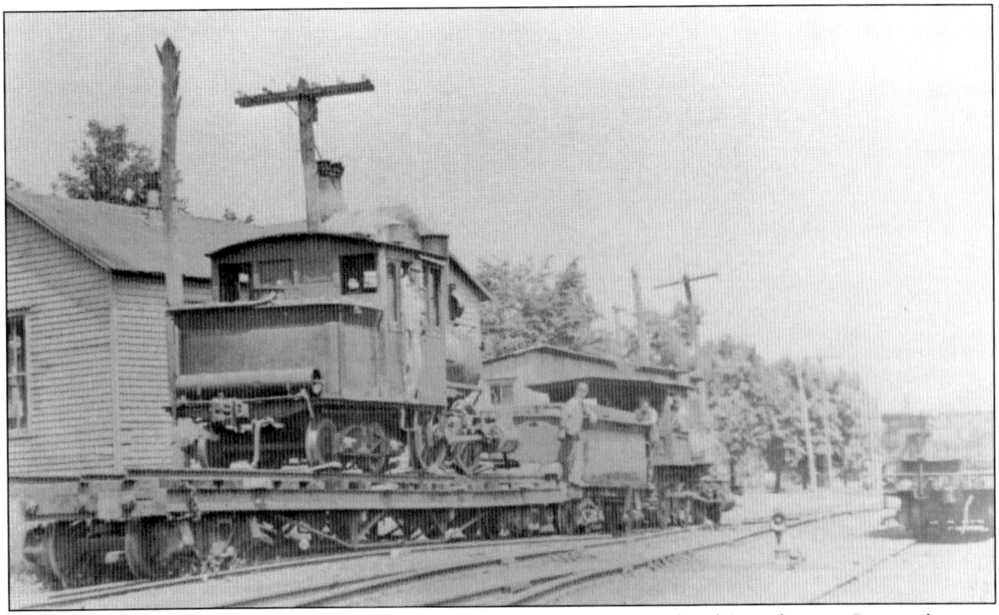

In 1905, the Shawmut had a bit of a railroad war in the borough of Smethport, Pennsylvania. It started in 1900 when the Shawmut built an at-grade crossing over the existing narrow-gauge Bradford, Bordell & Kinzua (BB&K) Railroad. Things were fine until 1905 when Elisha Kent Kane acquired the BB&K and merged it into his Kushequa Railroad. Kane's plan was to convert the BB&K to standard gauge to provide his Kushequa line with access to East Smethport. The Shawmut obtained a court injunction to prevent the crossing from being widened to standard gauge. Kane outsmarted the Shawmut and left the crossing as is, but converted the rest of the line to standard gauge. He then ferried (above and below) his standard-gauge cars across the Shawmut on top of little narrow-gauge flatcars. (Both, PS&NRRHS.)

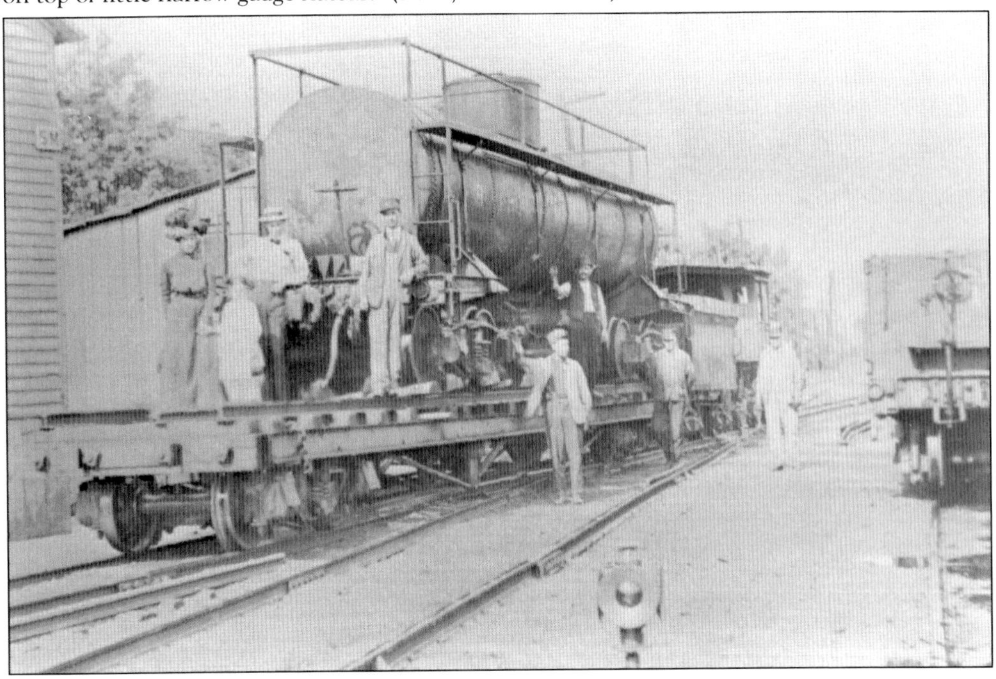

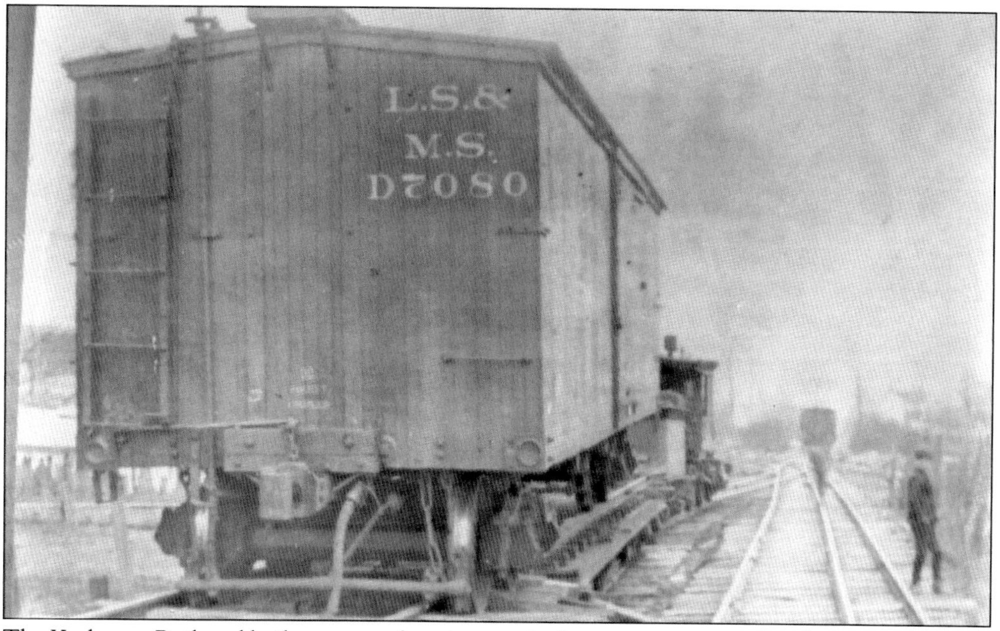

The Kushequa Railroad built ramps to ferry its standard-gauge cars across the Shawmut piggyback on narrow-gauge flatcars. Seen here is a Lake Shore & Michigan Southern boxcar being positioned by an ex-BB&K locomotive. This one-of-a-kind operation lasted until 1913, when the courts ruled that Elisha Kent Kane could cross the Shawmut as a standard-gauge railroad. (PS&NRRHS.)

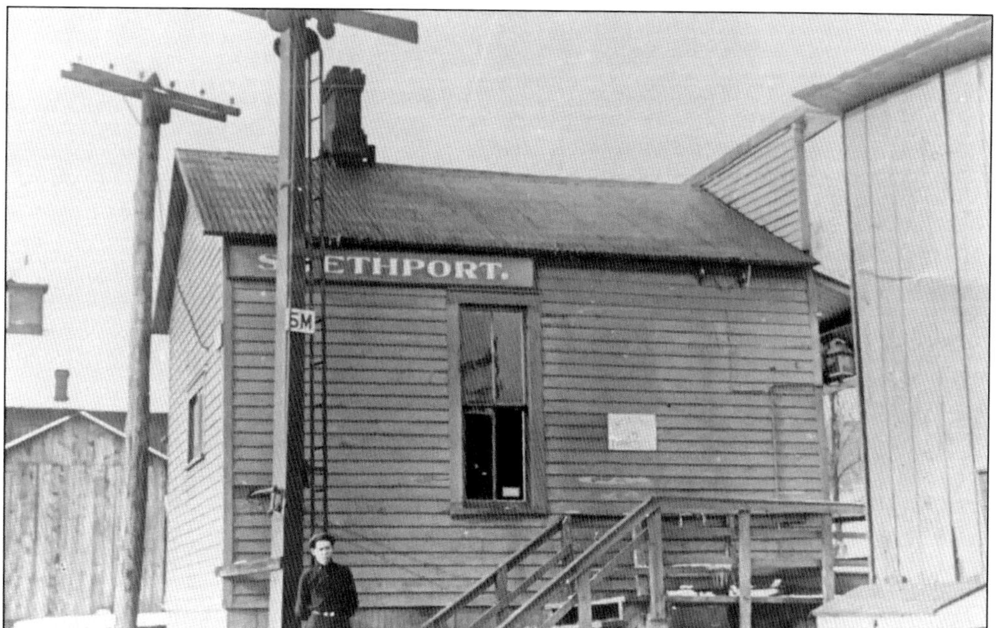

The Shawmut constructed its first depot in Smethport, Pennsylvania, at 116 Water Street; it had the telegraph call letters "SM." Not only did SM act as a train order and agency station, it doubled as the control point for the non-interlocked crossing between the Shawmut and the Kushequa Railroad. (SMHS.)

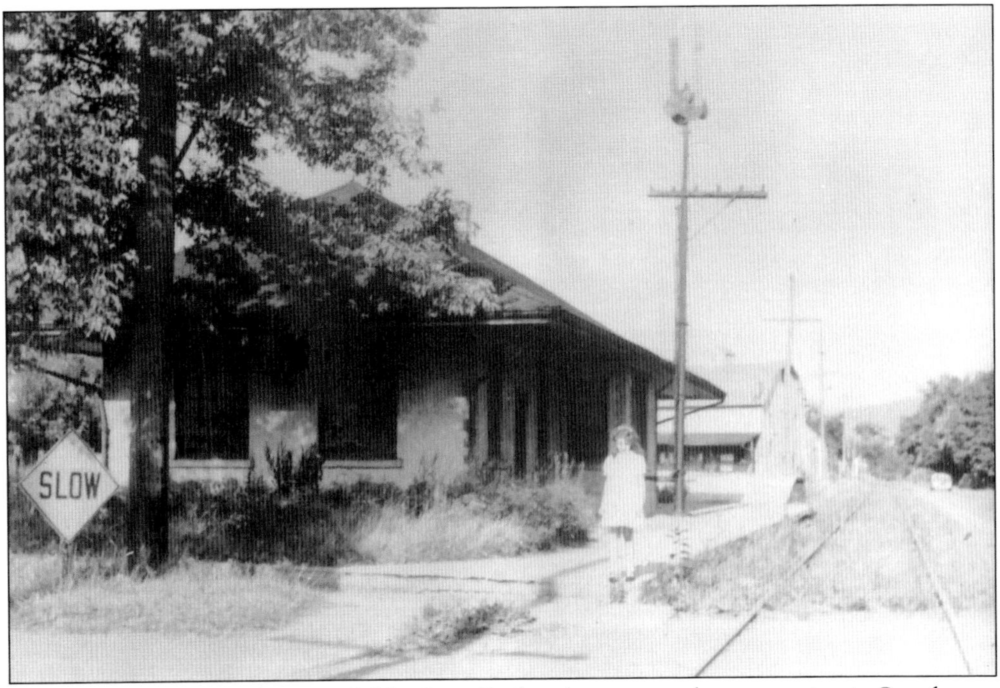

In 1928, the Pittsburg, Shawmut & Northern Railroad constructed a new station in Smethport, Pennsylvania. The structure, located at MP 88.4, was situated on the northeast corner of Mechanic and Water Streets. It was constructed in the Mission style with a beige stucco exterior and a red tile roof. (SMHS.)

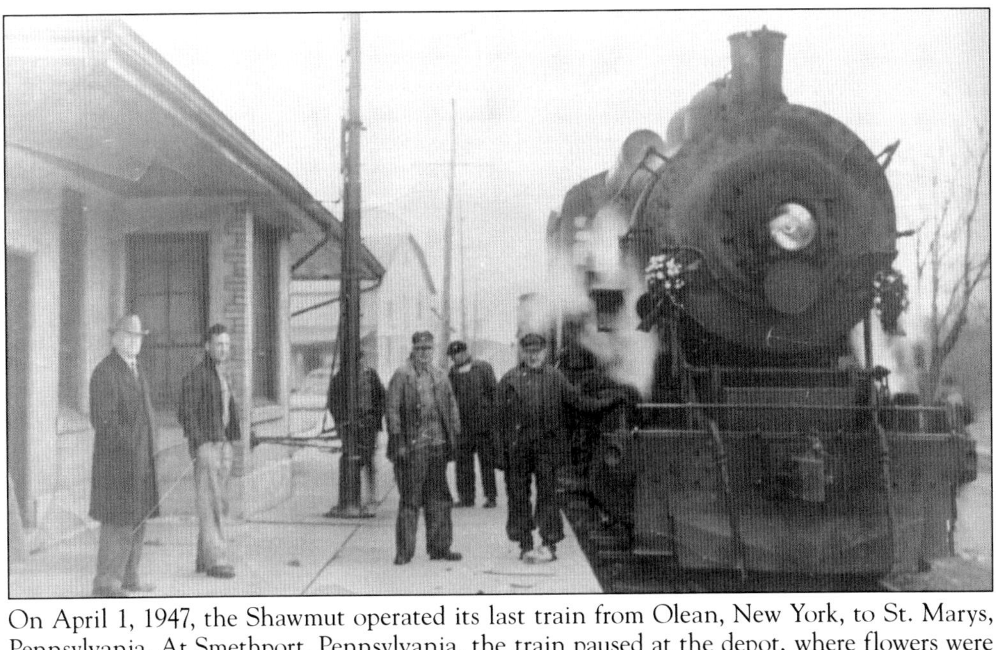

On April 1, 1947, the Shawmut operated its last train from Olean, New York, to St. Marys, Pennsylvania. At Smethport, Pennsylvania, the train paused at the depot, where flowers were hung on the front of engine No. 71. From left to right are two unidentified men, Tommy Johnson (behind signal mast), L.J. Lentz, Dave O'Dell, and George Starner. (PS&NRRHS.)

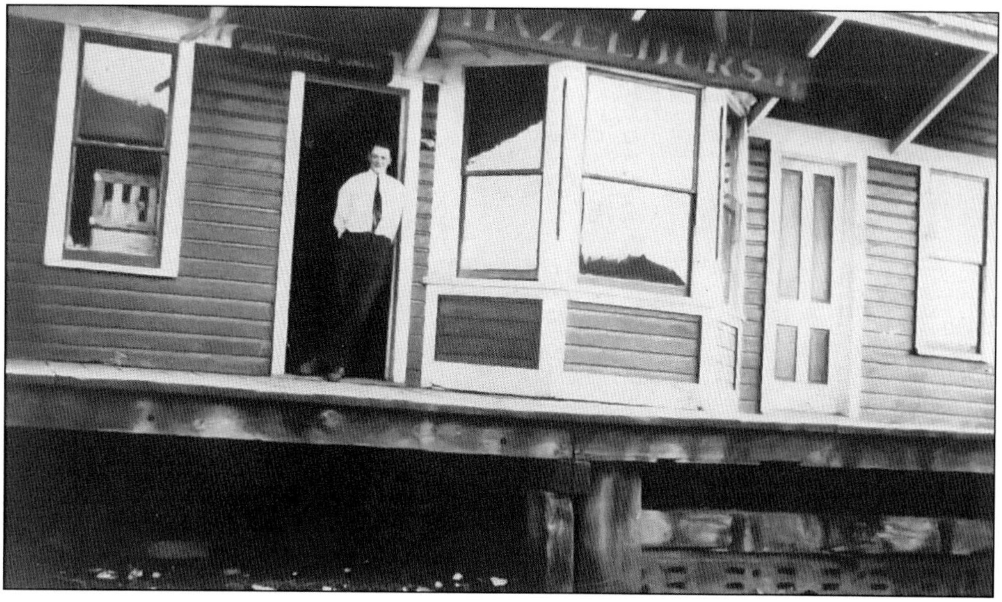

Hazelhurst (now Hazel Hurst), Pennsylvania, was located on the original Mount Jewett, Clermont & Northern Railroad. Once consolidated into the Shawmut, the line became its Mount Jewett Branch. Named after Bradford resident B.F. Hazelton, the hamlet was, by 1900, the center of glassmaking in McKean County. At its height, it had four glass factories: Interstate Glass Company, Keystone Glass Company, the Berny-Bond Glass Company, and Healy Glass Company. In the above photograph, taken sometime in the 1900s, freight and ticket agent M. Connor poses for his portrait at the depot. Below, the main track, seen from the depot in a view looking east, descends toward Kasson. (Above, SMHS; below, PS&NRRHS.)

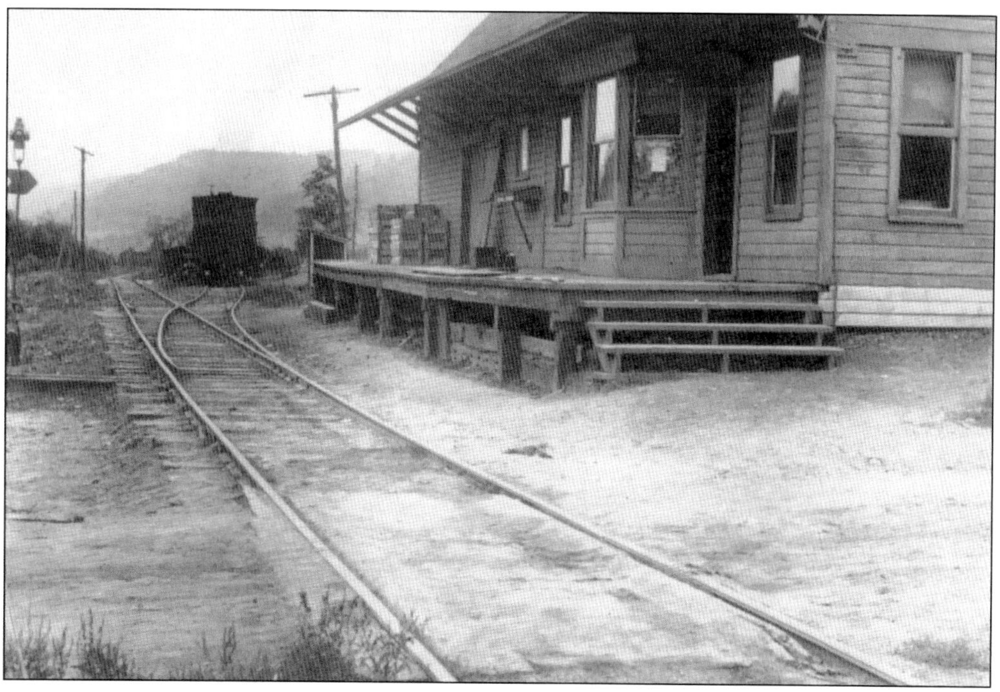

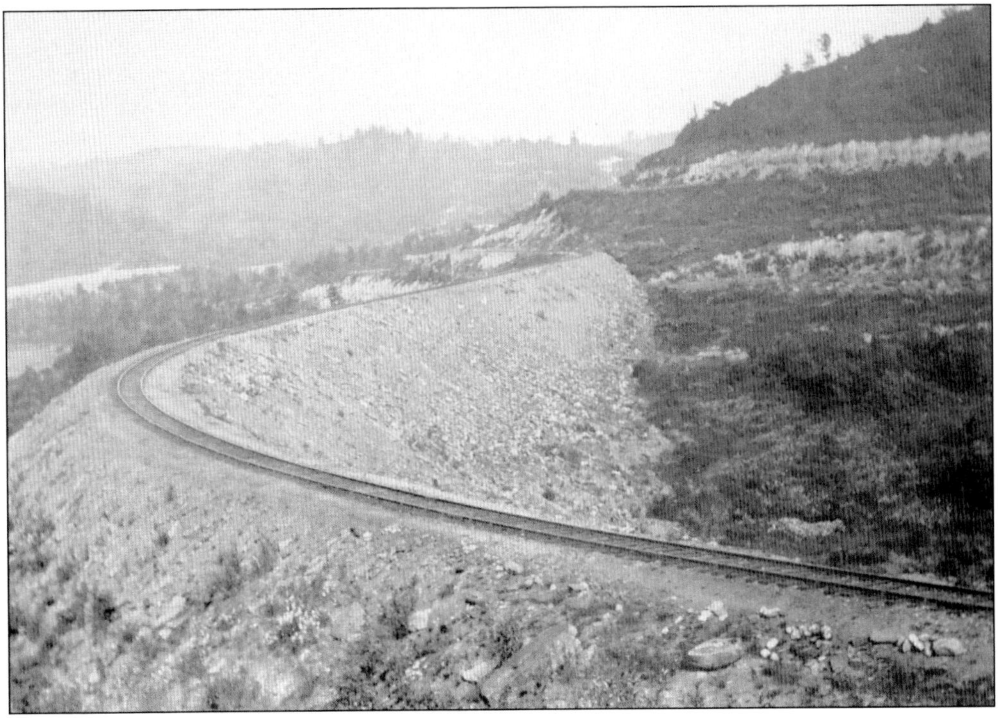

One of the big challenges faced by the young Shawmut was how to link its former Buffalo, St. Marys & Southwestern line at Clermont, Pennsylvania, with its former Mount Jewett, Clermont & Northern line at Kasson. Clermont is located on the "Big Level" with an elevation of 2,106 feet, while Kasson is in the valley at 1,581 feet—a difference of 525 feet in 7.6 miles. The solution was to build a series of fills and curves entirely out of earth and rock, save for a single bridge over a highway. On the main loop, long coal drags appeared to be passing themselves. (Above, SMHS; below, PS&NRRHS.)

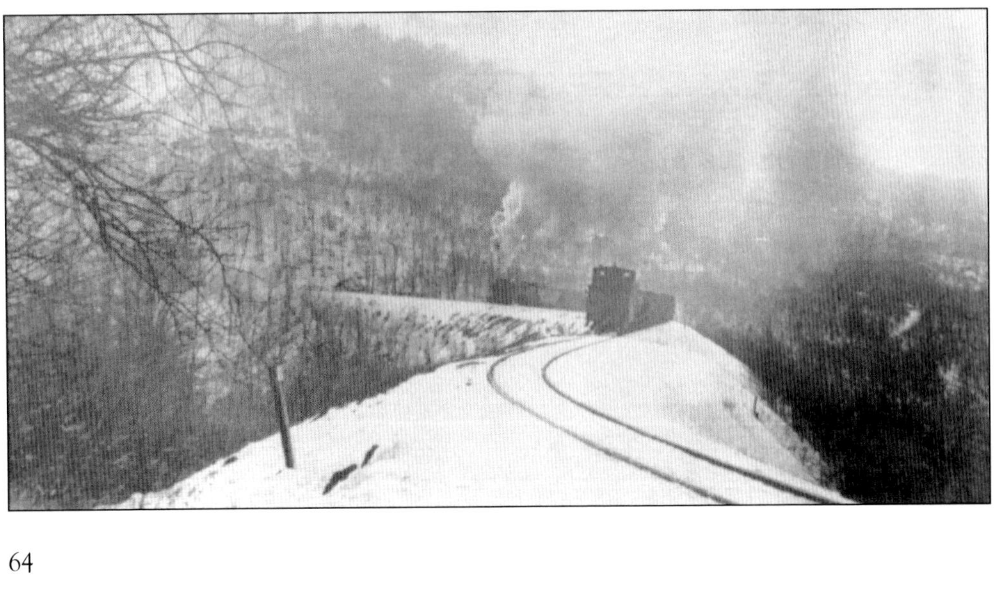

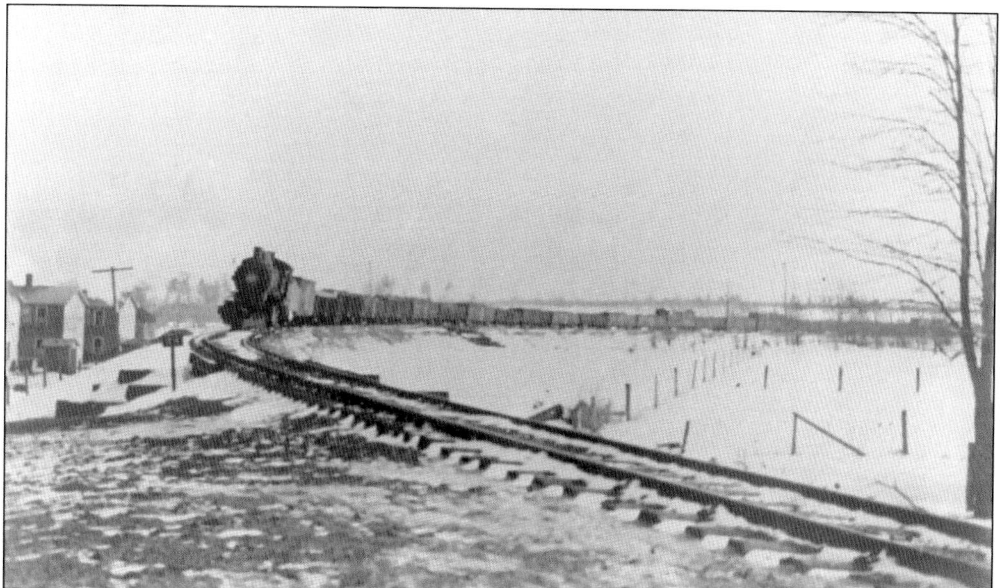

The hamlet of Clermont, Pennsylvania, located at MP 101.8, was the northern end of the original Buffalo and St. Marys Railroad. It was at this point where the coal traffic was turned over to the Pennsylvania Railroad. This photograph, taken in the 1910s, shows a northbound train on the new Shawmut track heading toward the big loop at Kasson. (PS&NRRHS.)

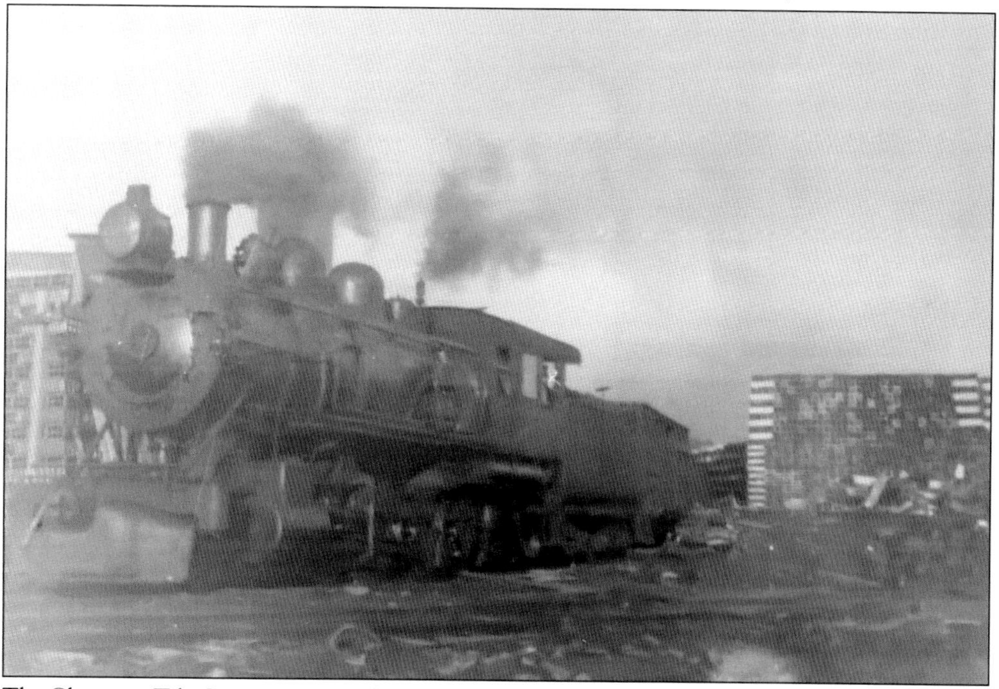

The Clermont Tile Company opened in 1901 at Clermont, Pennsylvania. It initially made building tile for walls, foundations, and flues. As these products were replaced by other materials, it changed to the production of drainage tiles and hot tops, large ceramic square shapes used by the steel industry in the casting of ingots. This undated photograph shows engine No. 51 switching the tile company. (PS&NRRHS.)

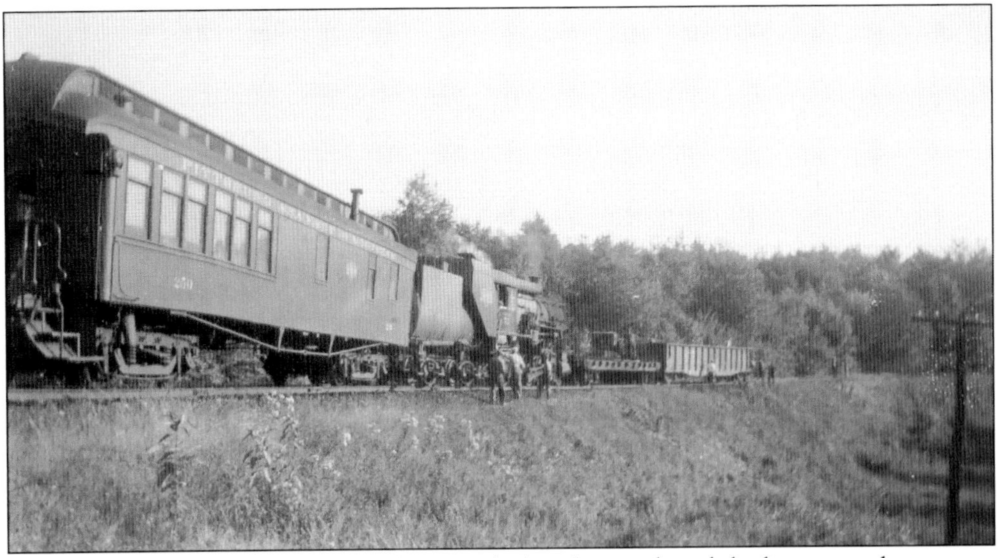

After the Shawmut was abandoned, the scrap dealer who purchased the line spent the summer of 1947 lifting the rails. This photograph shows the scrap train, powered by engine No. 72 and accompanied by combine No. 290, working at MP 119 in the vicinity of Bear Run, north of St. Marys, Pennsylvania. (SMHS.)

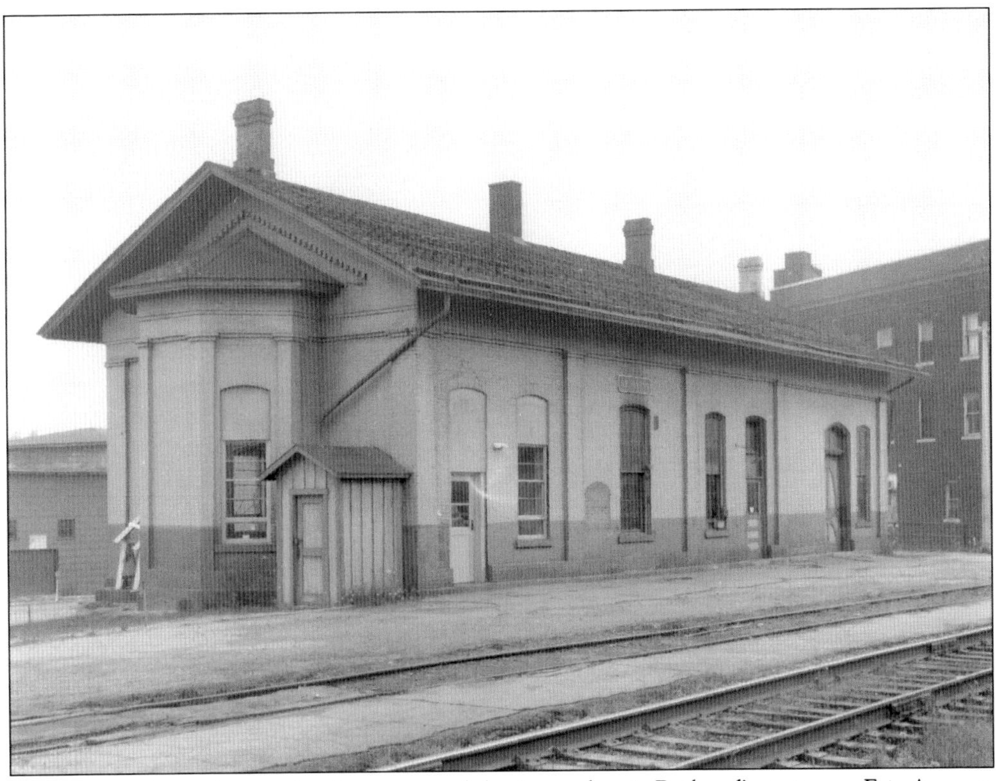

In St. Marys, Pennsylvania, the Shawmut used the Pennsylvania Railroad's station on Erie Avenue. The connection to the PRR depot was off the west leg of the wye at St. Marys Junction. As a result, one of the moves, either to or from the depot, was always a reverse move. (PS&NRRHS.)

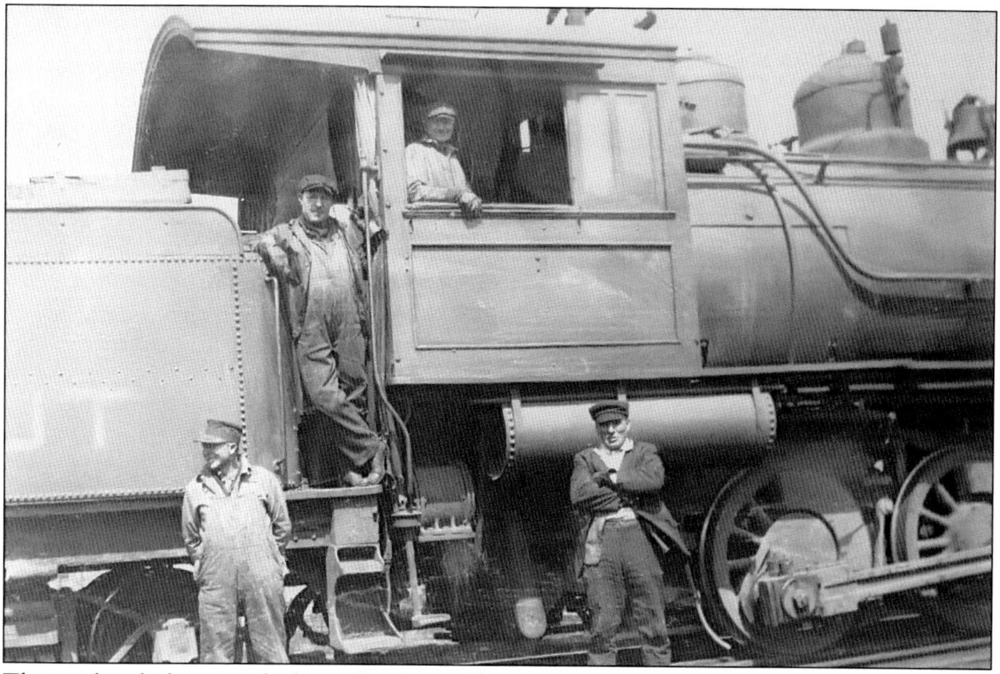

This undated photograph shows Pittsburg, Shawmut & Northern employees with one of the 0-6-0 switch engines, either No. 22 or 23. These little engines were nearly as powerful as the larger Consolidations. From left to right are Andy Herzing (brakeman), F. X. Hoffman (engineer), Charles Ehrensberger (engineer), and Joe Friedl (conductor). (SMHS.)

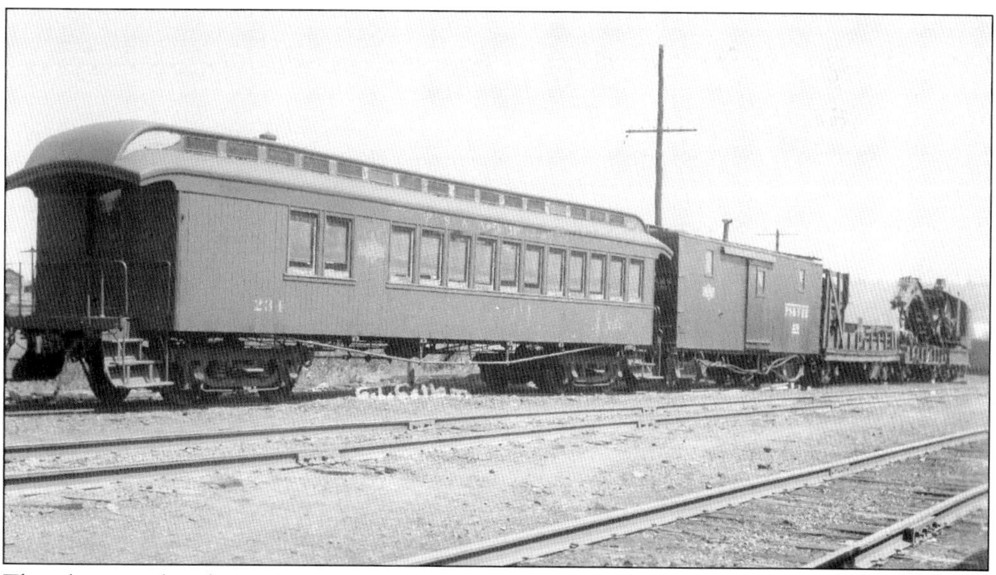

This photograph, taken on June 21, 1936, at St. Marys Junction, shows the Pittsburg, Shawmut & Northern Railroad wreck train. From left to right are crew car No. 234, tool and equipment car No. 230, rail and wheel car No. 263, idler flat car No. 281, and wrecking crane No. 244. (SMHS.)

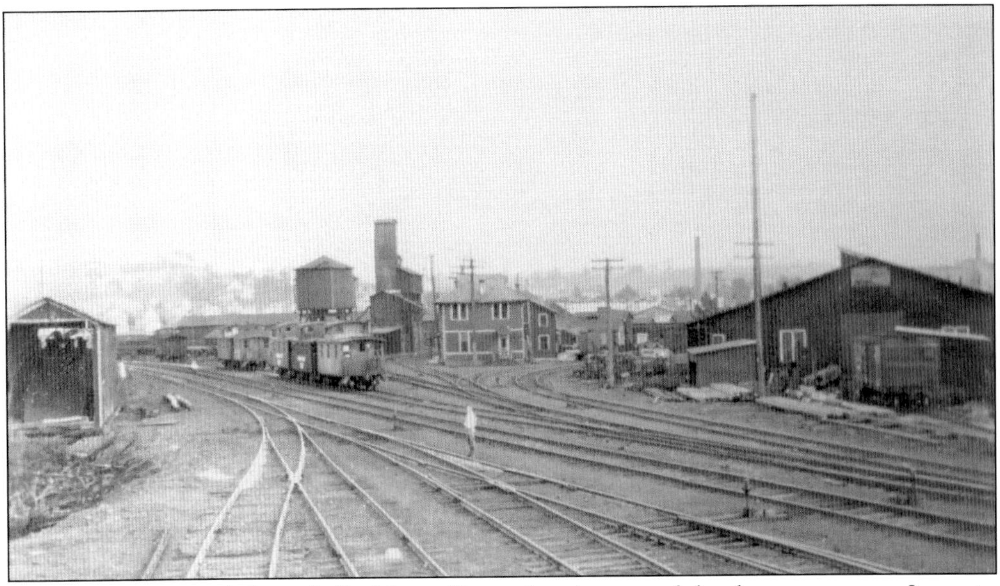

The Shawmut passed through St. Marys, Pennsylvania, east of the downtown area. Its main classification yard was located along Washington Street, and its shops originally stood along Depot Street. The south end of the yard, near Kaulmont where the wye led to the Depot Street shops and the PRR depot, was known as St. Marys Junction. The late 1920s photograph above of St. Marys Junction, with a view looking south, shows, from left to right, the snowplow shed, the caboose track, the water and coaling facilities, the yard office (call sign "JN"), and the woodworking shop. In about 1930, the original coaling tower was replaced by a coaling dock that crossed over top of the lead to the engine house. The coaling dock can be seen below in the right background of this undated photograph. (Above, PS&NRRHS; below, SMHS.)

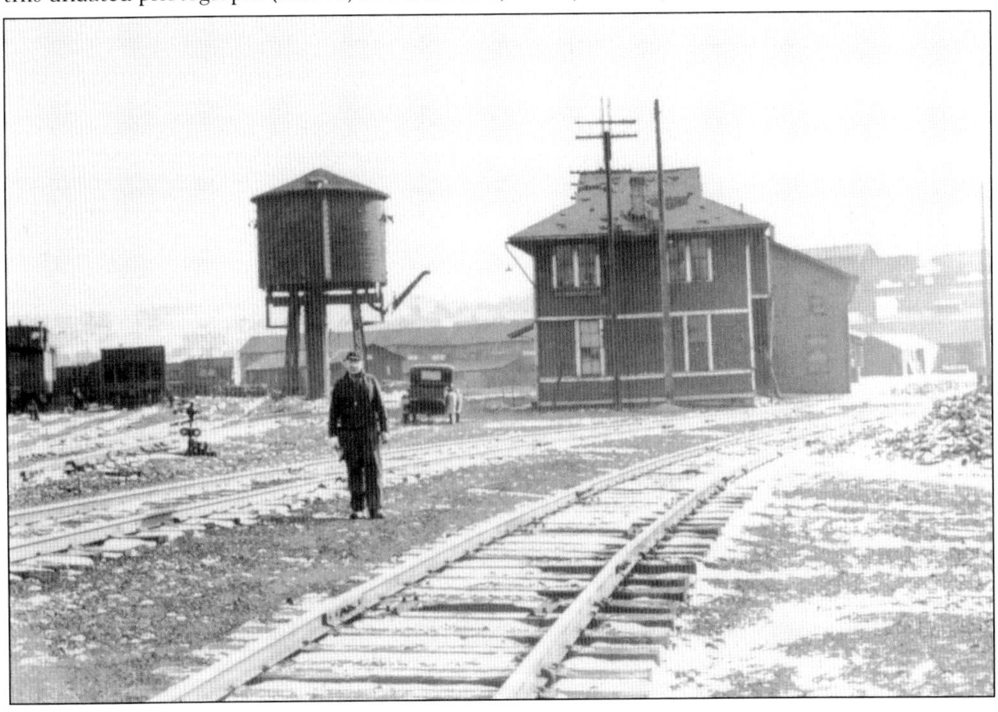

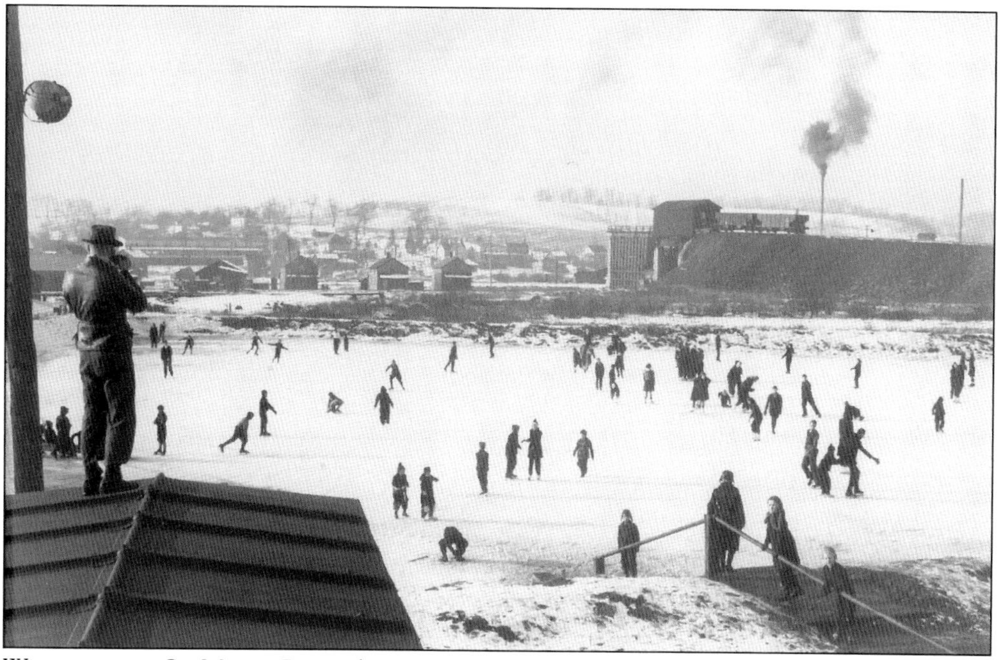

Wintertime in St. Marys, Pennsylvania, meant skating on the pond at Kaulmont. In the left background, some of the buildings of the Stackpole Carbon (nee Battery) Company can be seen. In the right background is the ramp leading up to the Shawmut's coaling dock, with smoke billowing out of the coach house of the Shawmut's shops beyond. (SMHS.)

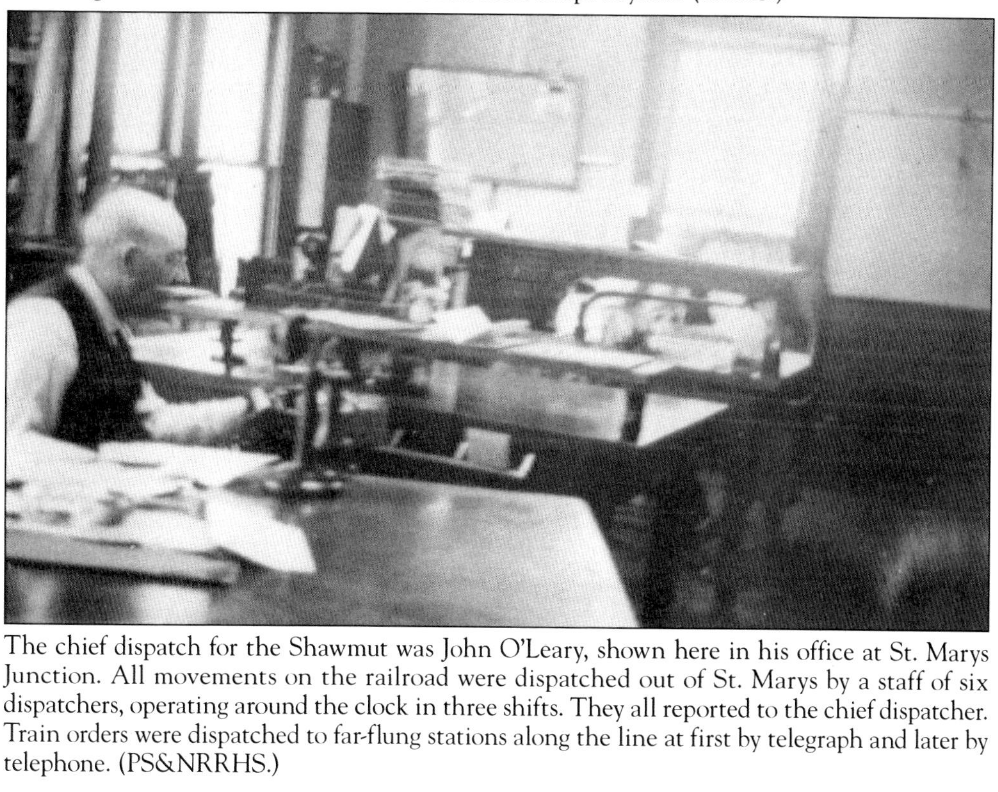

The chief dispatch for the Shawmut was John O'Leary, shown here in his office at St. Marys Junction. All movements on the railroad were dispatched out of St. Marys by a staff of six dispatchers, operating around the clock in three shifts. They all reported to the chief dispatcher. Train orders were dispatched to far-flung stations along the line at first by telegraph and later by telephone. (PS&NRRHS.)

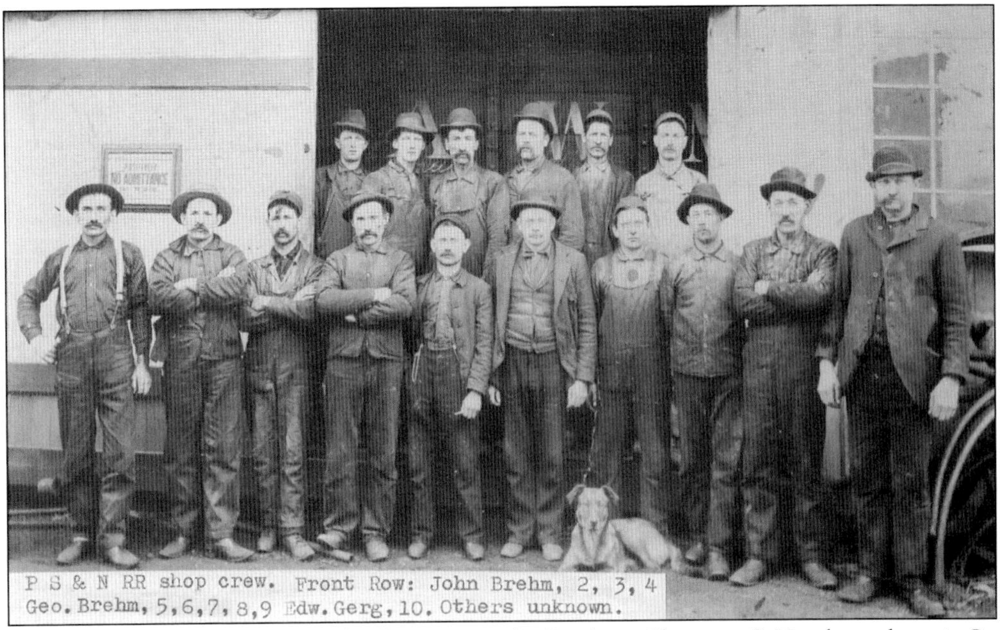

This undated photograph shows the shop crew at the Pittsburg, Shawmut & Northern shops in St. Marys, Pennsylvania. From left to right are (first row) John Brehm, two unidentified men, George Brehm, four unidentified men, Edward Gerg, and unidentified; (second row) all unidentified. The sign reads, "Positively no admittance. Call at office." (SMHS.)

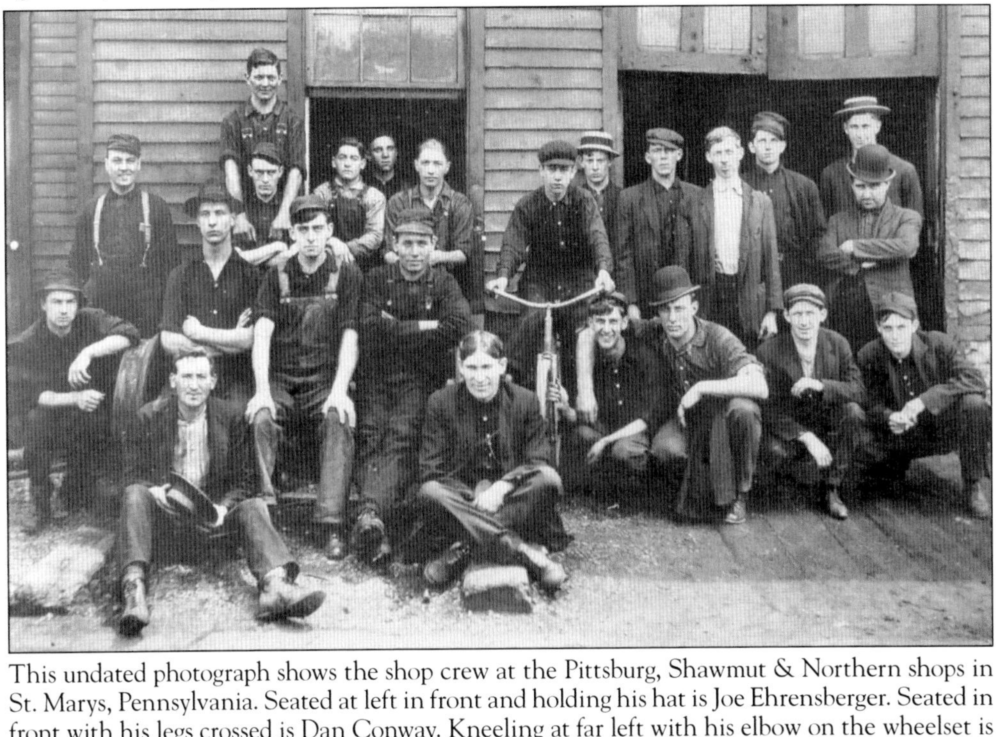

This undated photograph shows the shop crew at the Pittsburg, Shawmut & Northern shops in St. Marys, Pennsylvania. Seated at left in front and holding his hat is Joe Ehrensberger. Seated in front with his legs crossed is Dan Conway. Kneeling at far left with his elbow on the wheelset is Leo Werner. Kneeling at far right is Pat Higgins. Standing at far left is Taylor Garner. All others are unidentified. (SMHS.)

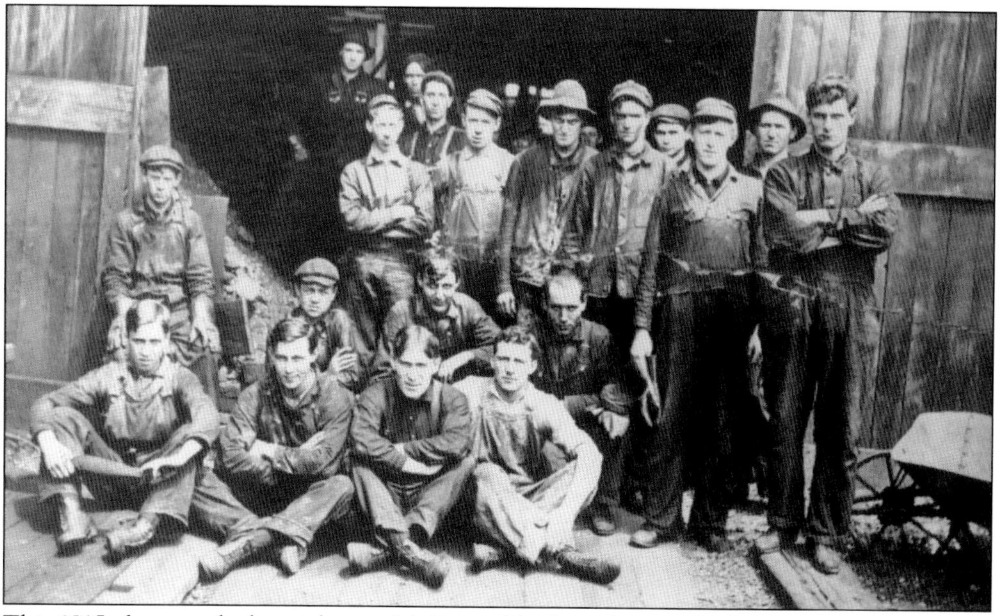

This 1915 photograph shows the machinists and boilermakers at the Depot Street shops in St. Marys, Pennsylvania. From left to right are (first row, seated) Joe Bauer, Ben Lawrence, Dan Conway, and Bert Keim; (second row, seated) Jesse Wallwork, Henry Ruhl, Richard Geyer, Scootie Herzing; (standing) Crusty Friedl, two unidentified men, Lawrence ?, ? Bauer, unidentified, Cy Geyer, Charles Simbeck, unidentified, ? Fehrenbach, Jake Rupp, and Henry Hoehn. (SMHS.)

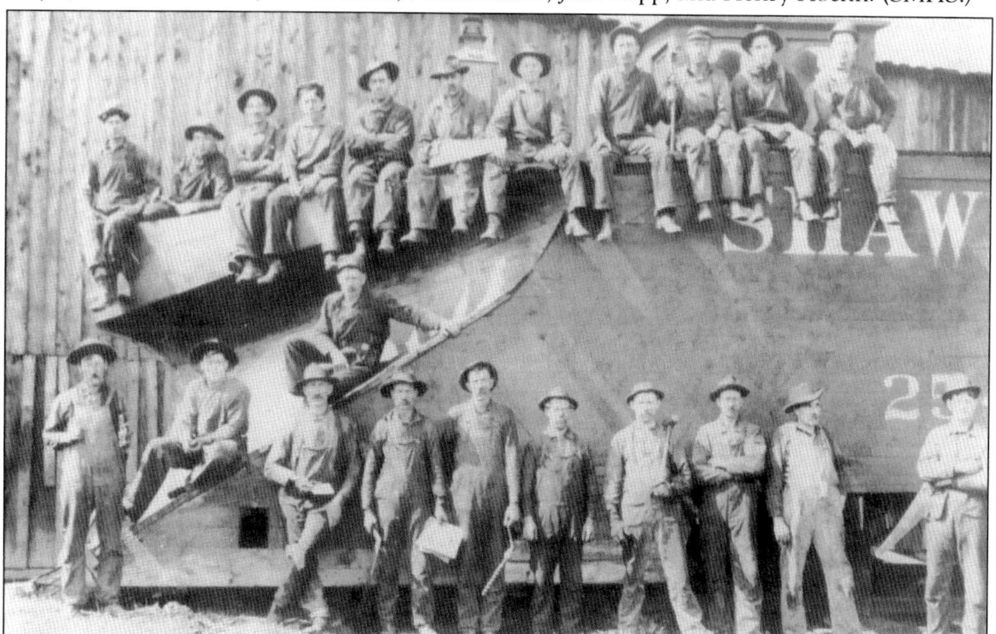

This photograph shows Shawmut shop workers posing on snowplow No. 254. From left to right are (first row) Frank Gerg, Joe Herzing, George Zwack, Red Herzing, Al Tyler, Oscar Willamee, John Schatz, Mike Proesl, George Cuneo, Al Hathorn, and Dave Williams; (second row) Tom Williams, Joe Glatt, Tony Gerg, unidentified, Frank Heath, John Kugler, Benny Frank, John Hoffman, unidentified, Frank Stauffer, and unidentified. (SMHS.)

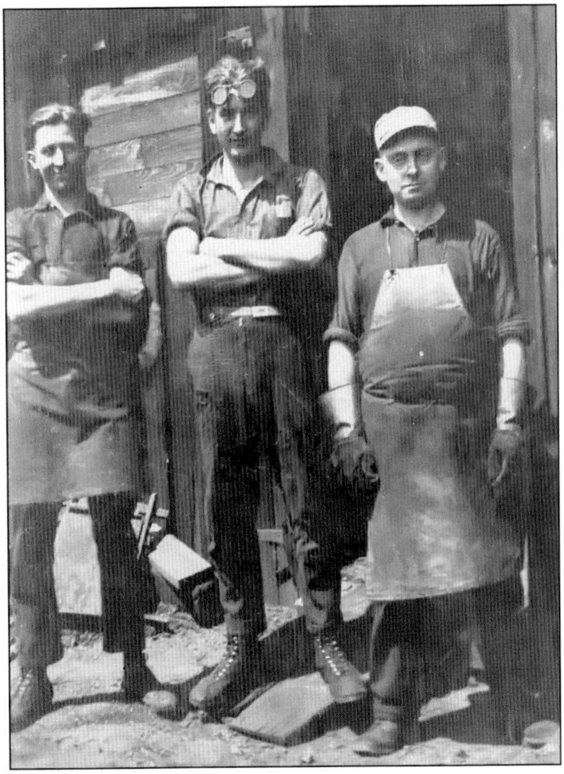

The engine shops of the Shawmut in St. Marys, Pennsylvania, had every trade necessary for repairing and rebuilding the line's locomotives. The blacksmiths were capable of fabricating nearly every replacement part that was needed. From left to right are Buck Nicklas (blacksmith helper), Tobo Gerg (blacksmith), and Frank Fodge (blacksmith). (SMHS.)

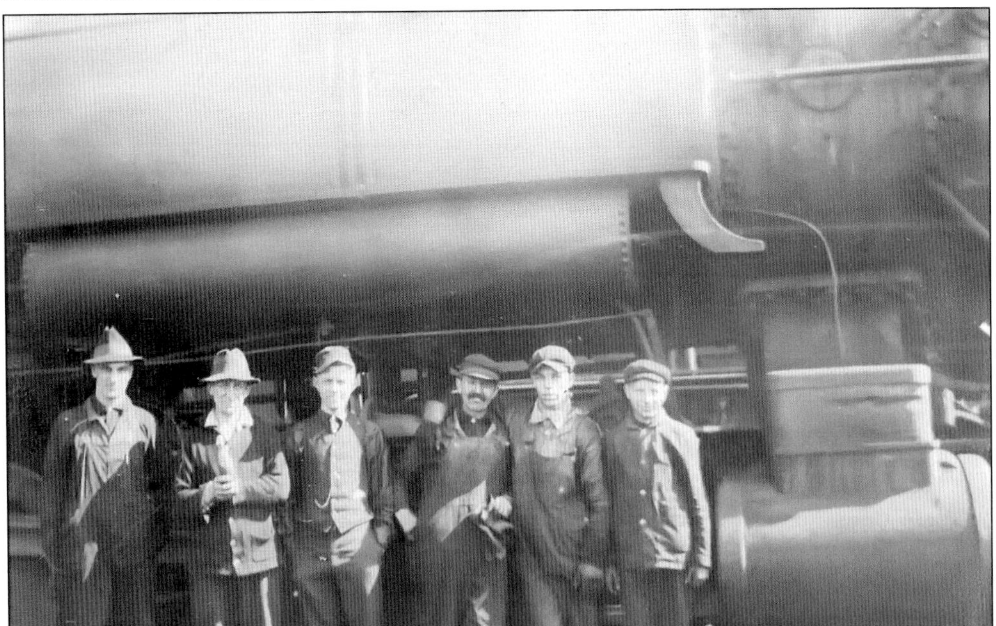

Shortly after the Shawmut constructed the Kersey Railroad, it purchased engine No. 98 to tackle the steep grade ascending out of the valley. This undated photograph shows the shop crew posing in front of No. 98. From left to right are Ed Eberl, Frank Daniels, two unidentified men, Amos Pontzer, and unidentified. (SMHS.)

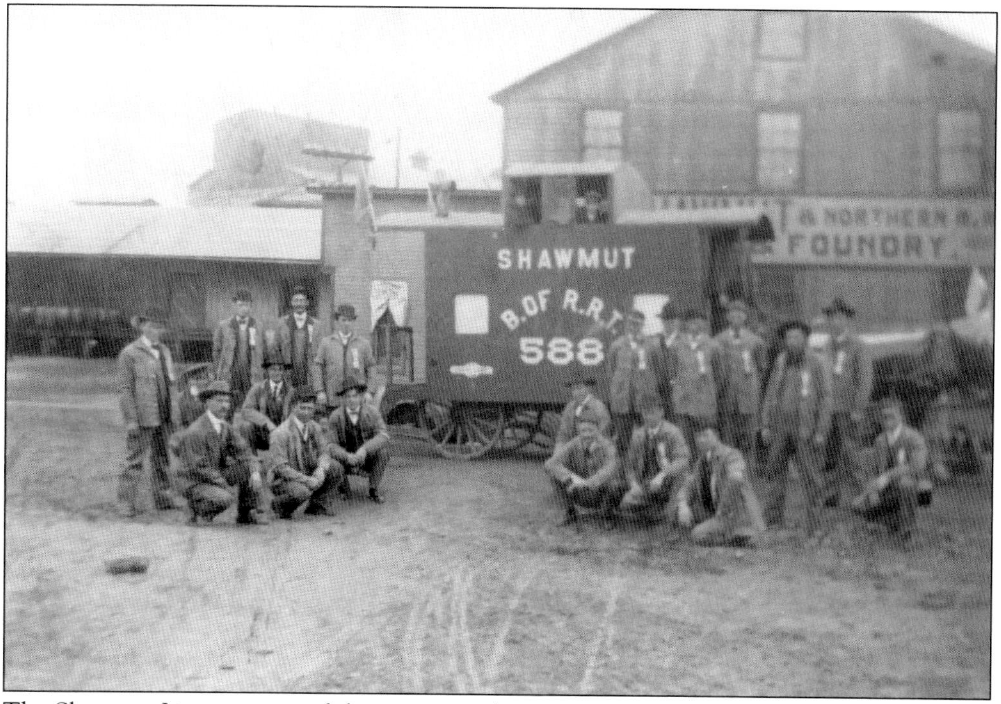

The Shawmut Line was one of the major employers in St. Marys, Pennsylvania. The railroad was always well represented in any parade staged within the borough. This photograph above, taken in the 1910s, shows the local shop crew posing in front of its horse-drawn float, a re-created caboose. "B. of R.R.T. 588" on the caboose stands for Brotherhood of Railroad Trainmen, Lodge 588, the union that represented these men. For the Fourth of July parade in 1935 pictured below, the crews built a one-third-size replica of a steel coal hopper. It was appropriately numbered 1776 and appears to have real chunks of coal on top of it. (Above, PS&NRRHS; below, SMHS.)

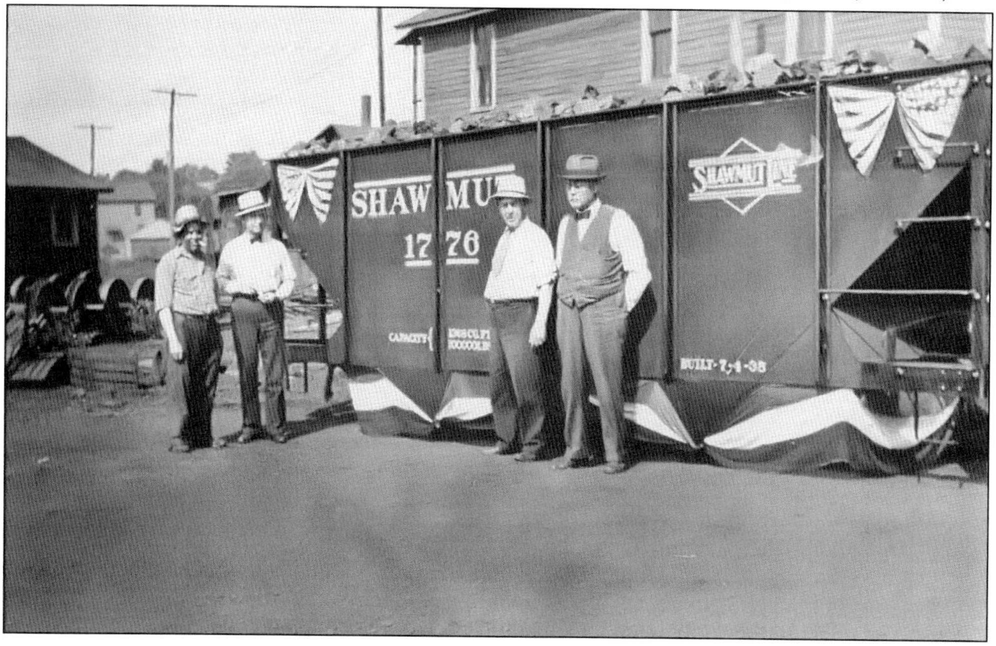

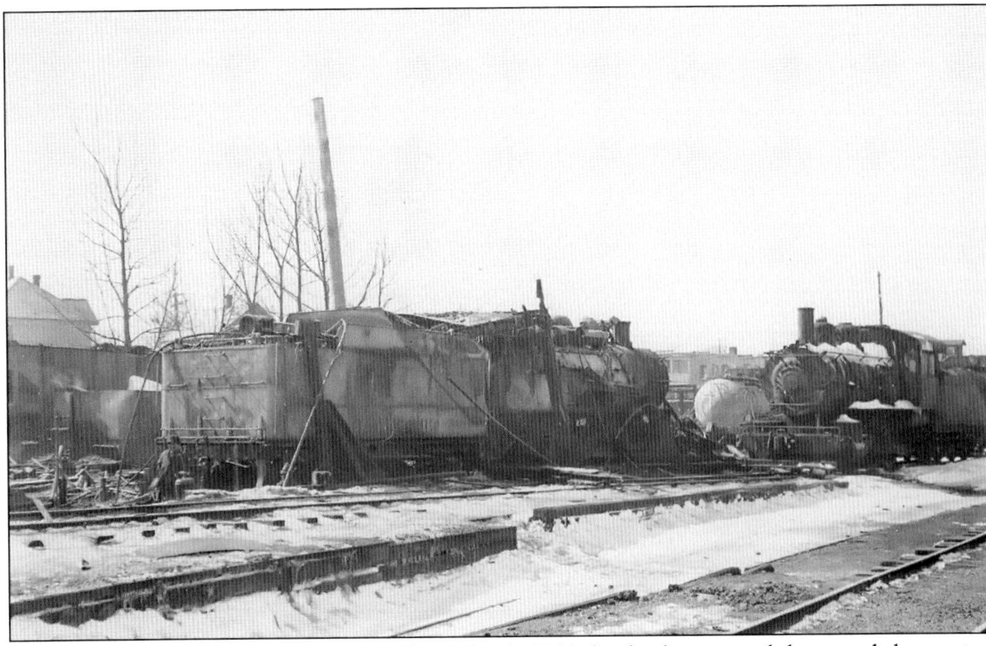

At about 5:00 p.m. on the afternoon of March 19, 1941, fire broke out and destroyed the engine house that stood on Depot Street in St. Marys, Pennsylvania. The cause was eventually traced to the explosion of an acetylene tank that was used for welding. The railroad lost three of its better locomotives, all of its tools, its shop equipment, and supplies. The estimated loss was put at $382,000. The photograph above shows engine No. 53 that was inside the engine house at the time of the fire; it was a total loss. Engine No. 23 (right) was on the siding next to the building; it was damaged but was repaired. The photograph below shows the remains of engines No. 70 and No. 74. (Both, SMHS.)

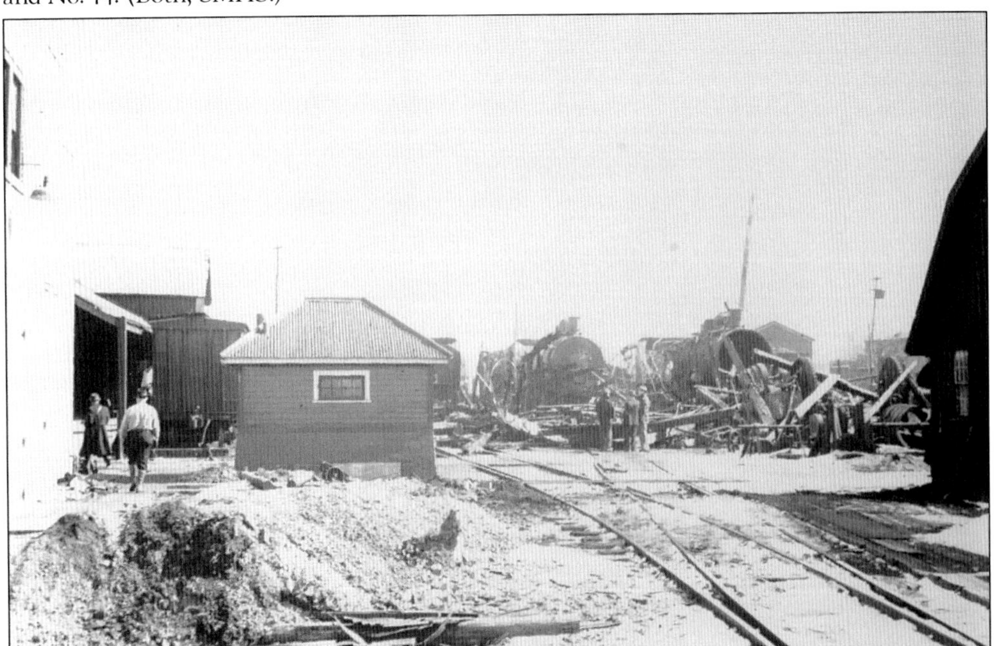

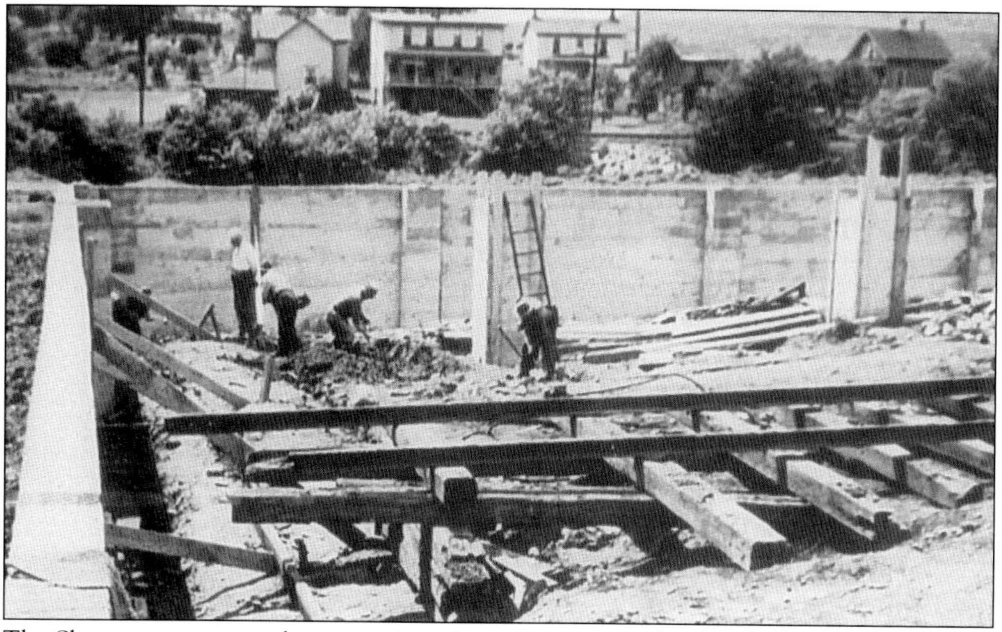

The Shawmut commenced construction of a replacement engine house in summer 1941. The decision was made to locate the new building near the other Shawmut facilities at St. Marys Junction. This eliminated the time and expense associated with ferrying the locomotives from the Junction to the Depot Street shops. This photograph above, taken by Walter Bickmire in 1941, shows the laying of the foundation for the new building. The undated photograph below, with a view looking east, shows the completed engine house (at lower left) at St. Marys Junction. Behind the new engine house is the woodworking shop; the caboose track is behind that. In the center are the yard office and the dispatcher's office. At far right is the coaling dock. (Both, SMHS.)

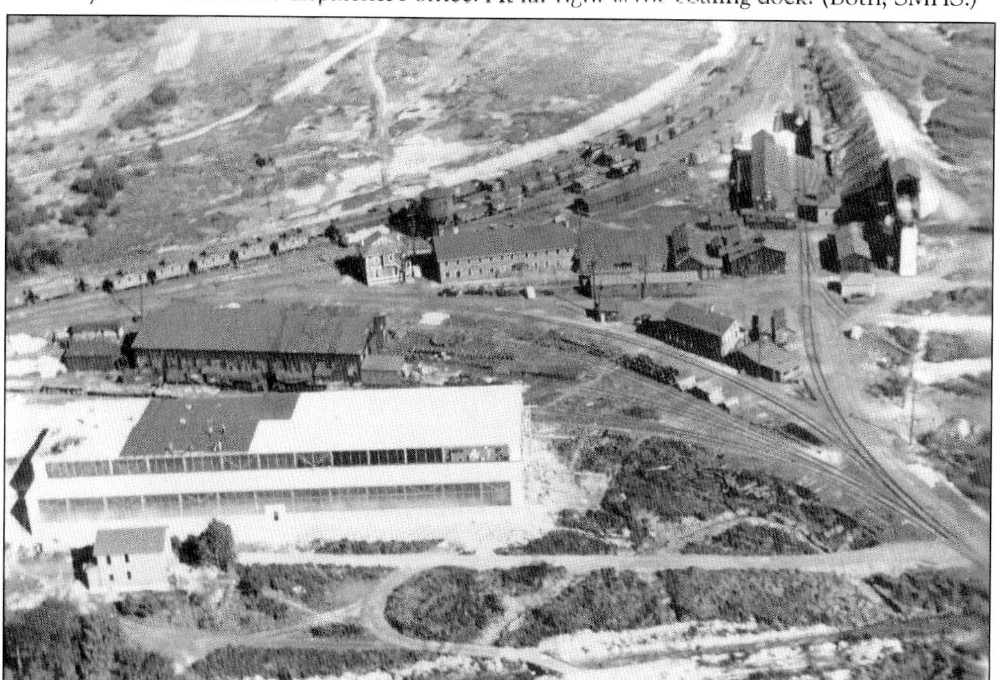

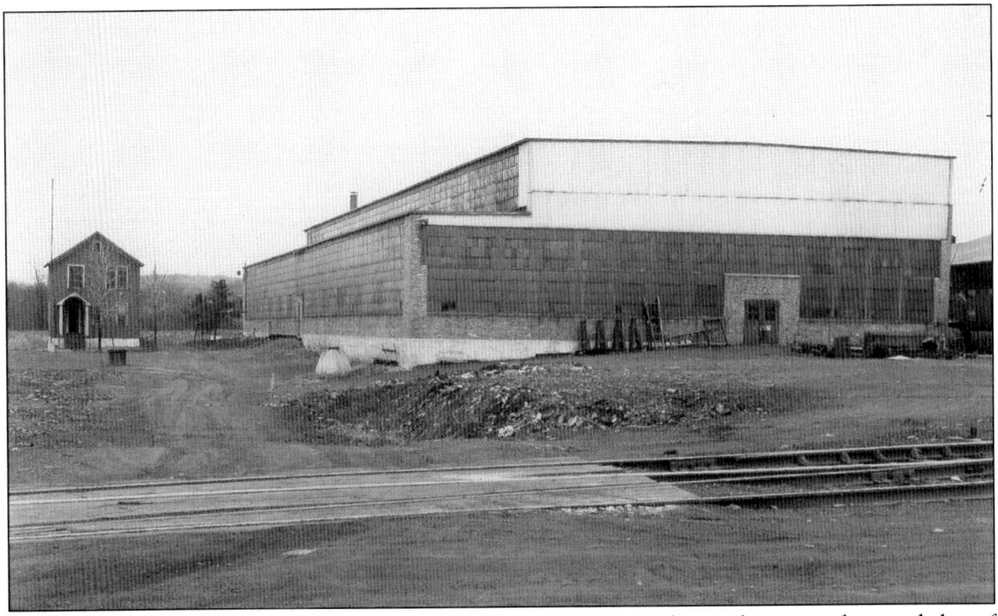

The replacement engine house in St. Marys, Pennsylvania, was located next to the north leg of the wye at St. Marys Junction. The superstructure was purchased secondhand. It was originally the Communications Building, also known as the Bell Telephone Building, at the 1939–1940 New York World's Fair. The building at left is the office of Fred E. Gerg, the superintendent of Motive Power. (SMHS.)

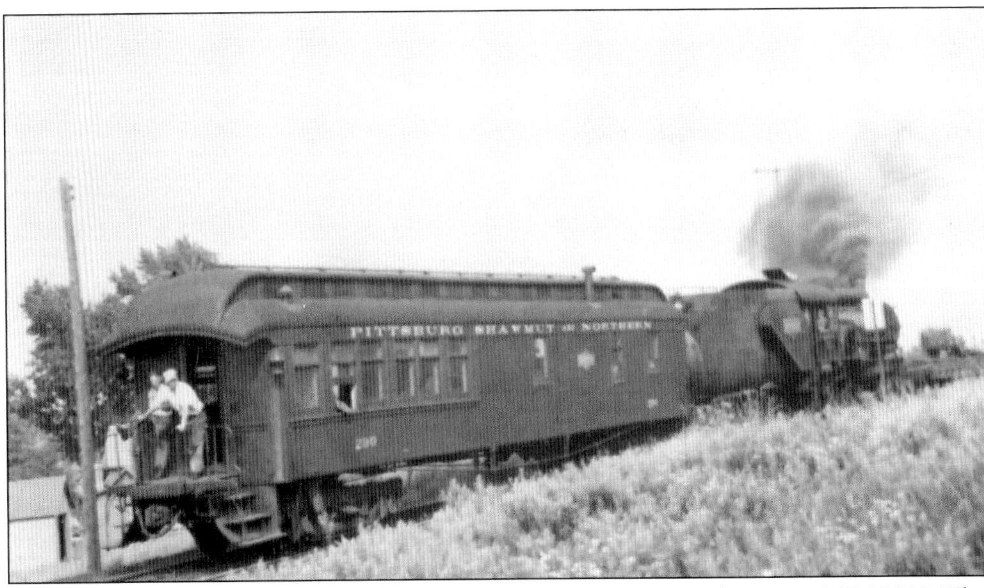

The Shawmut main line crossed Brussels Street in St. Marys, Pennsylvania, at MP 126.12. This summer 1947 photograph shows engine No. 72 and combine No. 290 on the scrap train approaching the Brussels Street crossing. The trackage within the borough of St. Marys was not scrapped; it was purchased and operated by the Pennsylvania Railroad. (SMHS.)

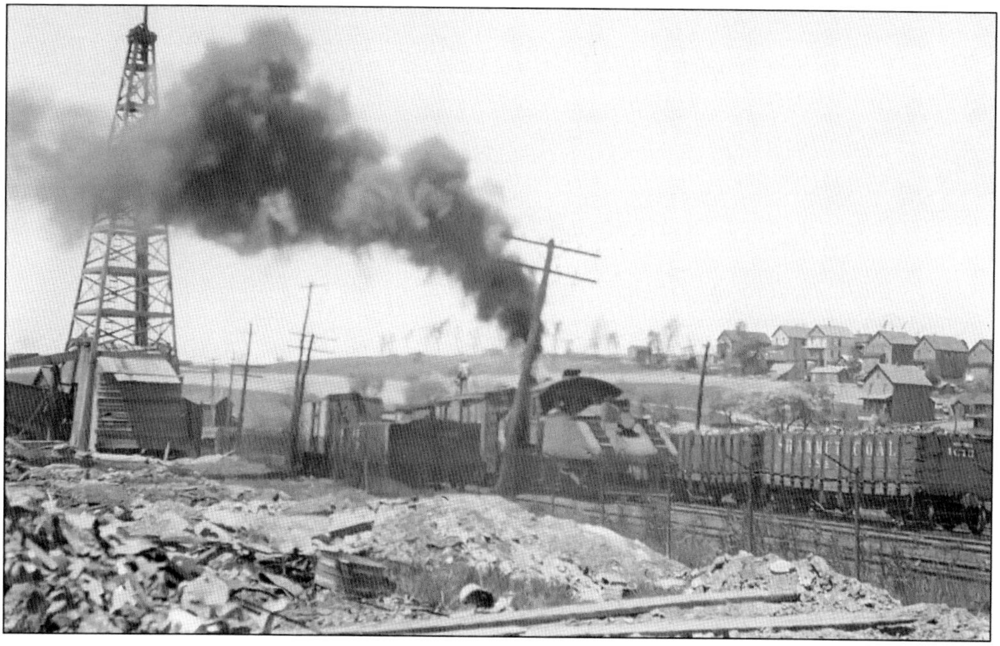

In 2015, the Pittsburg, Shawmut & Northern Railroad Historical Society obtained two rare, large-format, glass plate negatives from which these photographs were produced. These images, from 1920, were taken from the Speer Carbon Company property in St. Marys, Pennsylvania. This location, just east of the Theresia Street crossing, is at MP 125.8. The photograph above shows one of the 0-6-0 switch engines, either No. 22 or 23, shunting cars in the yard. The oil derrick (left) is one of many oil wells that were located along the Shawmut main line from here south to Detsch. The photograph below shows one of the ubiquitous Consolidations pushing hard against caboose No. 187, assisting a southbound up the grade to Paine Junction. (Both, PS&NRRHS.)

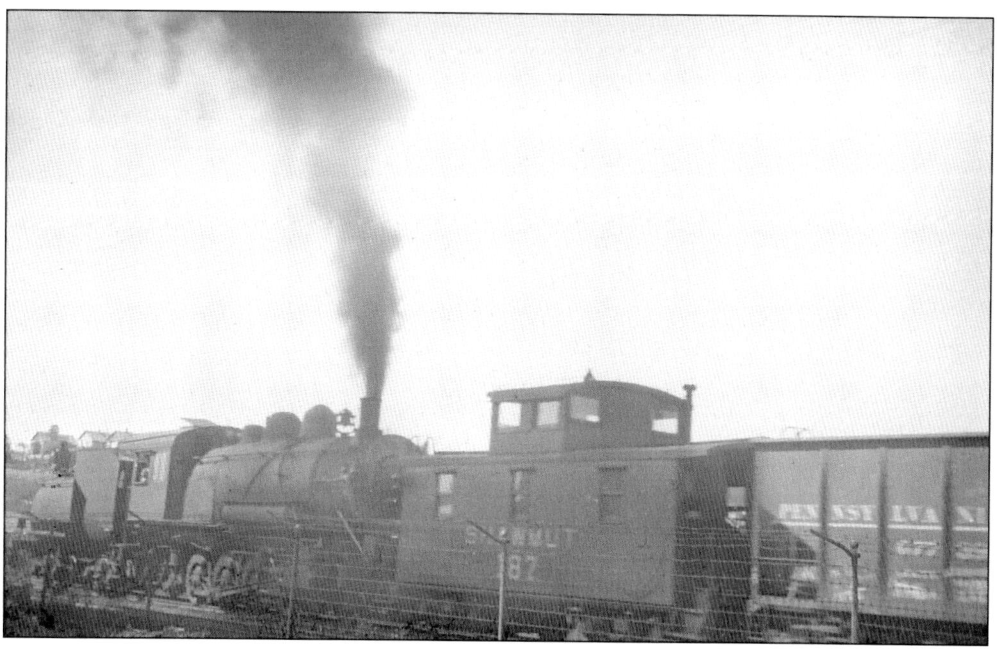

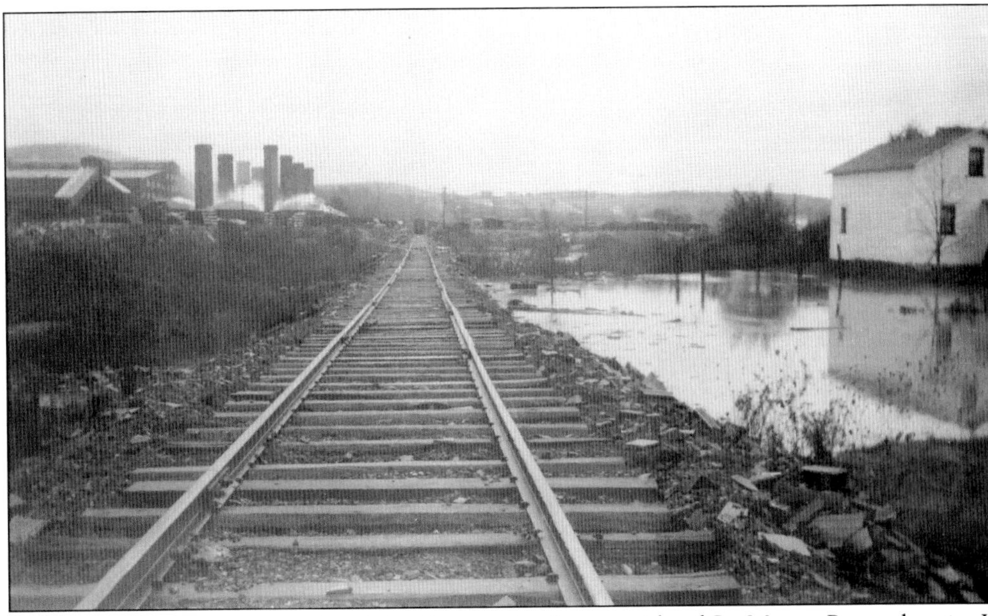

The Fireproof spur was an industrial siding on the far east side of St. Marys, Pennsylvania. It branched off the main line at MP 126.16 to serve the St. Marys Sewer Pipe Company and the Pennsylvania Fireproof Company. The view in this undated photograph looks west, with the St. Marys Sewer Pipe Company on the left. (SMHS.)

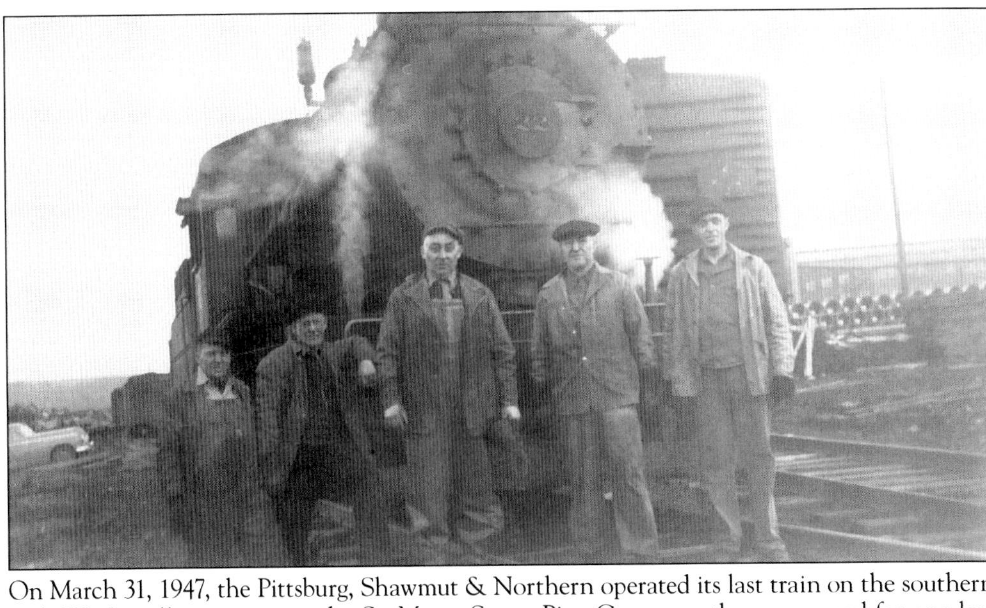

On March 31, 1947, the Pittsburg, Shawmut & Northern operated its last train on the southern end. While collecting cars at the St. Marys Sewer Pipe Company, the crew posed for one last photograph. From left to right are Dennis "Dewey" Moyer, Harry McGill, Ed Kraus, Larry Bucher, and William Friedl. (SMHS.)

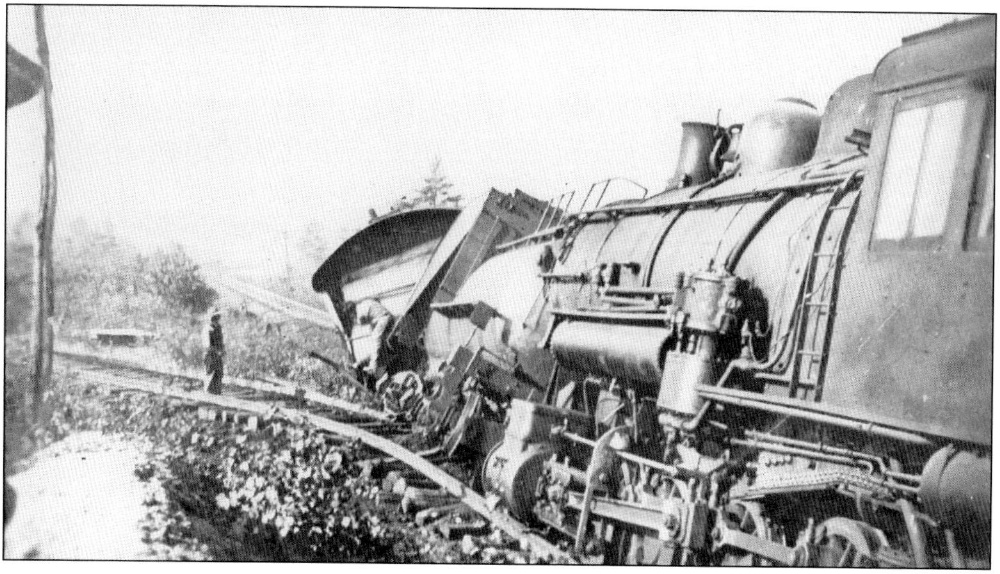

The top of the 1.9 percent grade that began at Theresia Street in St. Marys, Pennsylvania, leveled out at the St. Michael Road crossing at MP 127.6. The station at this crossing was known as Detsch. Just south of Detsch, at MP 128.5, was the McCullough Spur. The location of this switch was known officially by the railroad as Averyville and as "Star Switch" by the crews. This spur served the mine of the Star Coal & Clay Company as well as the McCullough No. 1 mine. These undated photographs show the result of vandals having thrown the switch, which caused a wreck of a southbound doubleheader. One can see above how the main line continues to climb the grade toward Paine Junction. Big Hook No. 244, seen below, works to put engine No. 75 back on the rails. (Both, SMI IS.)

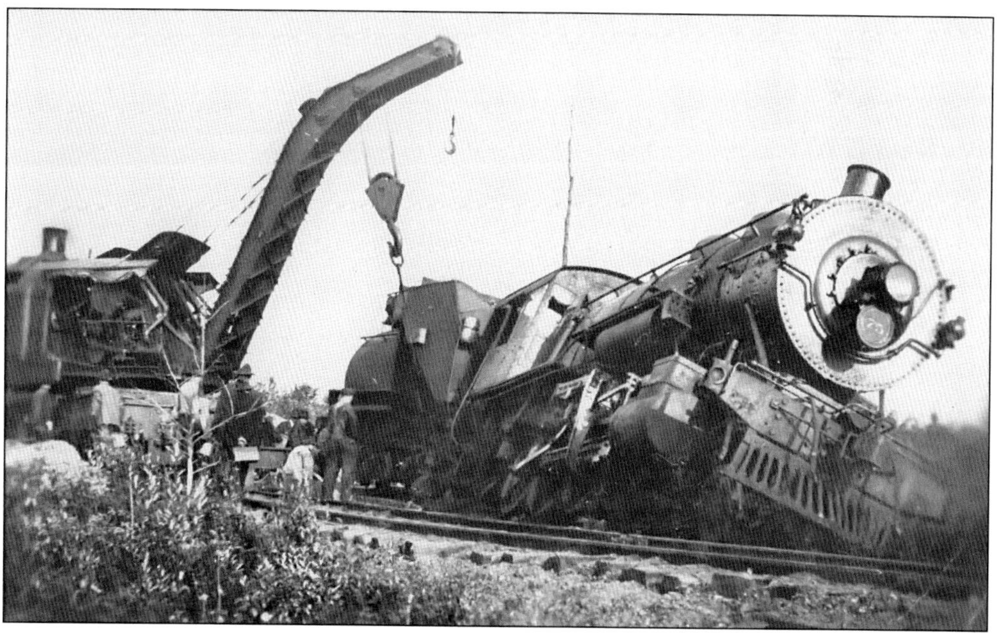

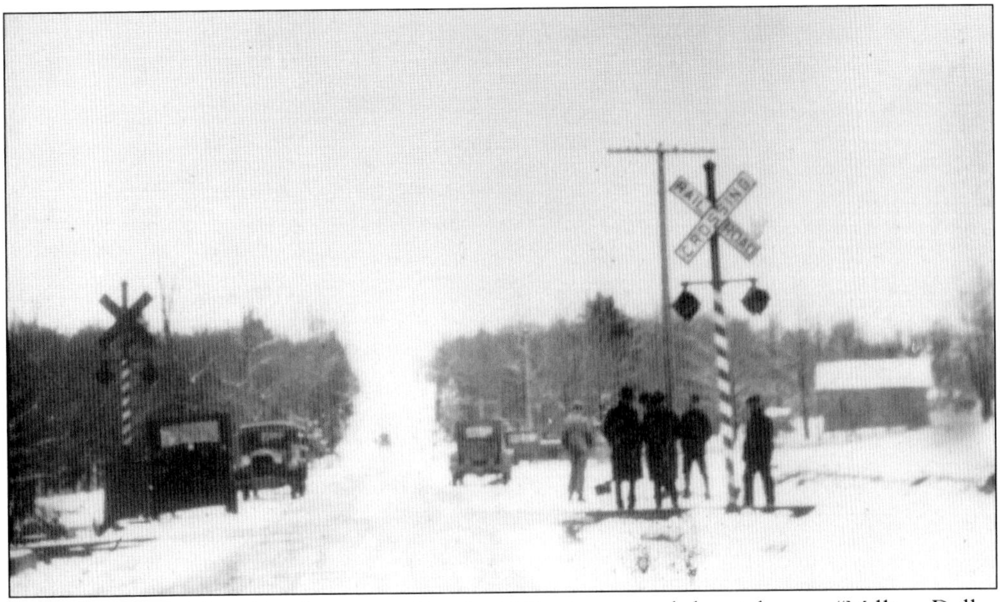

When South St. Marys Road was paved in the 1930s, it received the nickname "Million Dollar Highway." The highway, part of Pennsylvania Route 255, crossed the Shawmut main line at MP 131.5. The view in this photograph, from about 1930, is looking south and shows the automatic crossing signals that protected the crossing. There were a total of six crossings on the Shawmut that were equipped with automatic signals. (SMHS.)

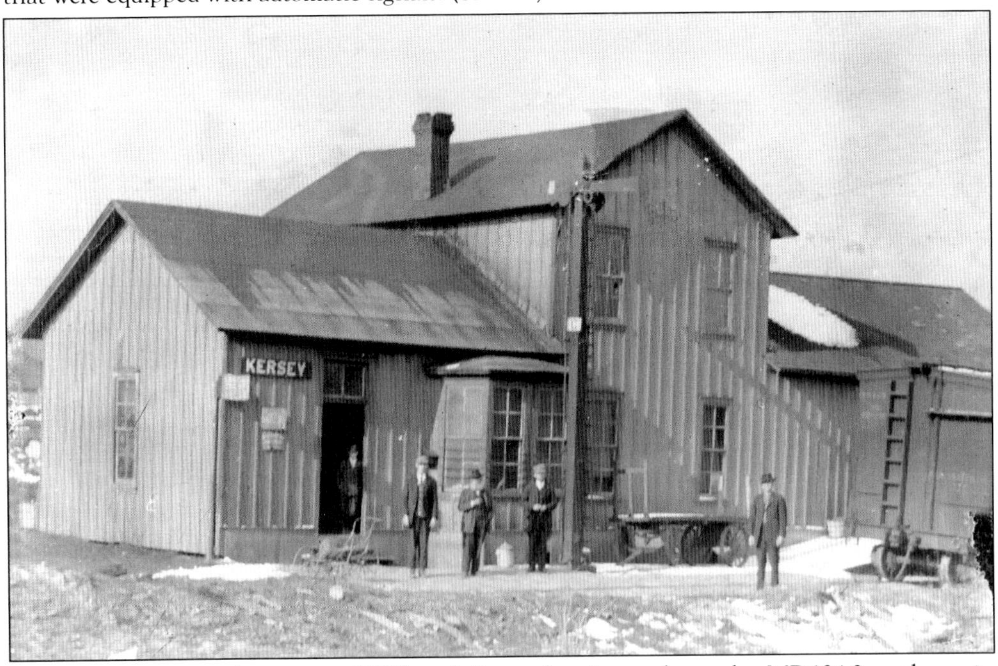

The hamlet of Kersey (pronounced KER-zee), Pennsylvania, was located at MP 134.0 on the main line. The wholly owned Kersey Railroad branched off the Shawmut main at Paine Junction, located at MP 132.4. The Kersey Railroad provided access to the Shawmut mines located in Byrnedale, Weedville, Force, and Tyler, Pennsylvania. This undated photograph shows the station at Kersey; its telegraph call letter was "C." (SMHS.)

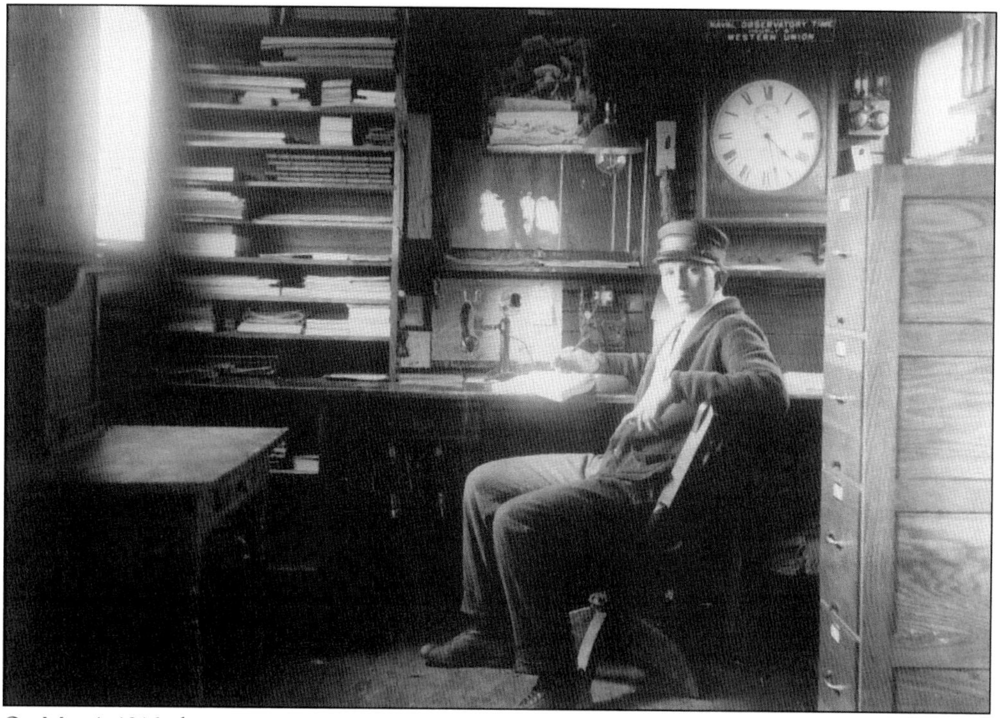

On May 1, 1916, the station agent manning the depot in Byrnedale, Pennsylvania, was 19-year-old William Foster. Although the telephone is now in use, the telegraph is still very much working "behind the scenes." The text above the clock on the wall reads, "Naval Observatory Time, hourly by Western Union," which came in automatically via telegraph. (SMHS.)

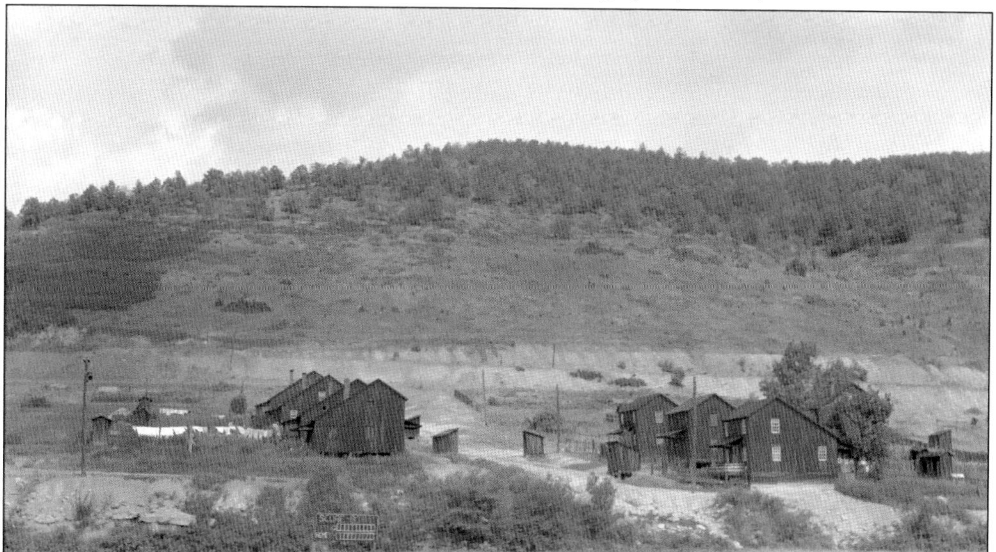

The hamlet of Byrnedale, Pennsylvania, located at MP 140.5 on the Kersey Railroad, was named after the first president of the railroad, John Byrne. All of the houses, churches, and the company store were owned by the Shawmut Commercial Company, in this typical coal-mining company town. This photograph, taken in September 1940, shows the typical company houses that the miners and their families lived in. (Library of Congress.)

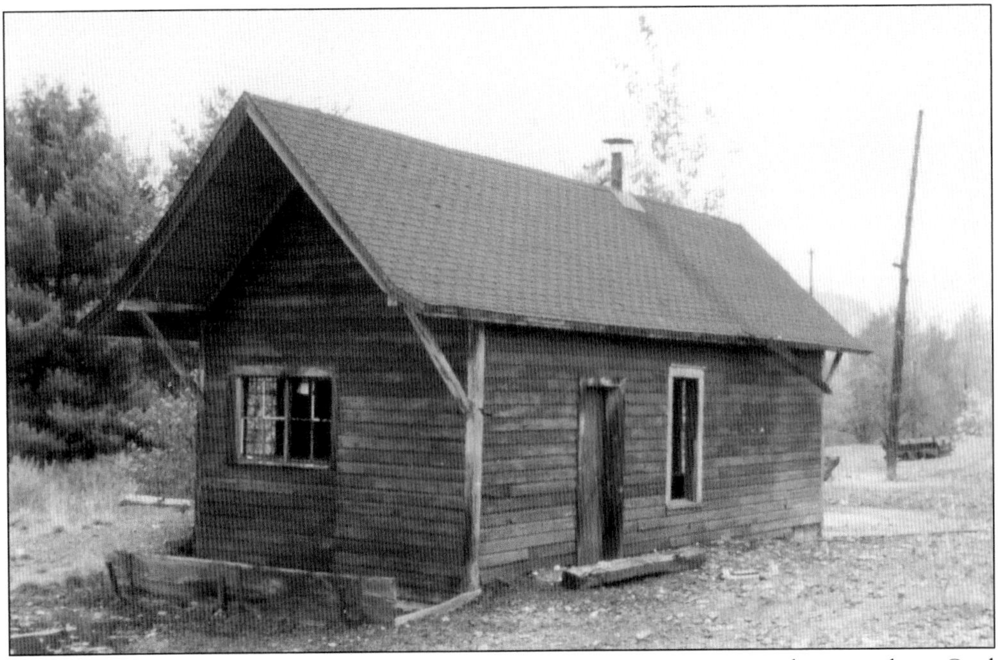

The depot at Brandy Camp, Pennsylvania, was located at MP 143.4 on the main line. Coal production and car loadings were so great at the No. 5 mine that the Shawmut erected this depot right in front of the mine. The view in this photograph, taken in the 1980s, is looking north. The Shawmut main line used to pass on the far side of the building. (SMHS.)

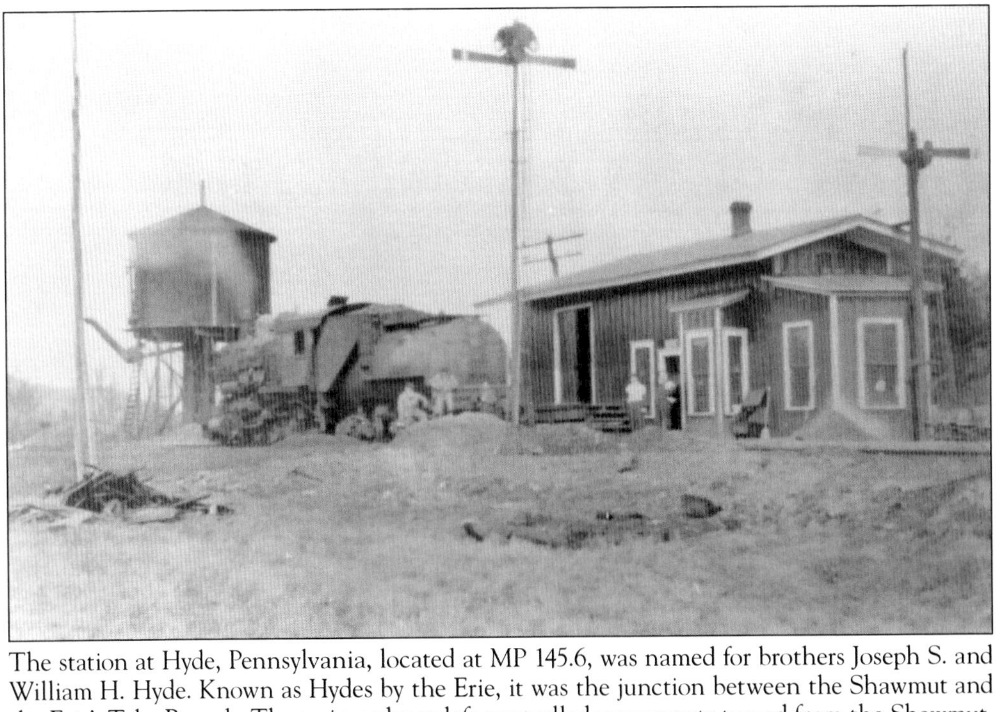

The station at Hyde, Pennsylvania, located at MP 145.6, was named for brothers Joseph S. and William H. Hyde. Known as Hydes by the Erie, it was the junction between the Shawmut and the Erie's Toby Branch. The train order at left controlled movements to and from the Shawmut. The train order at right controlled movements along the Erie's Toby Branch. (PS&NRRHS.)

Three

Motive Power and Rolling Stock

Most of the Shawmut's locomotives numbered below 40 were inherited from its predecessor lines. These tended to be the lighter locomotives of the American (4-4-0) and Mogul (2-6-0) wheel arrangements. They were typically assigned to passenger trains and finished their careers assigned to work trains.

Exceptions to the above statement were the two 0-6-0 yard switchers, Nos. 22 and 23. They were purchased new by the Shawmut in 1903 and 1905, respectively. Having all 70 tons on 51-inch drivers, they were nearly as powerful as the larger 2-8-0s. During most of their lives, one was assigned to Angelica and one was assigned to St. Marys.

Nos. 40–43 were "light" Consolidations (2-8-0s) purchased in 1899 by the Shawmut; Nos. 44 and 45, of a similar design, were inherited from the Buffalo, St. Marys & Southwestern.

The balance of locomotives (Nos. 50–75) were "heavy" Consolidations purchased from the Baldwin Locomotive Works between 1904 and 1911. These were the workhorses of the PS&N, many lasting until the very end.

There were two "monsters," relative to the other locomotives, that roamed the Shawmut. The first was No. 81, a Decapod (2-10-0) that was purchased secondhand from the Erie. This purchase was made to replace the several locomotives that were lost in the 1942 St. Marys engine house fire. The second was No. 98, a Santa Fe (2-10-2) that was purchased new from Baldwin. Neither of these locomotives was well liked. Their longer wheelbases were damaging to the Shawmut's light track work. As a result, the Consolidations were the mainstay of road power on the Shawmut.

In March 1925, the Shawmut purchased No. 90, a Model 75 gasoline railcar from the Brill Company of Philadelphia, Pennsylvania. By August, a second Model 75, No. 91, was also ordered. Affectionately named "Hoodlebugs" by crews and passengers alike, these self-contained passenger cars cut operating costs in half from that of the traditional steam-powered passenger trains.

The balance of this chapter deals with the freight, passenger, maintenance, and service cars operated by the Shawmut.

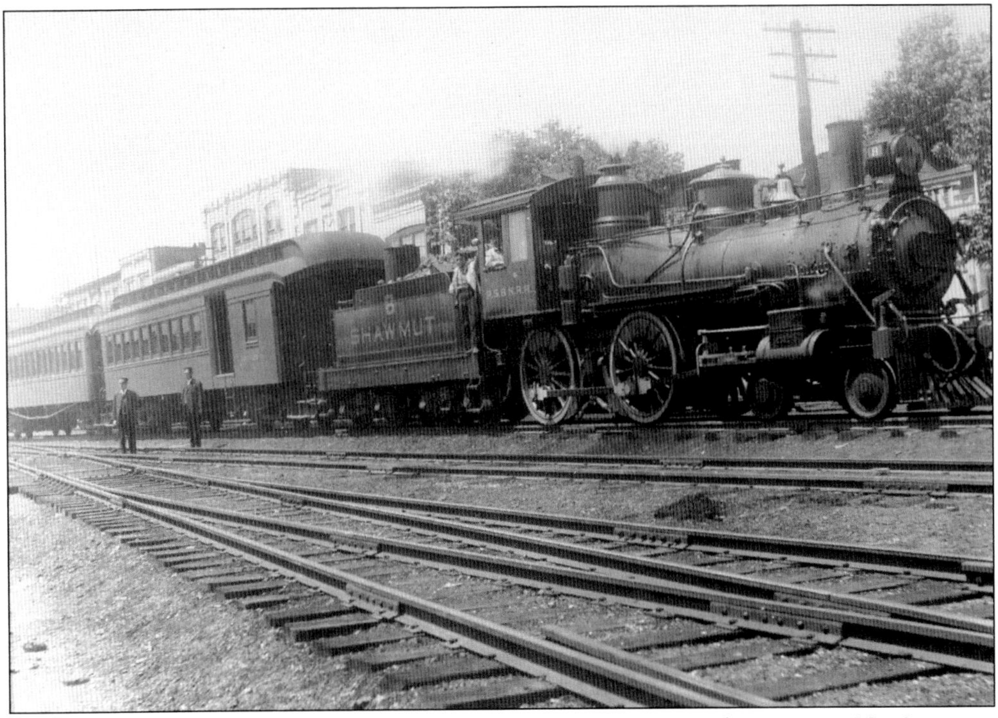

Taken about 1911, this photograph shows Pittsburg, Shawmut & Northern engine No. 8 waiting to depart from the Pennsylvania Railroad Station on Erie Avenue in St. Marys, Pennsylvania. The view in this photograph is looking north with Erie Avenue behind the train. The tracks in the foreground led to the Pennsylvania Railroad freight house. (SMHS.)

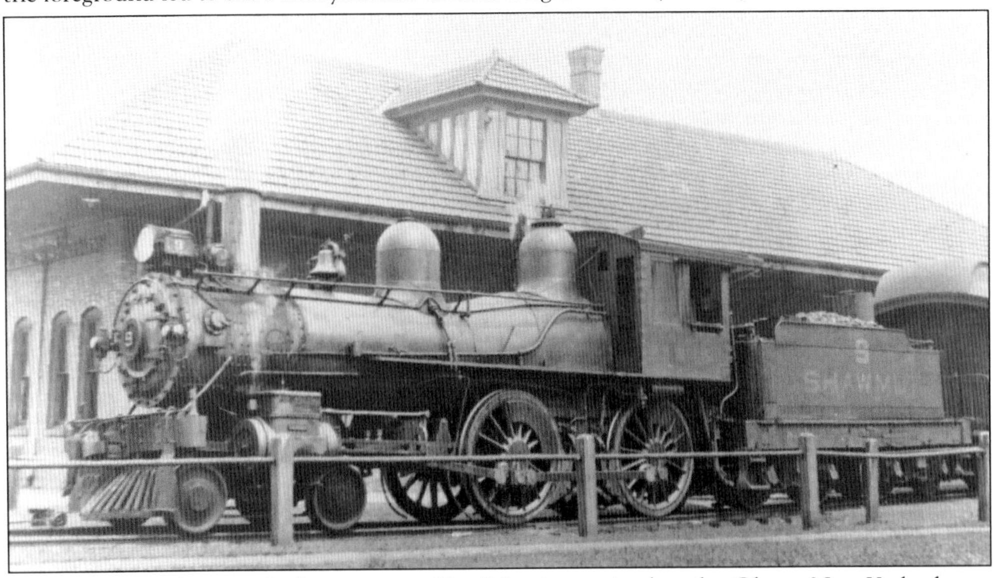

This July 1921 photograph shows engine No. 9 having arrived at the Olean, New York, depot. This locomotive was built by the Cooke Locomotive and Machine Works in Paterson, New Jersey, in 1886 for the Central New York & Western Railroad. The locomotive was scrapped in March 1928, by which time passenger serviced on the Shawmut had been replaced by the Brill gasoline motor cars called the Hoodlebugs. (PS&NRRHS.)

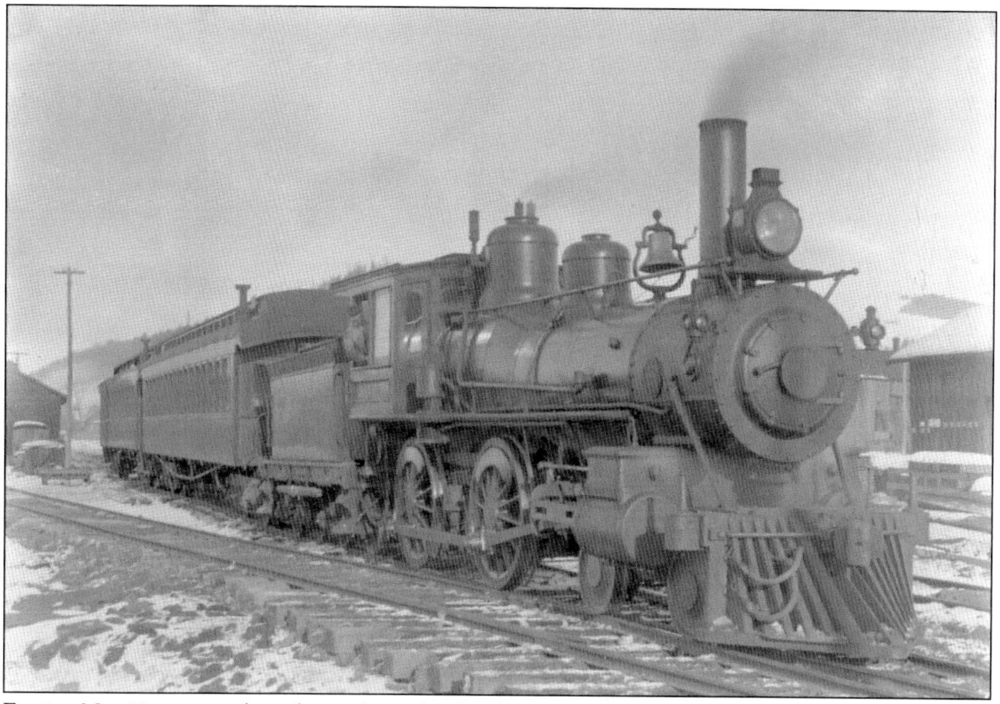

Engine No. 11 was purchased new from the Cooke Locomotive and Machine Works in Paterson, New Jersey, in 1889 by the Central New York & Western. Seen here sometime in the first decade of the 20th century, this handsome locomotive is leading a passenger train at Bolivar, New York. It was destroyed on September 22, 1912, in a wreck at Nile, New York. (PS&NRRHS.)

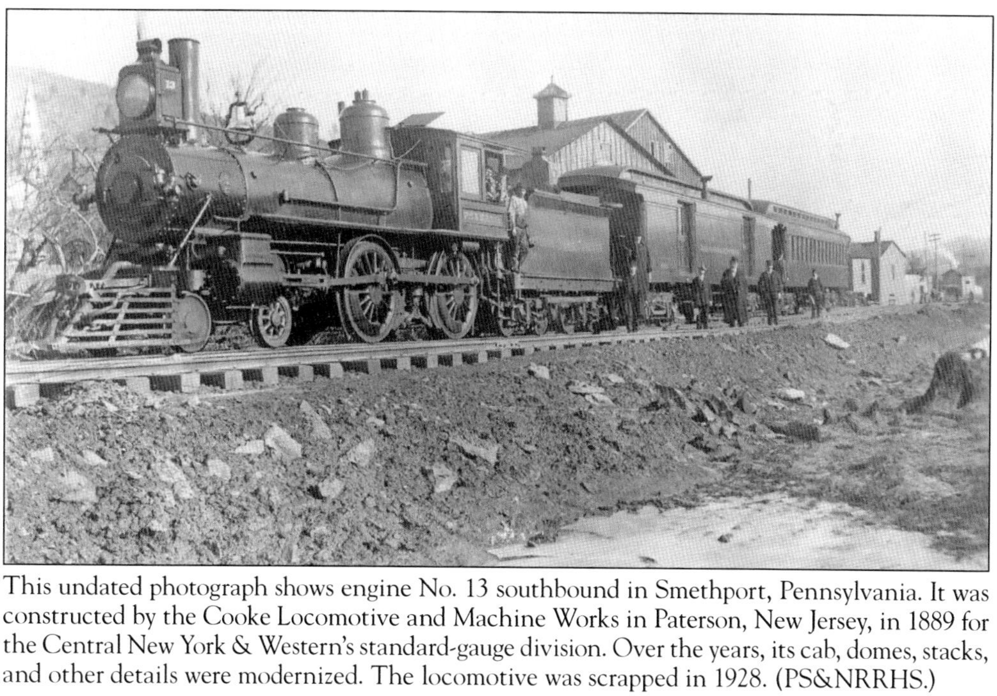

This undated photograph shows engine No. 13 southbound in Smethport, Pennsylvania. It was constructed by the Cooke Locomotive and Machine Works in Paterson, New Jersey, in 1889 for the Central New York & Western's standard-gauge division. Over the years, its cab, domes, stacks, and other details were modernized. The locomotive was scrapped in 1928. (PS&NRRHS.)

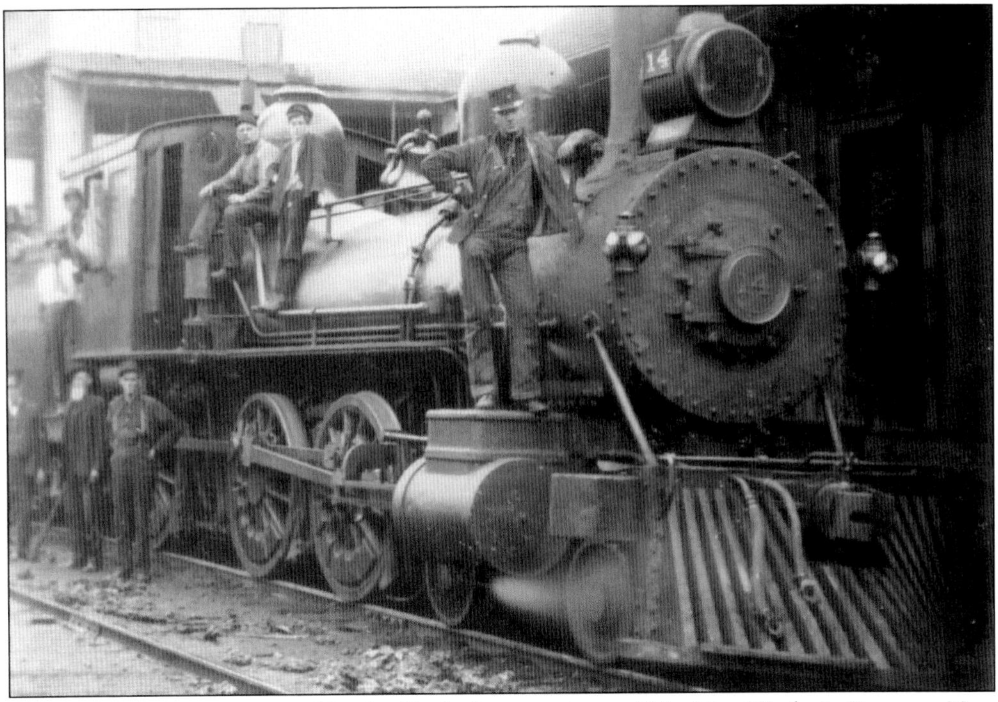

Engine No. 14 was constructed by the Cooke Locomotive and Machine Works in Paterson, New Jersey, in 1886 as Rochester, Hornellsville & Lackawanna No. 23. It was retired in 1916 and became the boiler for the coal hoist at Angelica, New York. This undated photograph was taken in Shawmut, Pennsylvania. (PS&NRRHS.)

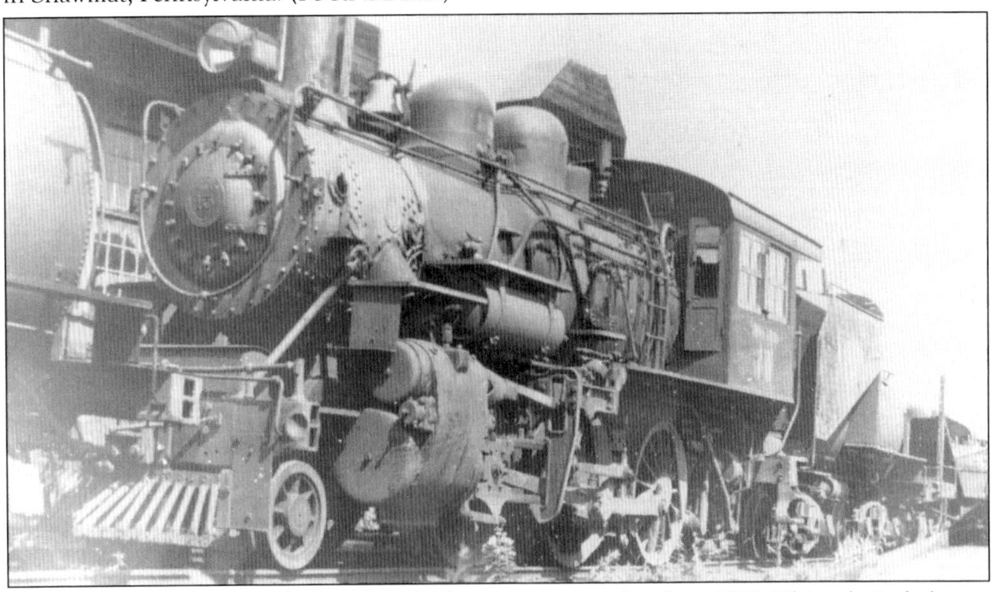

The second locomotive to be numbered 15 was constructed in late 1913. This relatively heavy 2-6-0 had 63-inch drivers and was designed as a dual-duty passenger and freight locomotive. Unfortunately, it was too light for freight service and too heavy to be economical on passenger runs. This 1935 photograph shows it in dead storage in Angelica, New York. It would be scrapped the very next year. (PS&NRRHS.)

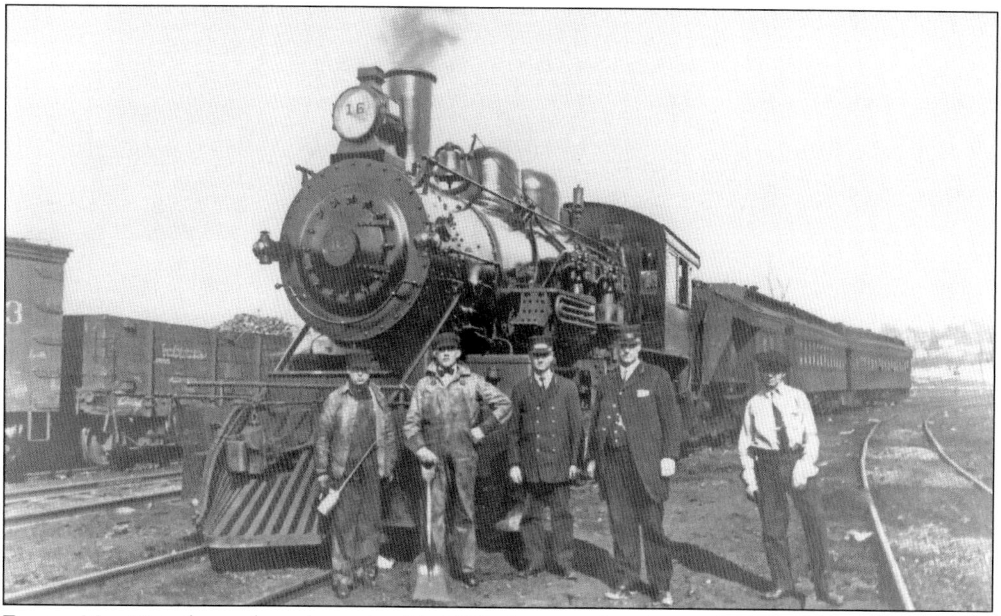

Engine No. 16 is shown brand-new in this 1913 photograph taken in St. Marys, Pennsylvania. It was ordered from the Baldwin Locomotives Works by the Shawmut, along with No. 17, to replace old or wrecked locomotives. Pictured here are, from left to right, Brownie Palmer, Jimmy Brynelle, Tom O'Conner, ? Rice, and Lew Storm. Engine No. 16 was scrapped in 1936. (PS&NRRHS.)

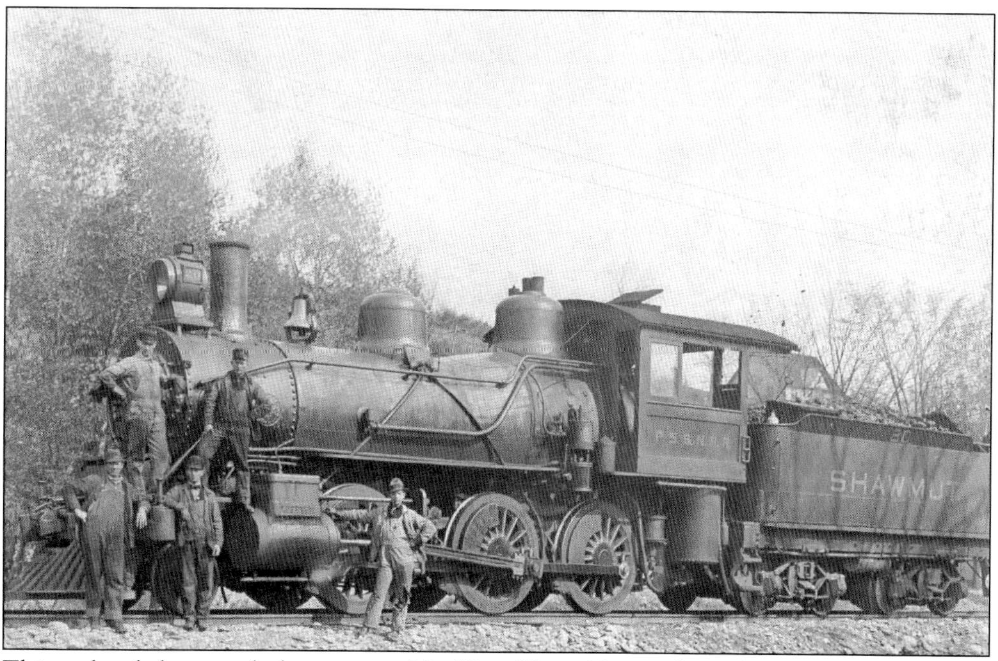

This undated photograph shows engine No. 20 at Olean, New York. At far left is Lawrence Kraus of Brookville, Pennsylvania. This 2-6-0 locomotive was built in 1897 by the Brooks Locomotive Works in Dunkirk, New York, for the Buffalo, St. Marys & Southwestern as its No. 5. The locomotive was scrapped in 1929. (SMHS.)

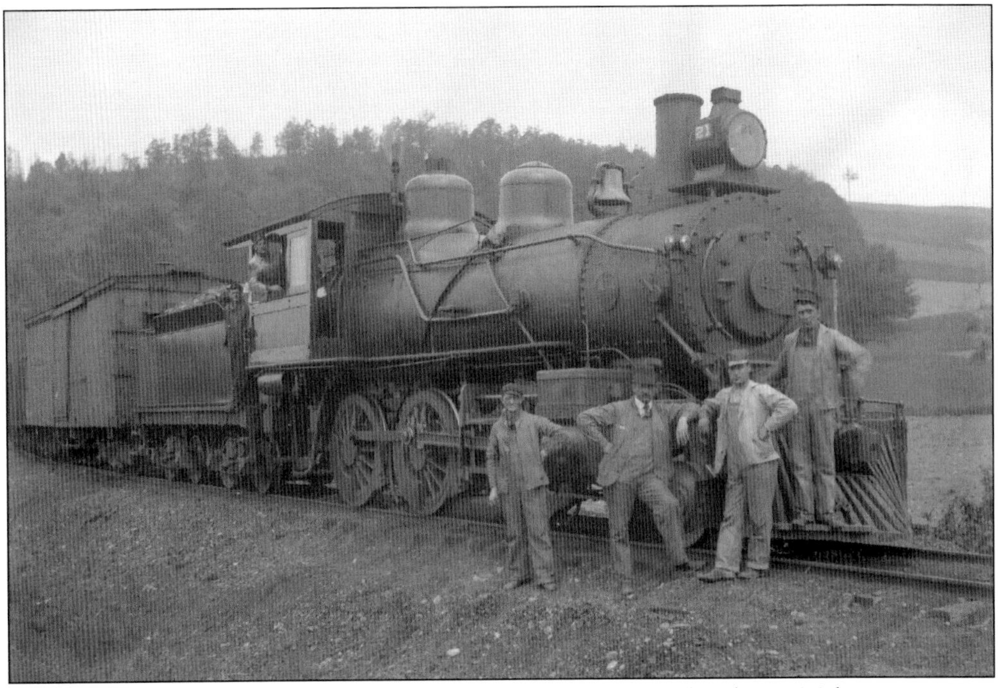

This 1901 photograph shows engine No. 21 near Ceres, New York. This 2-6-0 locomotive was built in 1897 by the Brooks Locomotive Works in Dunkirk, New York, for the Buffalo, St. Marys & Southwestern as its No. 11. It weighed approximately 55 tons and had 57-inch drivers. The locomotive was scrapped in 1924. (SMHS.)

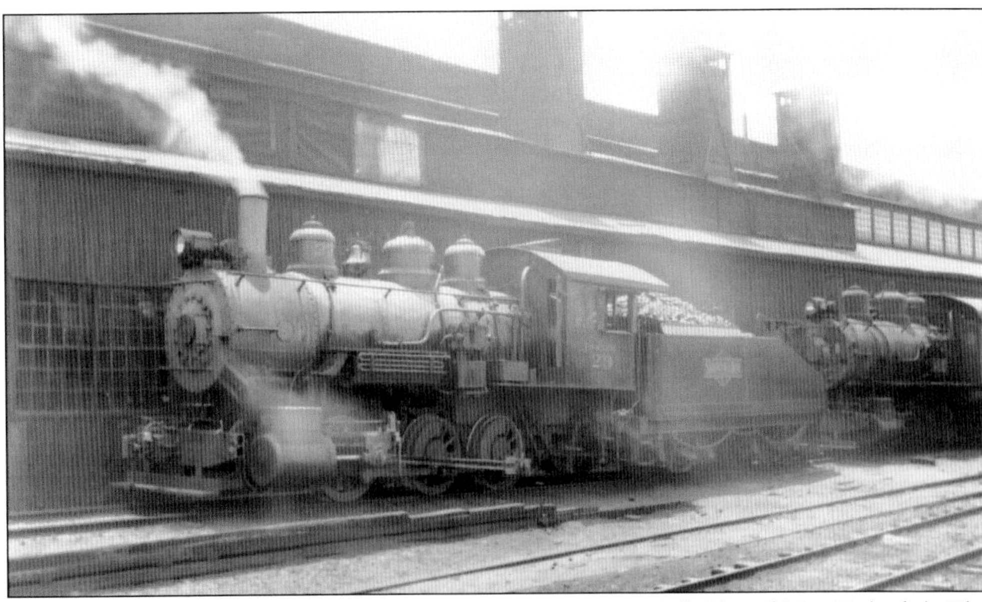

The two "yard goats" employed on the Shawmut were No. 23 (left) and No. 22 (right). The locomotives were built by the Baldwin Locomotive Works in 1905 and 1903, respectively. They were both of the 0-6-0 wheel arrangement. This undated photograph was taken next to the engine house in St. Marys, Pennsylvania. (PS&NRRHS.)

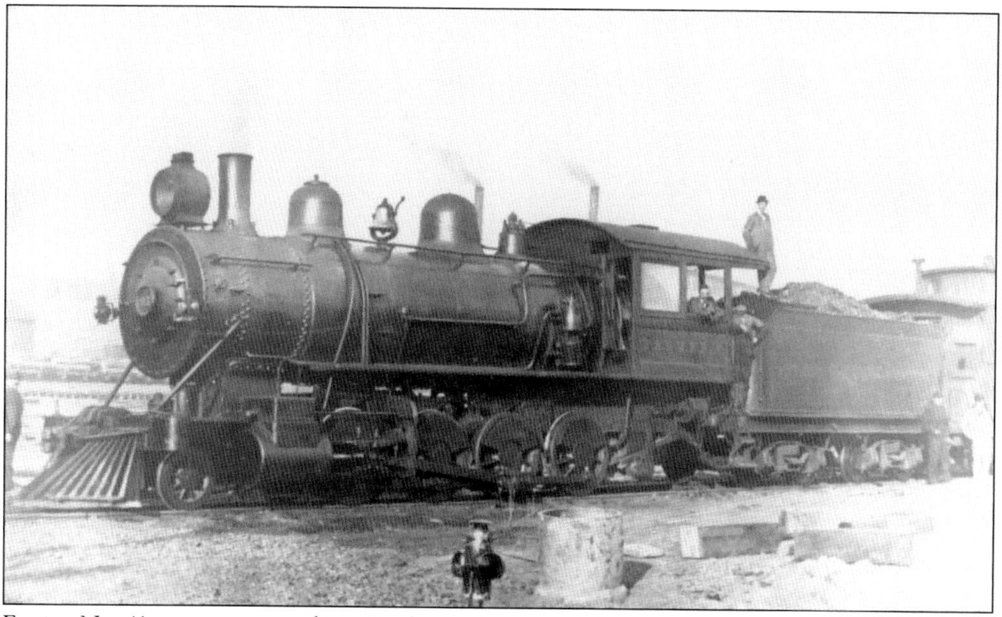

Engine No. 41 was constructed in 1899 for the Buffalo, St. Marys & Southwestern in anticipation of the Shawmut merger. Considered a light Consolidation (2-8-0), it was constructed by the Pittsburgh Locomotive Works. This undated photograph was taken at the Kaulmont station in St. Marys, Pennsylvania. Engine No. 41 was scrapped in 1924. (PS&NRRHS.)

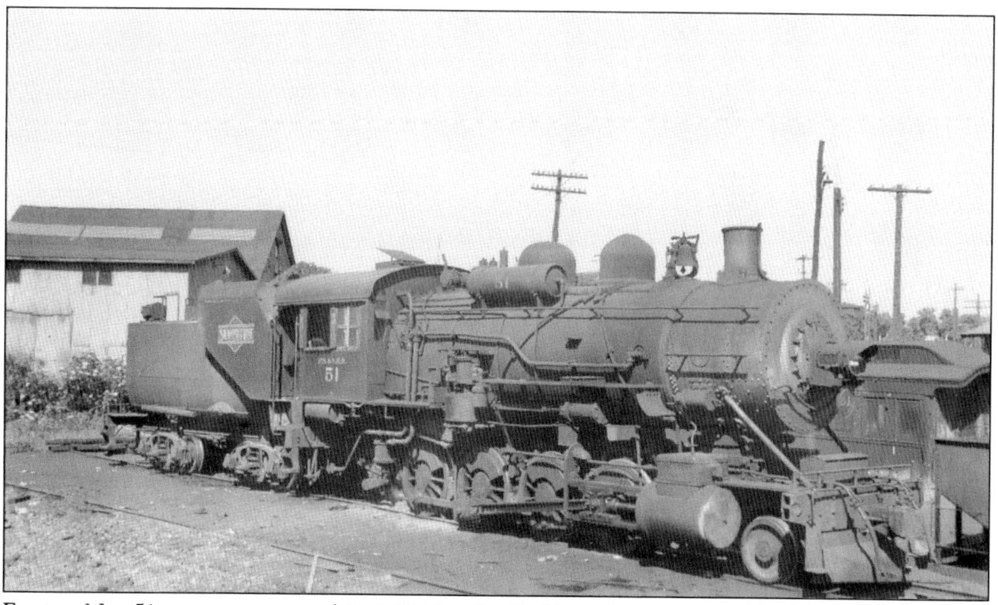

Engine No. 51 was constructed in 1904 by the Baldwin Locomotive Works of Philadelphia, Pennsylvania. It was part of the Shawmut's first order of heavy Consolidations (2-8-0s). They were well liked and remained the mainstay of Shawmut motive power. On July 4, 1946, No. 51 was at Olean, New York. (SMHS.)

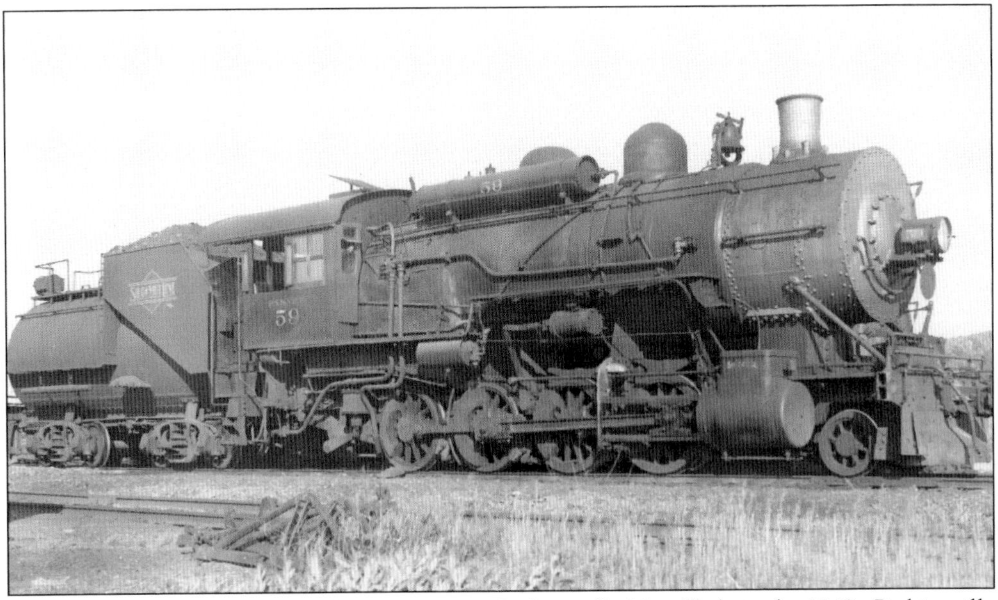

Engine No. 59 is shown tying up between runs at Perkinsville, New York, in the 1940s. Perkinsville was where the Shawmut maintained its engine servicing facilities on the far northern end of the railroad. Heavy grades on the Shawmut required additional air for the brakes. Shop forces added 10-foot-long air tanks on top of the boiler to supply the additional air. (PS&NRRHS.)

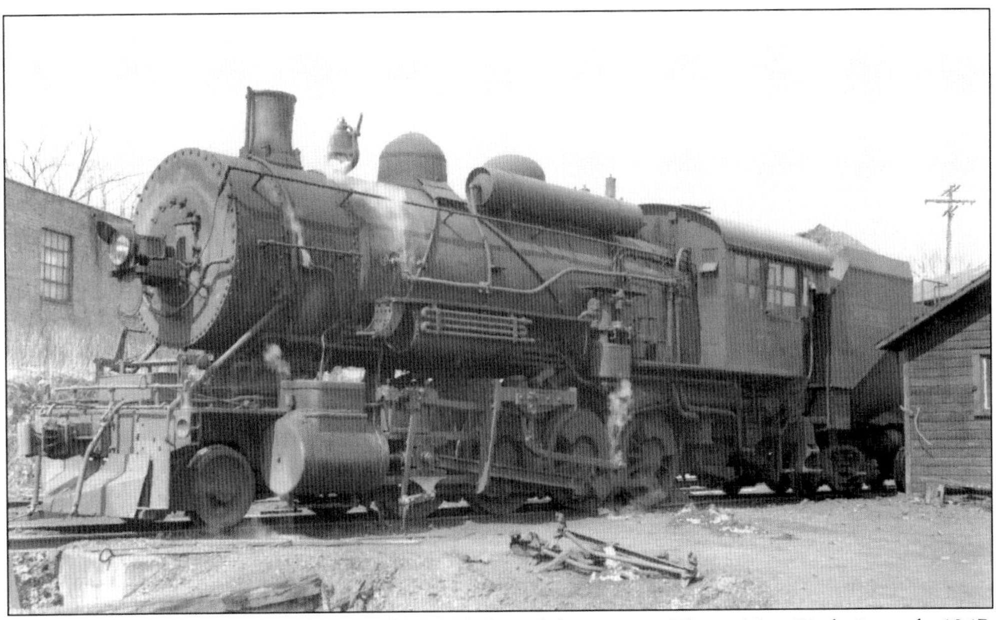

Engine No. 71 is shown standing on the south leg of the wye in Olean, New York, in early 1947. In the background (left) is the Market Basket warehouse building, which still stands today. The building at right is the section house where the Olean-based section gang stored its tools and "speeder car" used to maintain the track. (PS&NRRHS.)

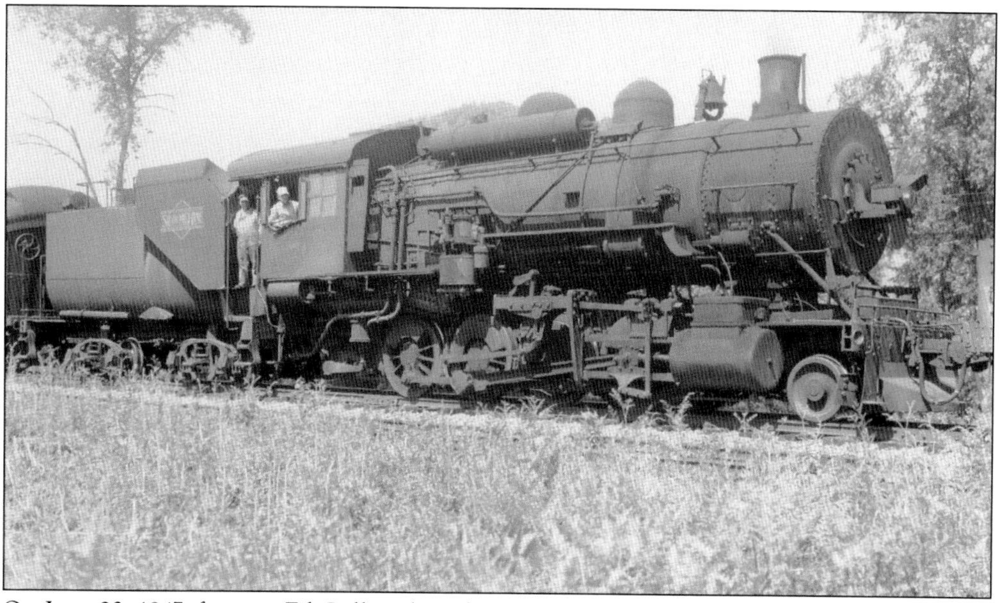

On June 23, 1947, fireman Ed Collins (standing) and engineer Layton "Doc" Rowe pause for a photograph on engine No. 71 while manning the scrap train south of Bolivar, New York. The brass number plate that hung beneath the headlight on No. 71 was rescued by Doc Rowe prior to its scrapping. It is now on display at the society's museum in Angelica, New York (see page 127). (PS&NRRHS.)

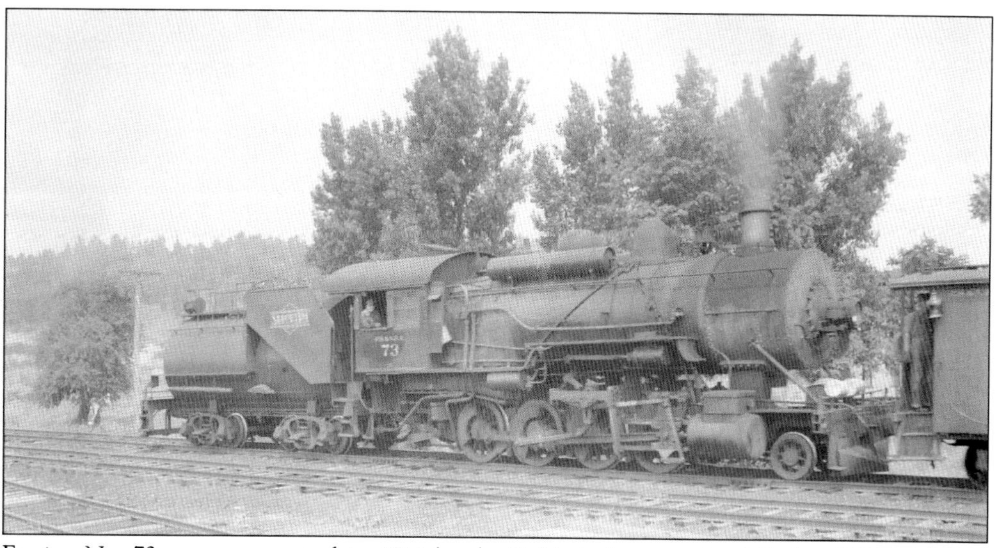

Engine No. 73 was constructed in 1911 by the Baldwin Locomotive Works of Philadelphia, Pennsylvania. It was part of the last order of new locomotives ever purchased by the Pittsburg, Shawmut & Northern. This photograph, taken August 3, 1940, shows No. 73 in pusher service at Angelica, New York. (PS&NRRHS.)

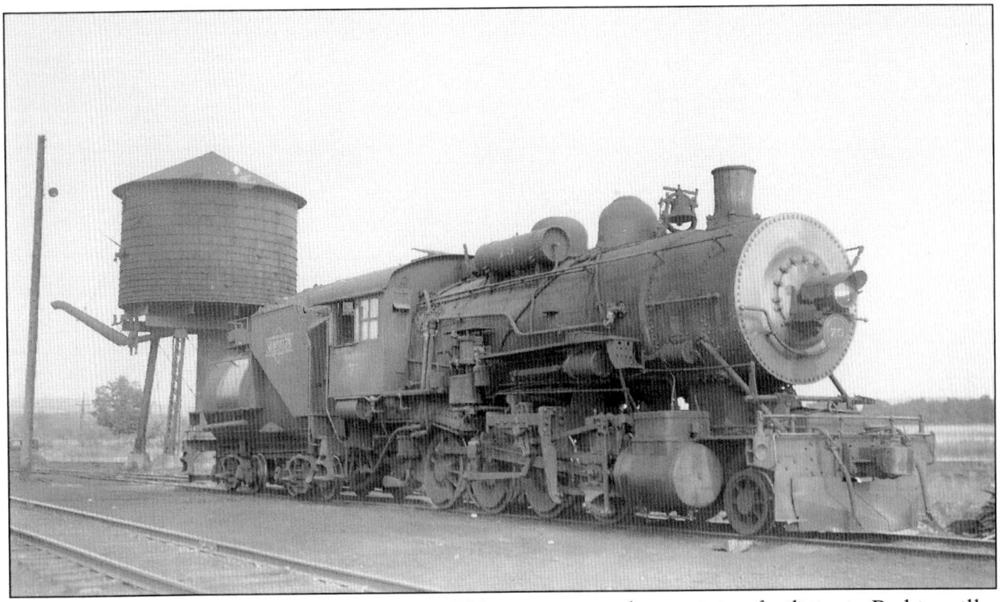

This undated photograph shows engine No. 75 laying over at the servicing facilities in Perkinsville, New York. Like most of the heavy Consolidations owned by the Shawmut, No. 75 is equipped with a Vanderbilt tender. Compared to rectangular tenders, these cylindrical tenders were stronger, lighter, and held more fuel in relation to their surface area. (SMHS.)

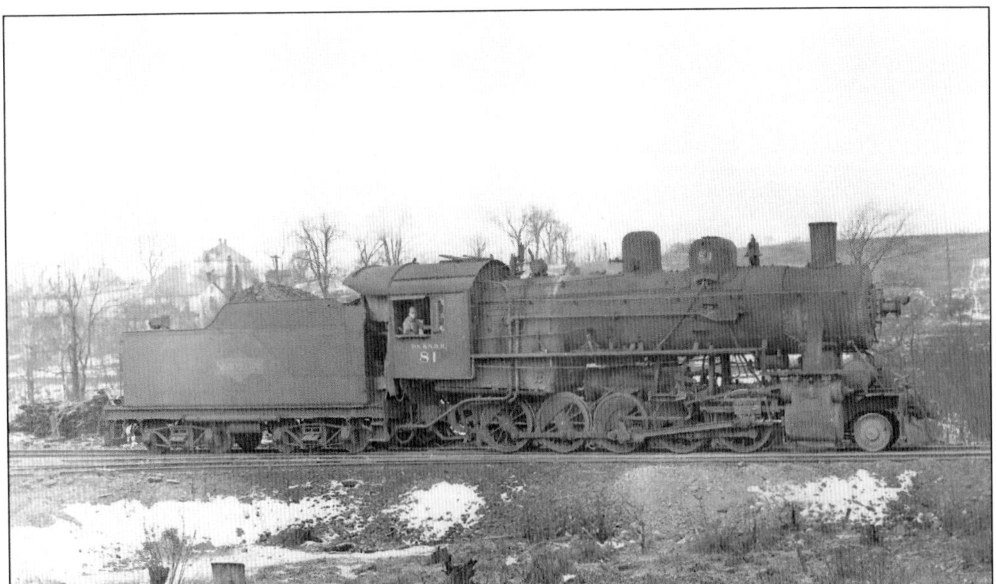

Engine No. 81 was purchased secondhand from the Erie Railroad in 1941 to replace some of the capacity of the engines that were destroyed in the St. Marys engine house fire (see page 74). It was constructed in 1918 by the Baldwin Locomotive Works of Philadelphia, Pennsylvania. The locomotive was scrapped in May 1944 due to a cracked cylinder. (PS&NRRHS.)

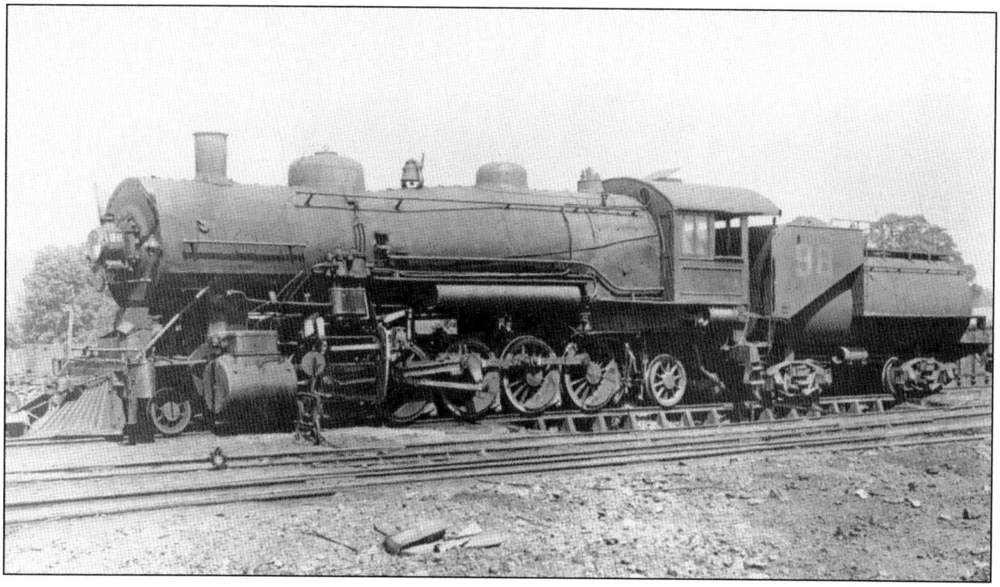

Above, engine No. 98 is shown standing over the ash pit in Angelica, New York, in 1916. Built in 1907 by the Baldwin Locomotive Works of Philadelphia, Pennsylvania, it was originally intended to operate on the Kersey Branch. Having a 2-10-2 wheel arrangement, it was huge compared to all other Shawmut locomotives. It was too destructive on the tracks on the Kersey Branch and spent much of its career in pusher service between Bolivar, New York, and Friendship. It was derided by both crews and railroad officials alike as the "curve straightener." No. 98, seen below, served as a prop for a photograph of the Angelica shop force. (Both, PS&NRRHS.)

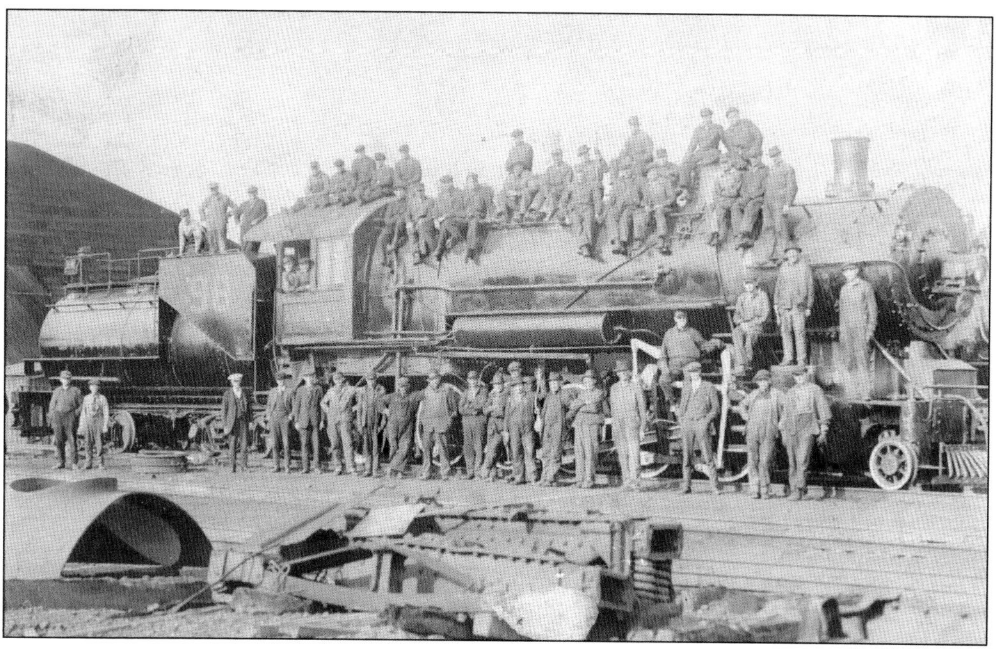

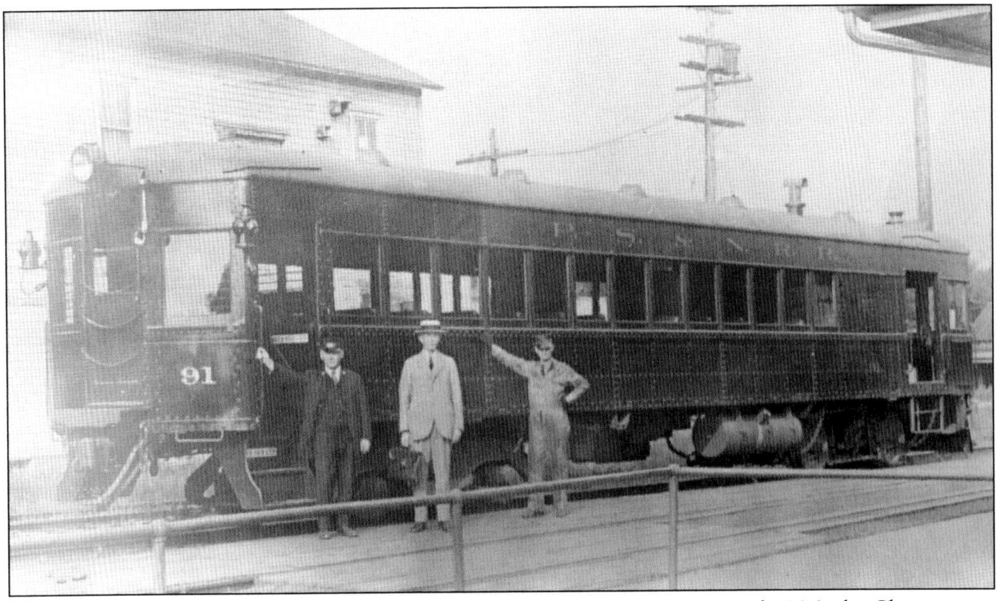

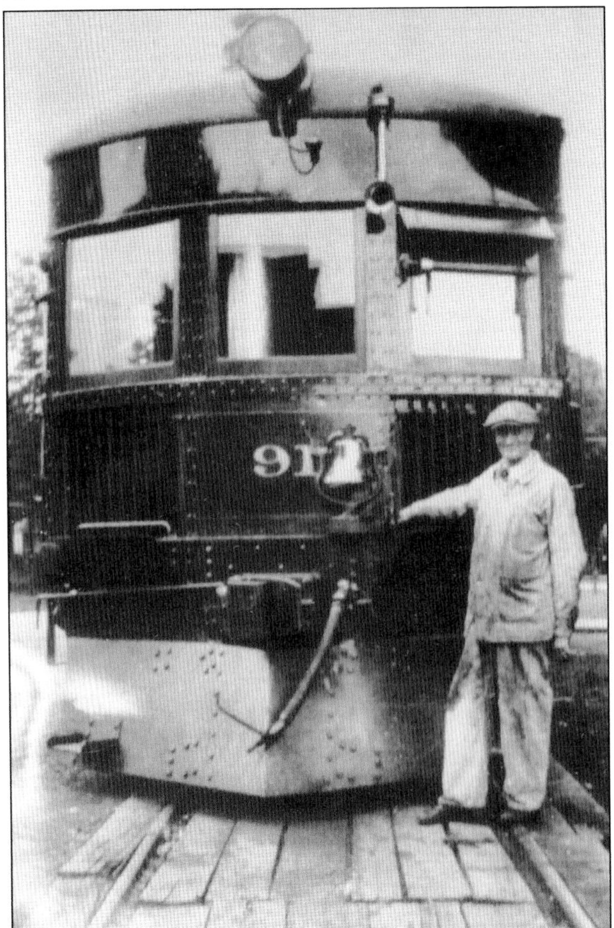

In 1925 and 1926, the Shawmut purchased two Model 75 gasoline motor cars from the Brill Company of Philadelphia, Pennsylvania. Numbered 90 and 91, respectively, they were affectionately known as Hoodlebugs. Each were operated by a two-man crew, compared to the four men required to operate a traditional steam-powered passenger train. Shown above sometime in the 1930s in front of the Angelica, New York, depot, from left to right are, Tom O'Connor (conductor), attorney John D. Dickson (receiver of the Shawmut), and Henry Mead (motorman). The photograph to the left is of engineer Charles Ehrensberger with car No. 91 in St. Marys, Pennsylvania. (Above, PS&NRRHS; left, SMHS.)

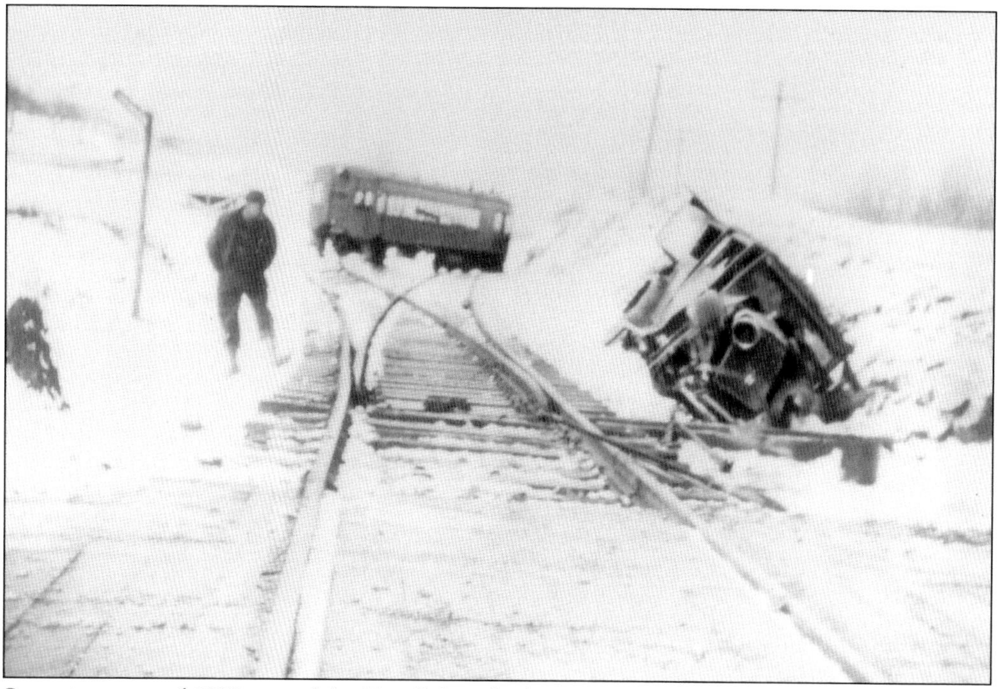

Sometime around 1930, one of the Hoodlebugs had a sparring match with a heavy touring car at the grade crossing at Gillen Station. Located at MP 131.5, this was the crossing of Pennsylvania Route 255 south of St. Marys, Pennsylvania (see page 80). By the looks of the touring car above, which had spun completely around, it lost the fight. The force of the impact of the touring car against the rear truck of the Hoodlebug was enough to shove the truck off the track. It picked the switch of the Gillen team track, seen below, causing it to split the switch. (Both, SMHS.)

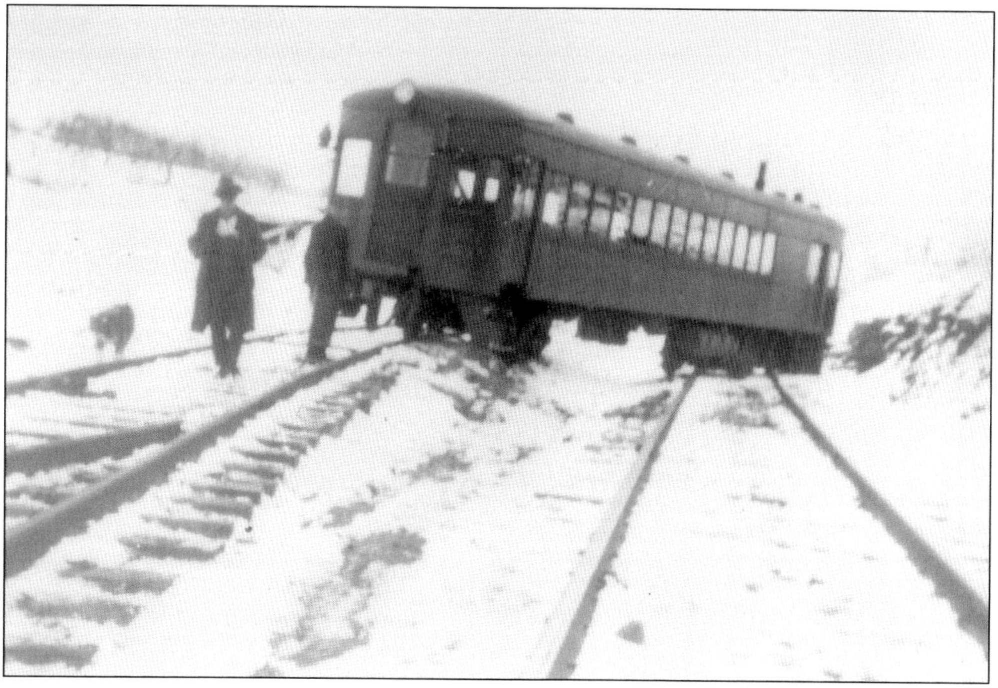

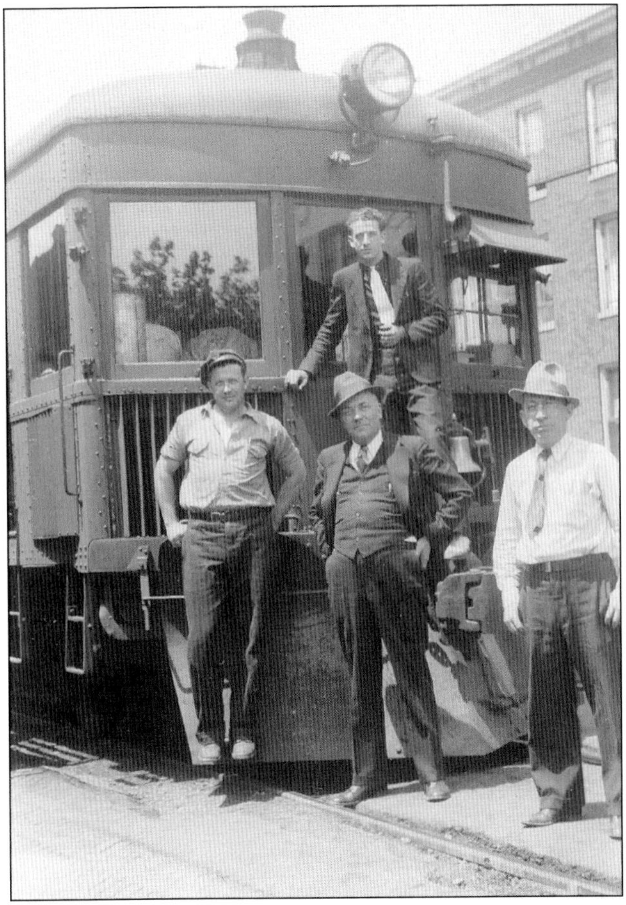

Unlike most other gasoline-powered railcars that used an electric transmission, the Hoodlebugs came with a five-speed mechanical transmission built into the front truck. This photograph of car No. 90 was taken in St. Marys and shows, from left to right, (first row), John S. Hauber, ? Roberts, and Ike Severin; (second row) James Lecker. (SMHS.)

In 1933, after a series of grade crossing accidents, the Shawmut painted the front ends of its Hoodlebugs with a series of stripes to increase visibility. This 1936 photograph shows car No. 91 in Hoboken, New Jersey, after being sold. It is en route to its new owner in Havana, Cuba. (PS&NRRHS.)

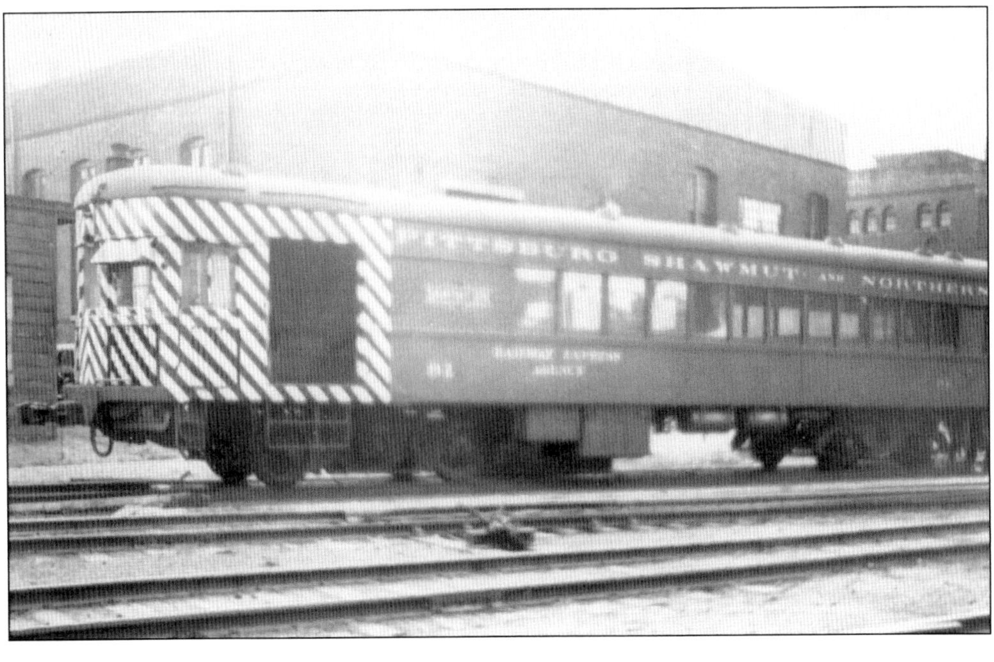

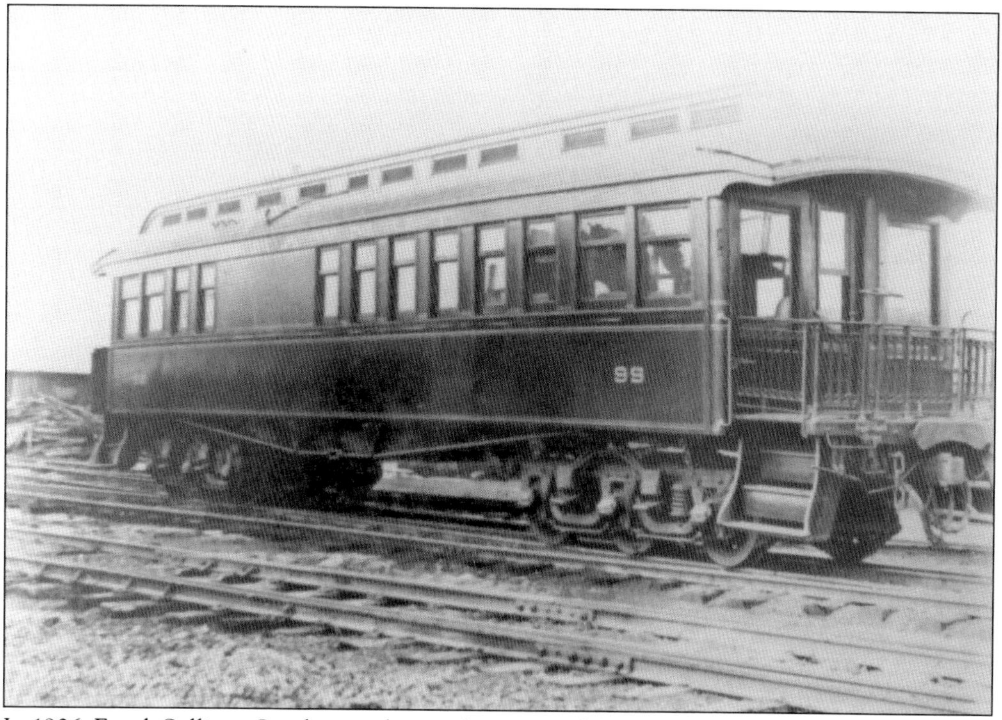

In 1906, Frank Sullivan Smith, president and receiver of the Shawmut, decided that the railroad needed a business car. Car No. 502 was purchased secondhand from the Chicago and Alton Railroad. Constructed by the Pullman Company on December 19, 1883, it was renumbered into the PS&N passenger car series as No. 99. At his expense, Smith had the car refurbished and re-equipped. It was repainted and the mahogany interior was re-oiled. Named for his wife, Clara Higgins Smith, the *Clara* was presented to her as a birthday present. This car is now preserved at the PS&NRRHS museum in Angelica, New York (see page 127). (Both, PS&NRRHS.)

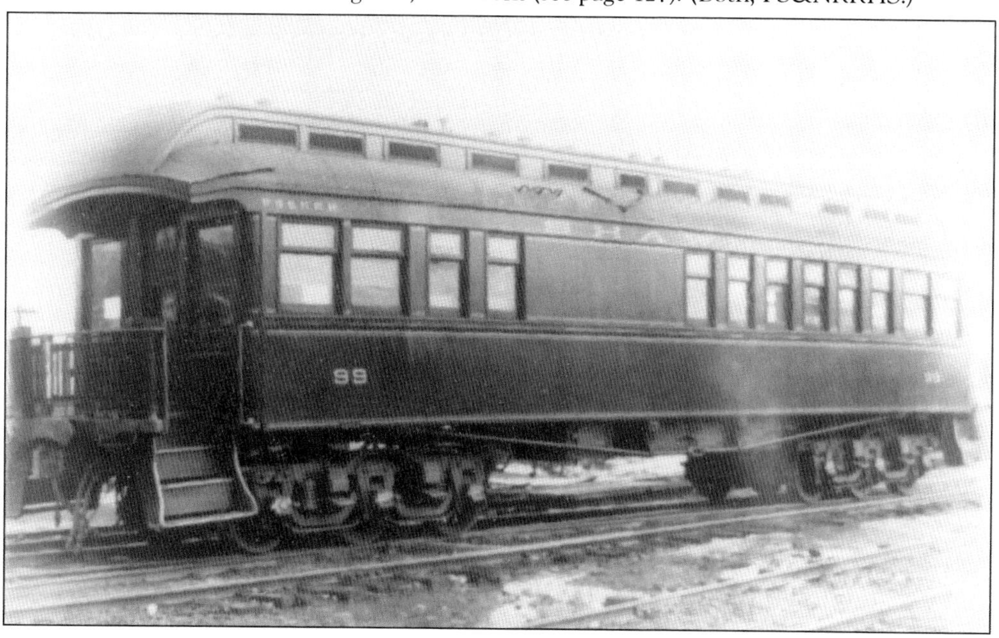

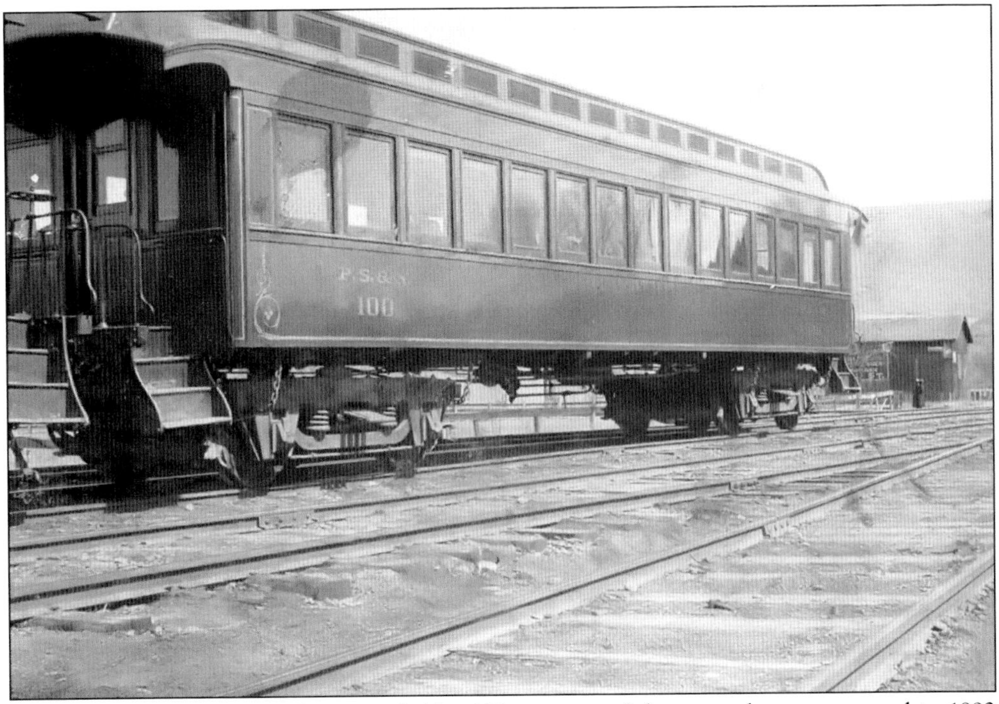

Pittsburg, Shawmut & Northern coach No. 100 was one of three coaches constructed in 1893 by the Jackson & Sharp Company for the Central New York & Western Railroad. It seated 56 passengers in 14 rows and included one washroom and one coal stove. The washroom is located closest to the photographer. (SMHS.)

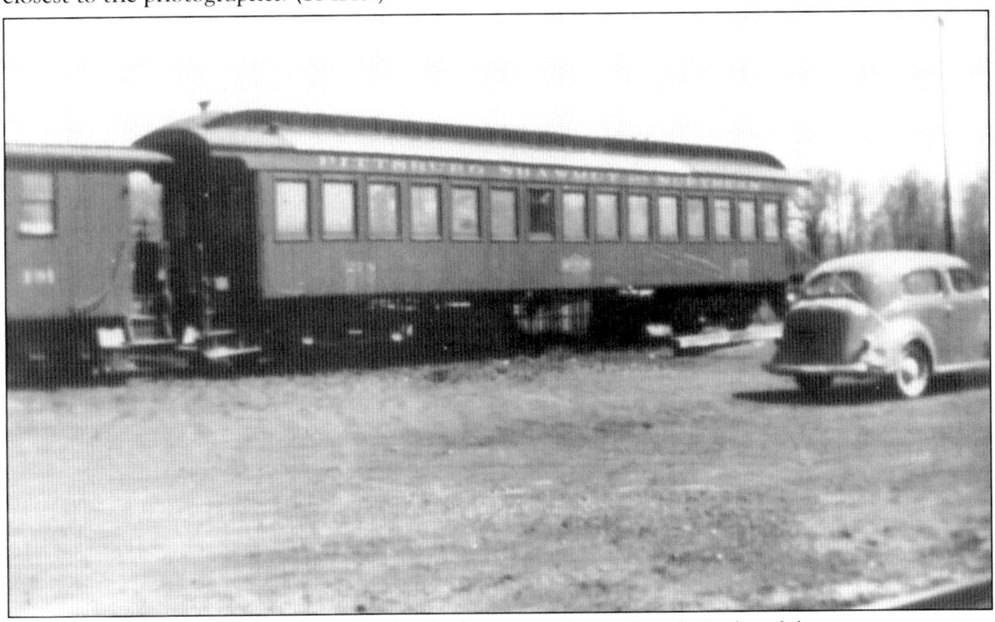

Coach No. 104 was purchased new by the Lackawanna & Pittsburgh Railroad, but its construction date and builder are unknown. It seated 56 passengers. With the end of passenger service, the 104 was renumbered into the work car series as 278. This car is now preserved at the PS&NRRHS museum in Angelica, New York (see page 127). (PS&NRRHS.)

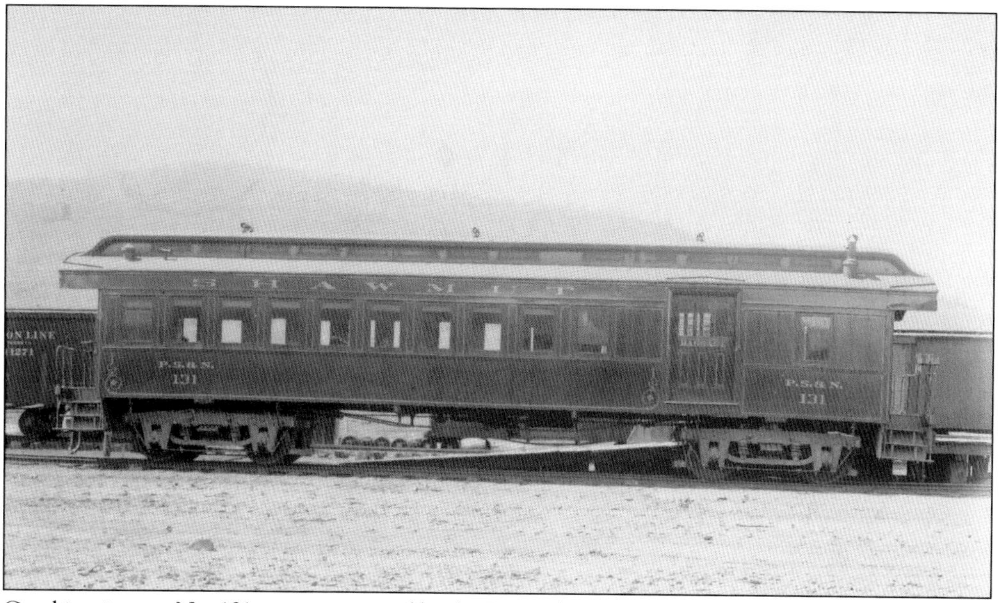

Combination car No. 131 was constructed by the Pennsylvania Railroad at its Altoona, Pennsylvania, shops. It was purchased in 1896 by the Central New York & Western Railroad. It is unclear whether the railcar was purchased new or used. This undated photograph was taken in Smethport, Pennsylvania, behind the County House. (SMHS.)

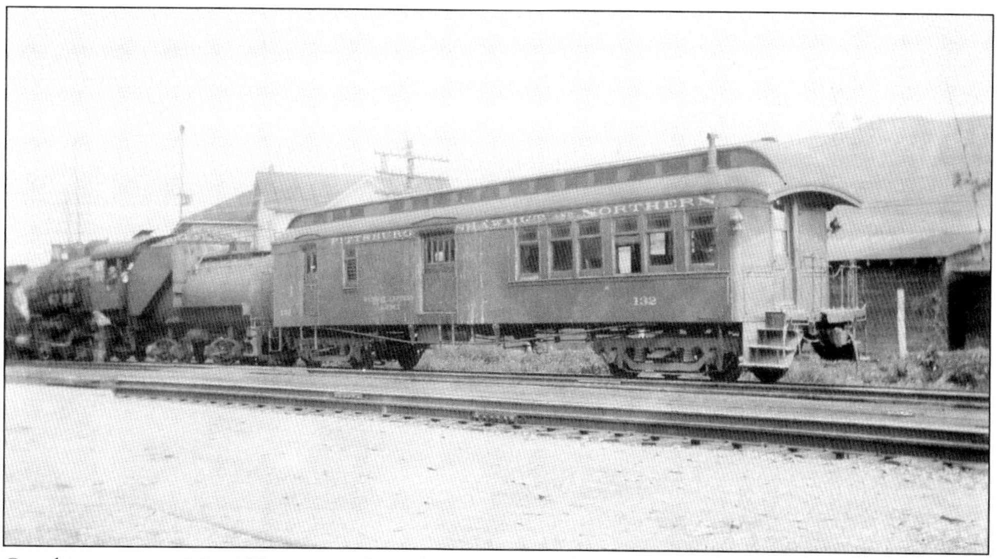

Combination car No. 132 was purchased new in 1905 from the Barney & Smith Car Company of Dayton, Ohio. It combined passenger, baggage, and railway post office functions into a single car. It had a seating capacity of 20 passengers. With the end of passenger service, the 132 was renumbered into the work car series as 286. (SMHS.)

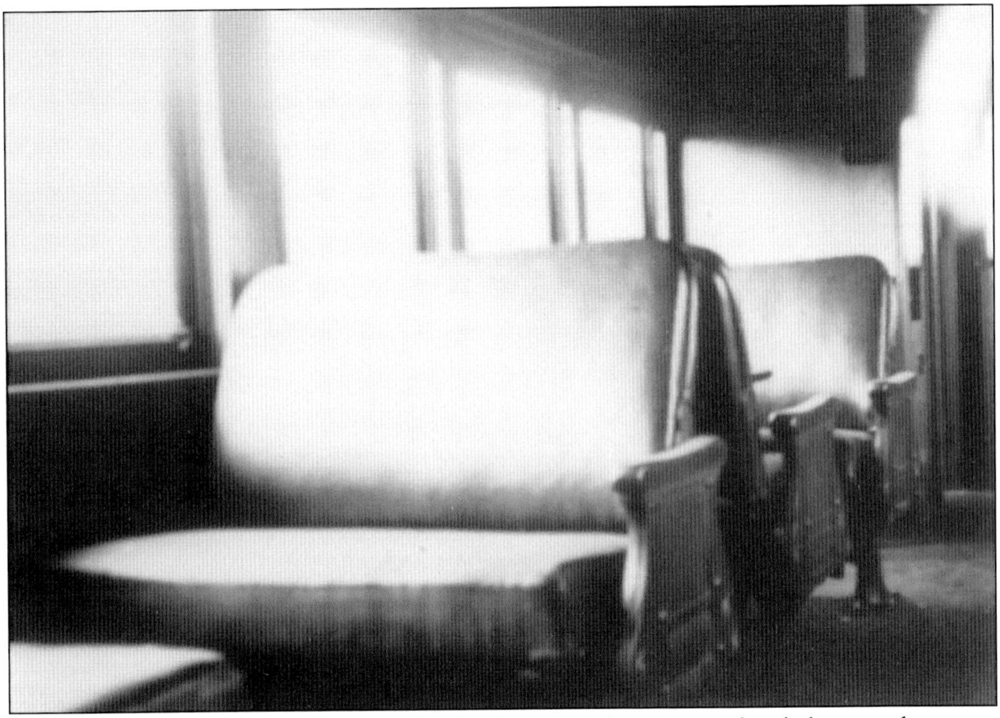

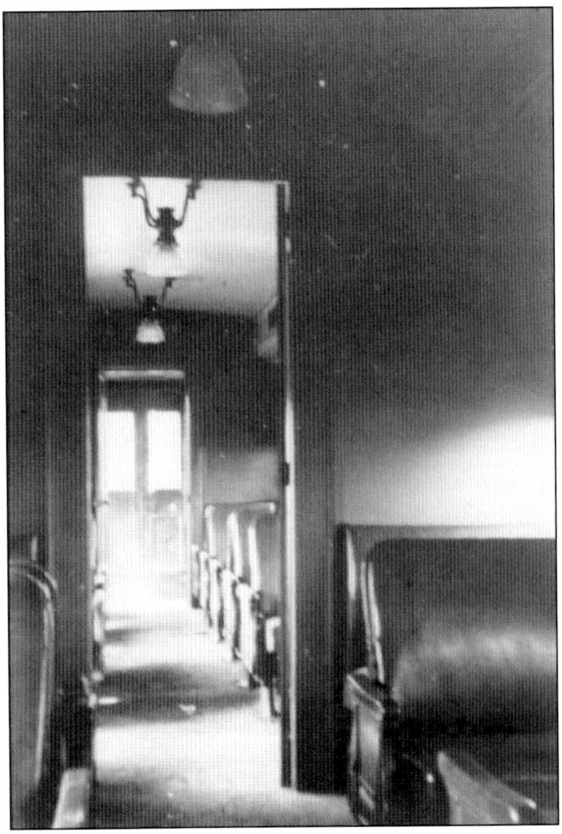

These two undated photographs are the only known images of interiors of Pittsburg, Shawmut & Northern passenger cars. The identity of the exact car is unknown; however, the photograph to the left is of a combination car with two passenger compartments. The passenger seats pictured above were upholstered in leather. When the Shawmut was abandoned in 1947, the remaining passenger cars had all of their interior fixtures stripped for salvage purposes. In the mid-1980s, four complete seats (sans upholstery) turned up in a garage sale in Bolivar, New York, and the PS&NRRHS was able to acquire them. They have been restored and are now in place in coach No. 278 at the PS&NRRHS Museum in Angelica, New York (see page 127). (Both, SMHS.)

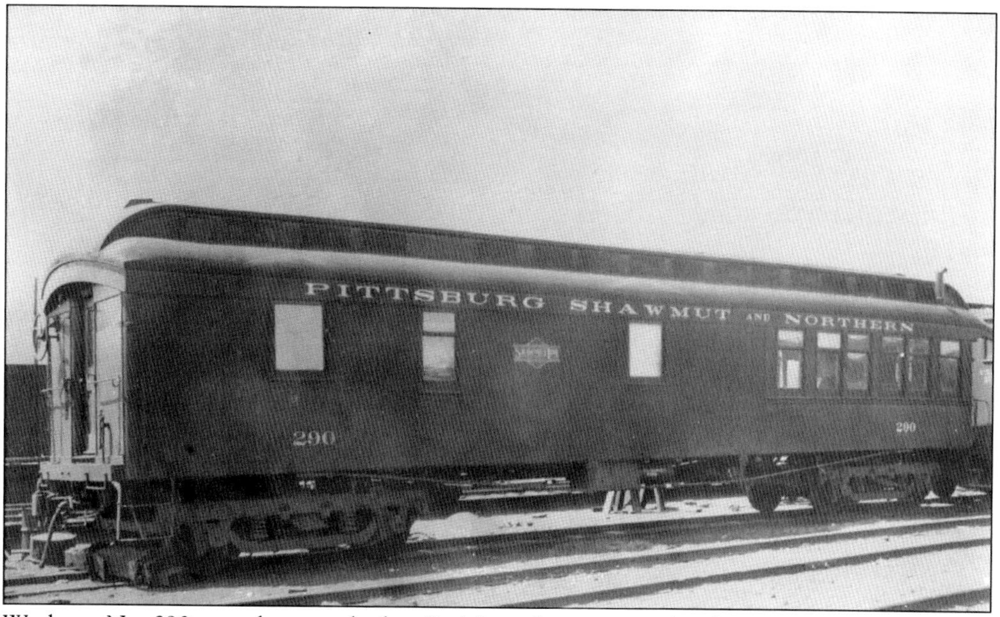

Work car No. 290 was photographed at St. Marys Junction on April 13, 1947. It was originally constructed for the Shawmut in 1905 by the Barney & Smith Car Company of Dayton, Ohio, as combination car No. 133. Like its sister No. 132, it combined passenger, baggage, and railway post office functions into a single car. (SMHS.)

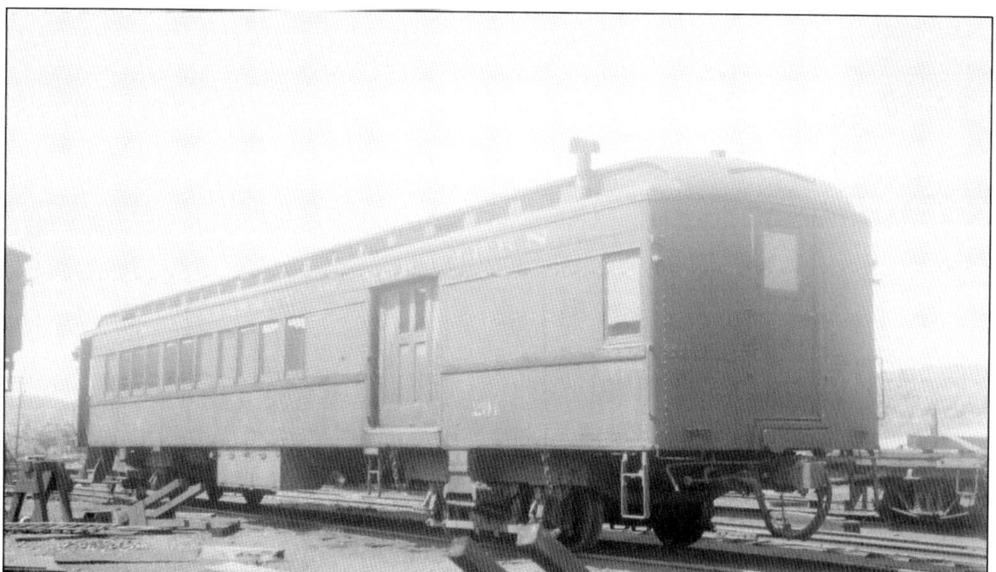

Work car No. 291 was photographed at St. Marys Junction on June 29, 1947. It was originally purchased secondhand from the Pennsylvania Railroad and operated as combination car No. 135. It was similar in construction to the PRR's P70 coaches. It was often paired with business car No. 299, the *Janelyn*. (SMHS.)

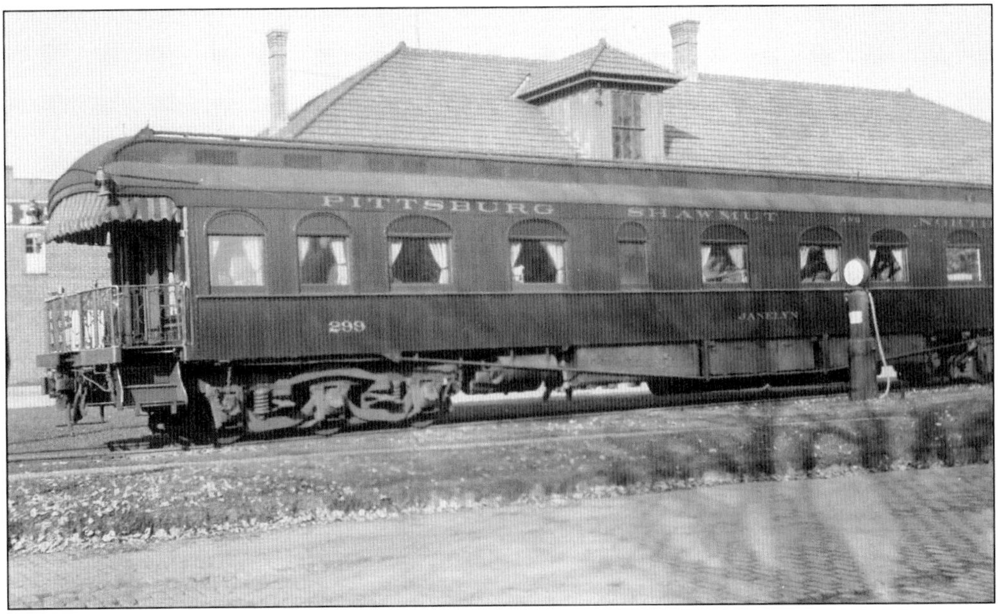

Business car No. 299 was built by Pullman in 1902 and operated on the Missouri, Kansas & Texas (also known as the Katy Line.) Damaged by a fire in its dining room, the railcar was purchased secondhand by the Shawmut in April 1930 for $4,400. It was rebuilt and refurbished in the St. Marys shops at a cost of $10,600 and was named the *Janelyn* by Receiver John Dickson after his two daughters. Seen above in the mid-1930s is the *Janelyn* at the Olean, New York, depot. When not out on the road, the *Janelyn*, also seen below, was stored at the St. Marys shops. (Both, SMHS.)

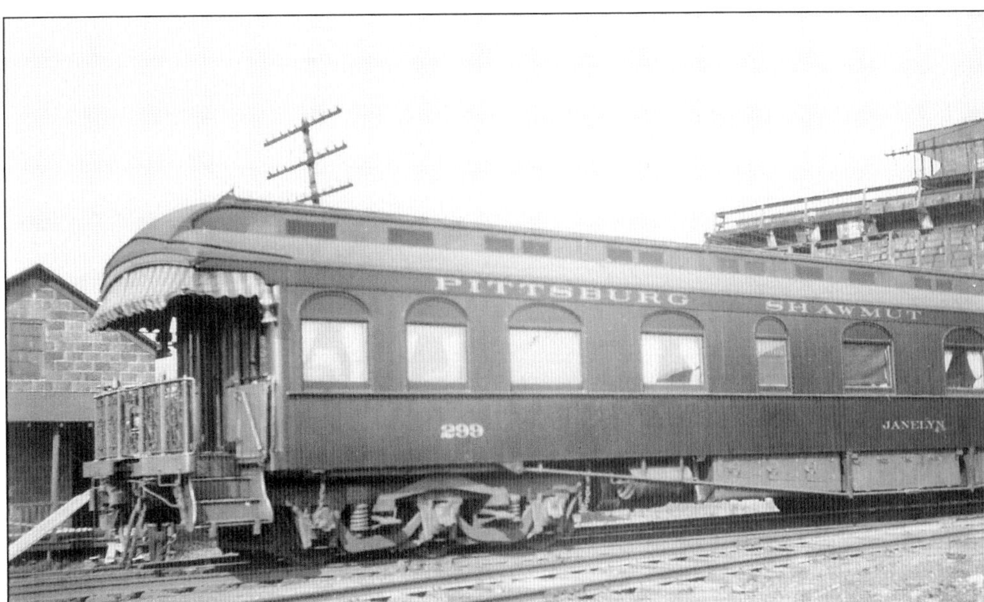

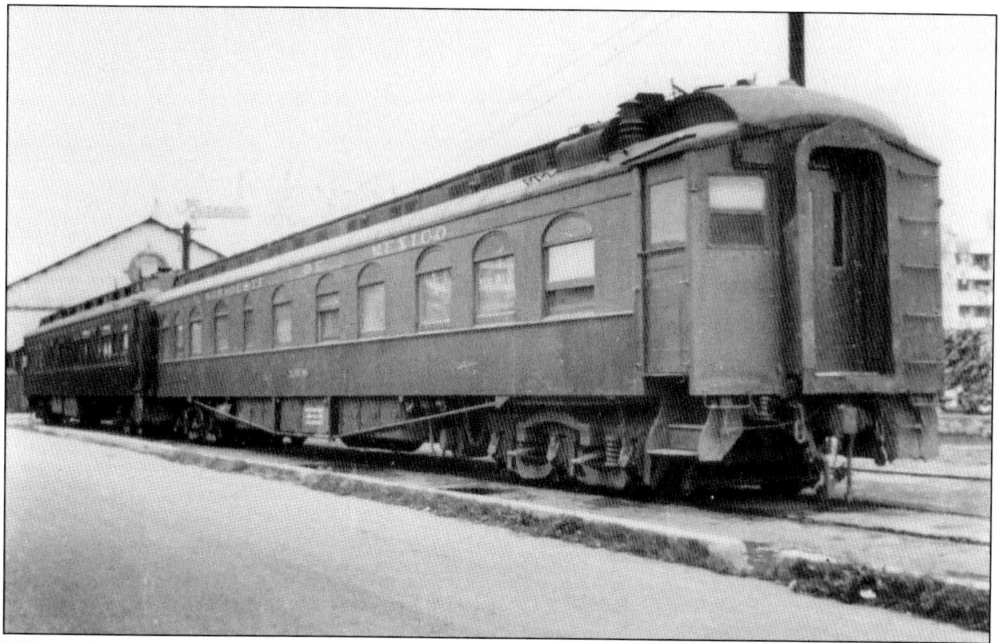

When Thomas Buchanan and Robert Sproul became the receivers of the Shawmut in 1946, one of their first acts was to put business car No. 299, the *Janelyn*, up for sale. In June 1946, it was sold to P. Pettler & Son, a "dismantling firm" from Beaver Falls, Pennsylvania. Events happened quickly, and the railcar left Shawmut property, headed for the Chicago firm of Purdy Company, a used equipment dealer. Seen above and below, it turned up in the 1950s, named the *Aros* on the Nor-Oeste de México. The car was last seen as the *Rocohuaina* in the 1980s at the La Junta, Mexico, shops of the Chihuahua al Pacífico. (Both, PS&NRRHS.)

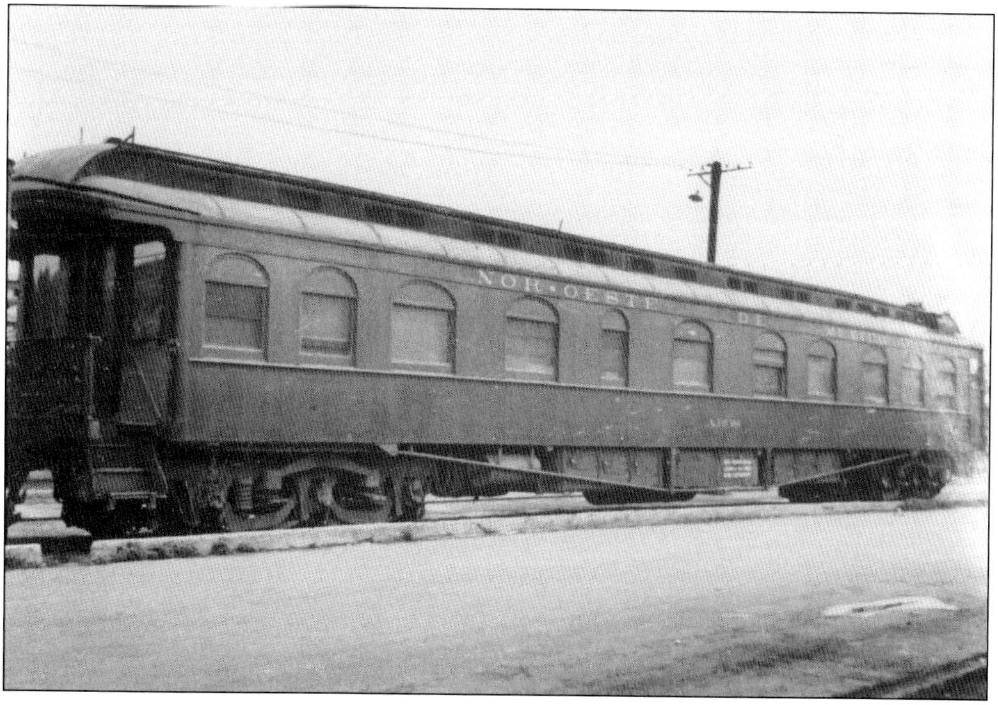

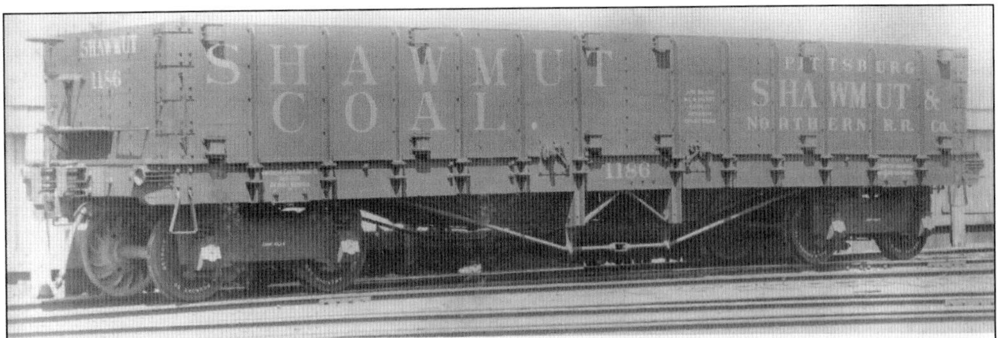

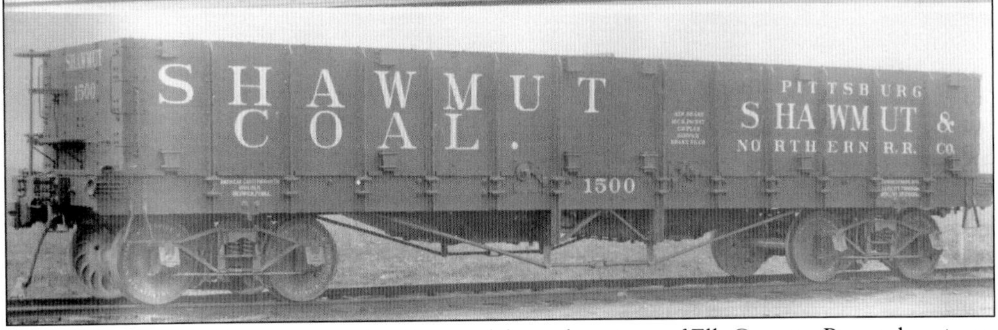

The lifeblood of the Shawmut was hauling coal from the mines of Elk County, Pennsylvania, to markets in New York State. Prior to the 1920s and the advent of steel hoppers, wooden hoppers were the norm. Wooden hopper No. 1186 was constructed by American Car & Foundry in 1899 and was equipped with Fox trucks. Hopper No. 1500 was constructed in 1901 and was equipped with archbar trucks. No. 2075 was similar to No. 1500 but had a different side-stake configuration. No. 4402 was constructed in 1899 and like the 1186 was equipped with Fox trucks. (Both, American Car & Foundry archives.)

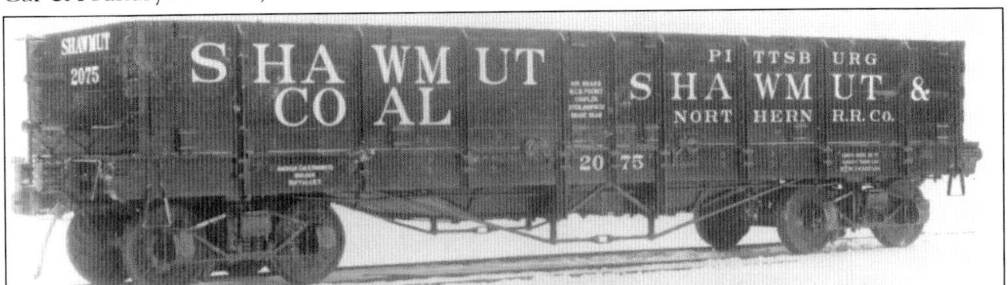

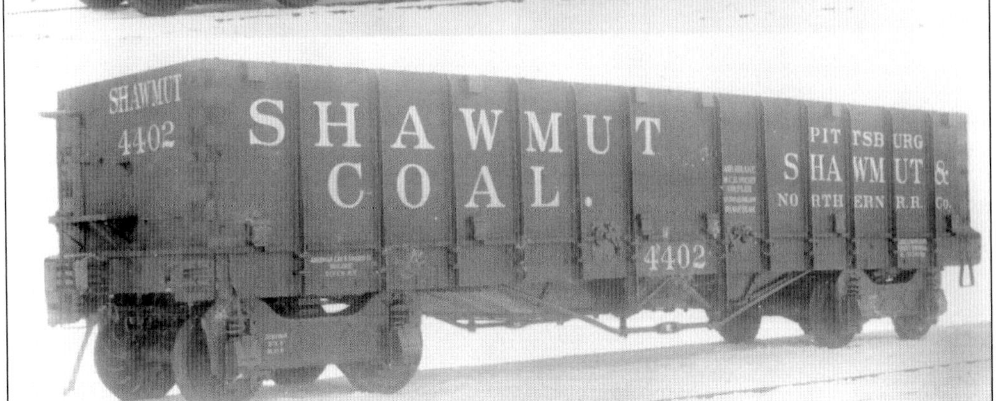

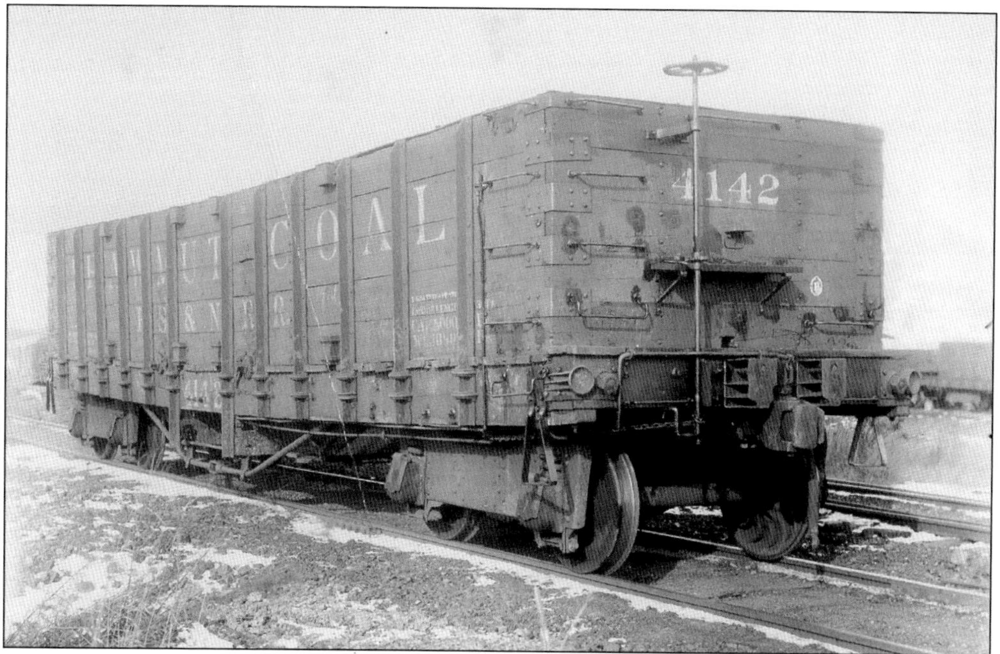

Wooden hopper car No. 4142 was constructed in 1899 by the American Car and Foundry Company at its Depew, New York, plant. It was one of 500 cars that were ordered at a cost of $480 each. Notice that these cars were one board higher than the cars in the 1000 and 2000 series. Most of these cars were scrapped by 1922. (SMHS.)

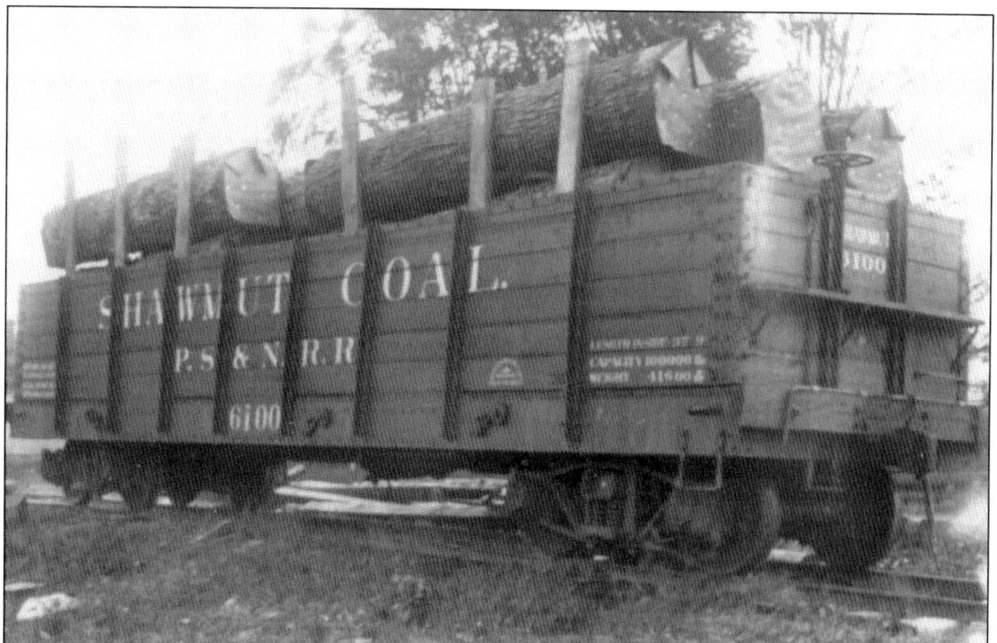

Hopper car No. 6100 was part of a 500-car order constructed in 1906–1907 by the Barney & Smith Car Company in Dayton, Ohio. Each car cost $989. This car represents the transition era from wooden-underframe cars to all-steel cars; it has a fully steel frame with wooden sides. These cars lasted into the 1930s. (PS&NRRHS.)

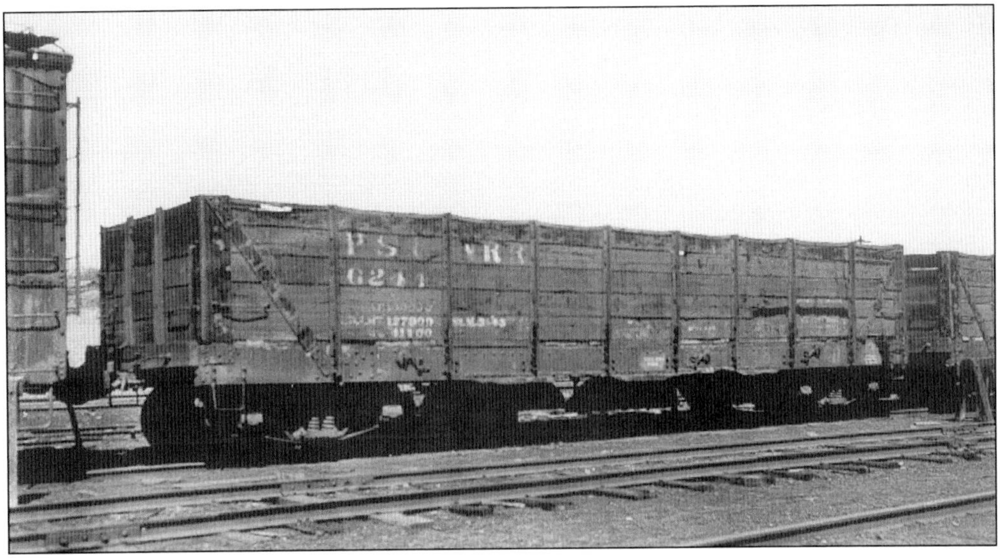

By the time wooden hopper cars 6244 (above) and 6365 (below) were photographed at St. Marys Junction by Robert W. Richardson, in either 1947 or 1948, they were retired and destined to be scrapped. Their dilapidated condition is indicative of the Shawmut's financial distress. They were equipped with archbar trucks, a style that was bolted together. The bolts tended to loosen over time; as a result, the Interstate Commerce Commission prohibited their use in interchange between railroads after December 31, 1939. In 1936, in preparation for the ban, the Shawmut was given the opportunity to swap one of the Hoodlebugs for enough Bettendorf trucks to upgrade its entire fleet. With mounting debt, Receiver Dickson was forced to sell the Hoodlebug for cash. After the ban, these cars could only be used for delivery to local Shawmut customers. (Both, SMHS.)

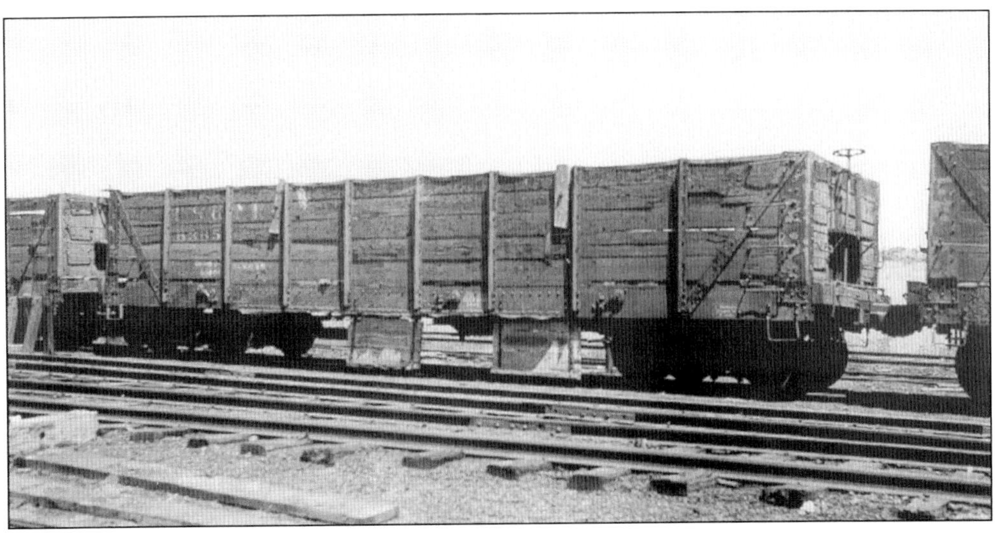

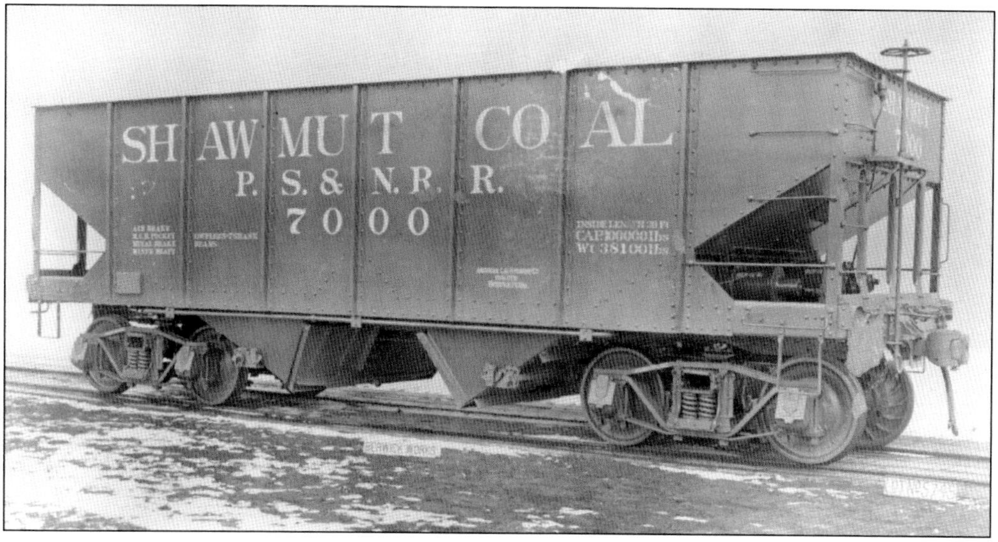

Between 1909 and 1911, the American Car & Foundry Company built 250 all-steel hoppers for the Shawmut at its Berwick, Pennsylvania, plant. Numbered 7000–7249, they each cost $1,053. Their interior length was 30 feet and their capacity was 50 tons. This builder's photograph above shows the first car in the series. During the 1930s, some of these cars (fewer than 100) were rebuilt and renumbered into the 7500 series. The undated photograph below shows hopper car No. 7522 at Olean, New York. By 1947 and its demise, the Shawmut listed 78 of these cars on its roster. (Above, PS&NRRHS; below, SMHS.)

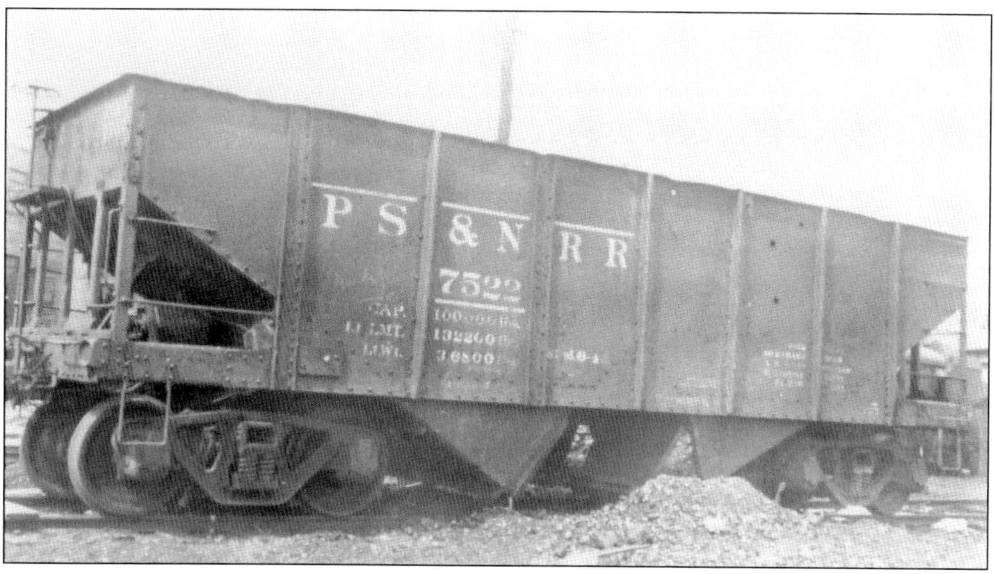

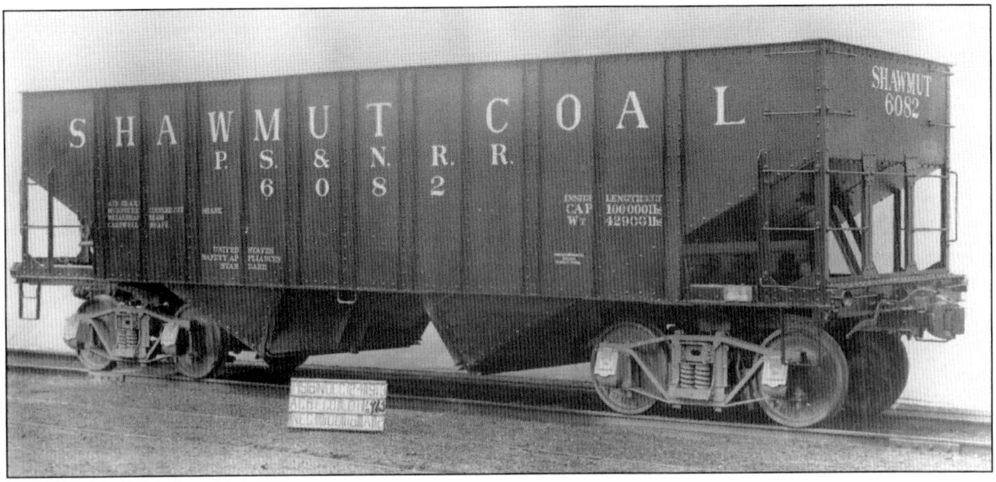

In 1913, with increasing coal traffic originating on the Pittsburg & Shawmut, the Pittsburg, Shawmut & Northern—which was leasing the P&S—placed another order for 500 steel hoppers with the American Car & Foundry Company. With the PS&N already in receivership, financing for these cars came from Thomas H. Hubbard, the majority owner of the P&S. When the P&S severed the lease in 1916, these cars were conveyed to the P&S. They were quickly renumbered by adding a "1" in front of the existing numbers. Hence, PS&N 6082, seen above, became P&S 16082. In 1947, after the abandonment of the Shawmut, Clayton Wise photographed the "funeral train" of hopper cars, seen below, at St. Marys Junction. They would soon be heading to Bethlehem Steel for scrapping. (Above, PS&NRRHS; below, SMHS.)

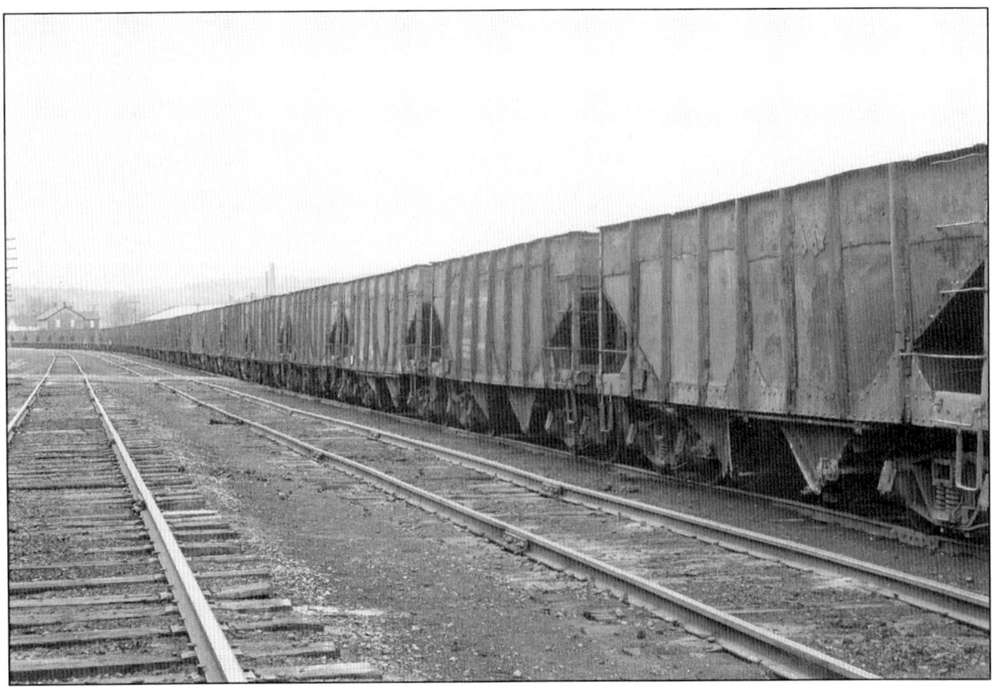

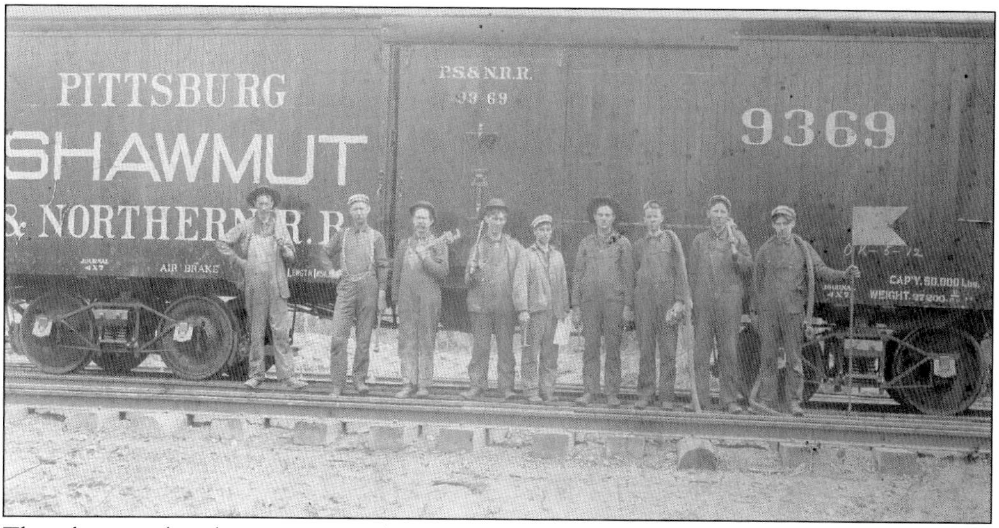

This photograph, taken sometime after 1912, shows Pittsburg, Shawmut & Northern Railroad employees standing in front of wooden, single-sheathed boxcar No. 9369. This car was constructed in 1893 by the Detroit Car Works of Detroit, Michigan. The men, based on the tools they have, worked out in the freight yards. They were referred to as car toads and car knockers. (SMHS.)

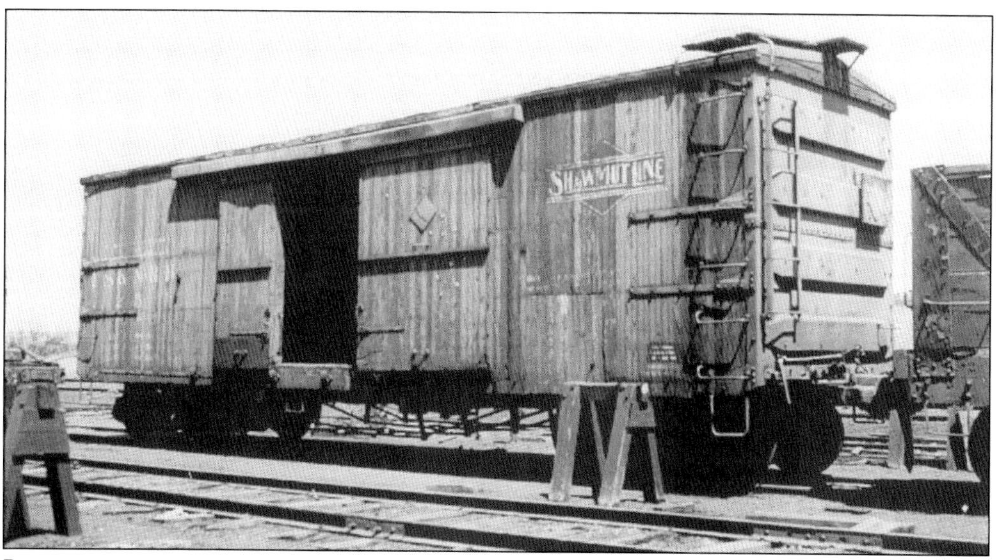

Boxcar No. 9625 was one of 19 used steel-underframe cars that were purchased by the Shawmut in 1932. The origin of these cars is uncertain. However, the New York Central and its subsidiaries had the only known cars of identical dimensions—nearly 10,000 of them. The Shawmut's cars were rebuilt with unique Hutchins corrugated-steel ends. (SMHS.)

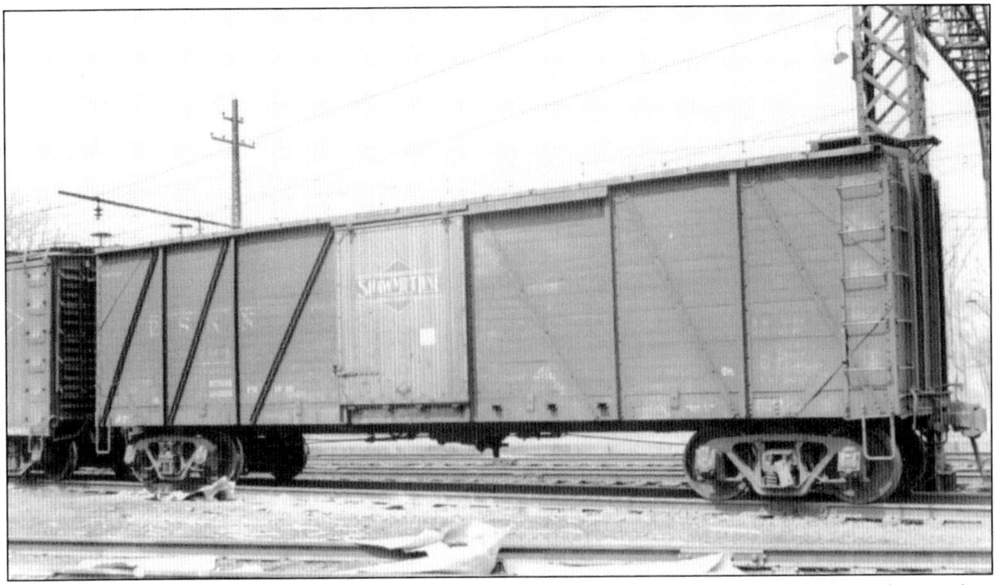

Steel-underframe outside-braced boxcar No. 9794 was one of 100 such cars leased from the Mather Stock Car Company of Chicago, Illinois. This undated photograph was taken on the electrified Niagara Junction Railway in Niagara Falls, New York. The Stackpole Carbon Company in St. Marys produced a great deal of carbon electrodes used by the many chemical companies located in Niagara Falls. (PS&NRRHS.)

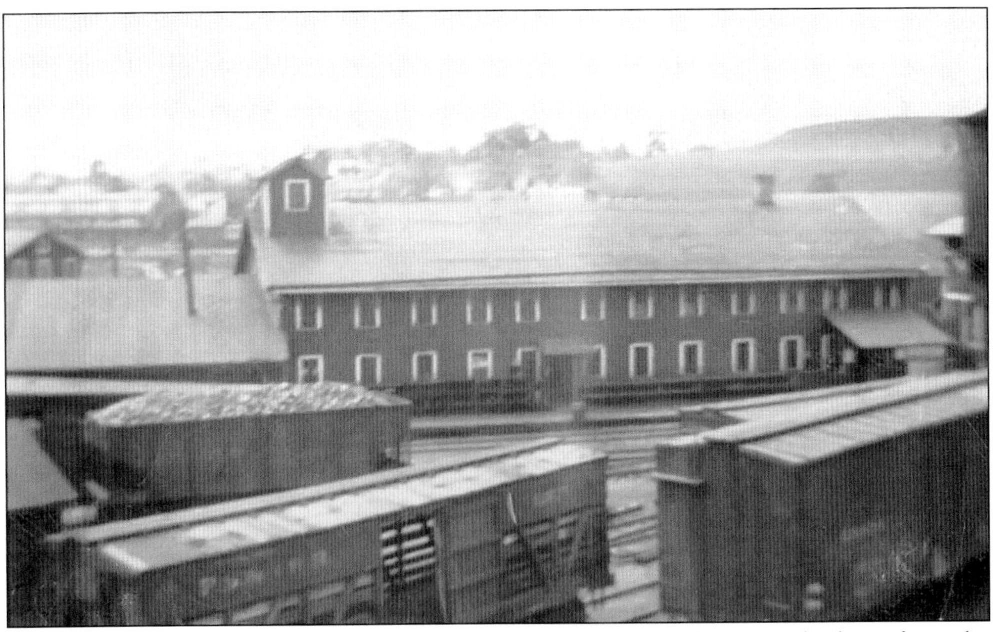

During the 1910s, the Shawmut briefly operated a series of stock cars under lease from the Standard Steel Car Company of Butler, Pennsylvania; they were numbered 12000–12399. Stock cars were a special type of louvered freight car specifically designed to carry livestock from farms to meatpacking houses. This undated photograph, taken at St. Marys Junction, is the only known photograph of a Shawmut Line stock car. (PS&NRRHS.)

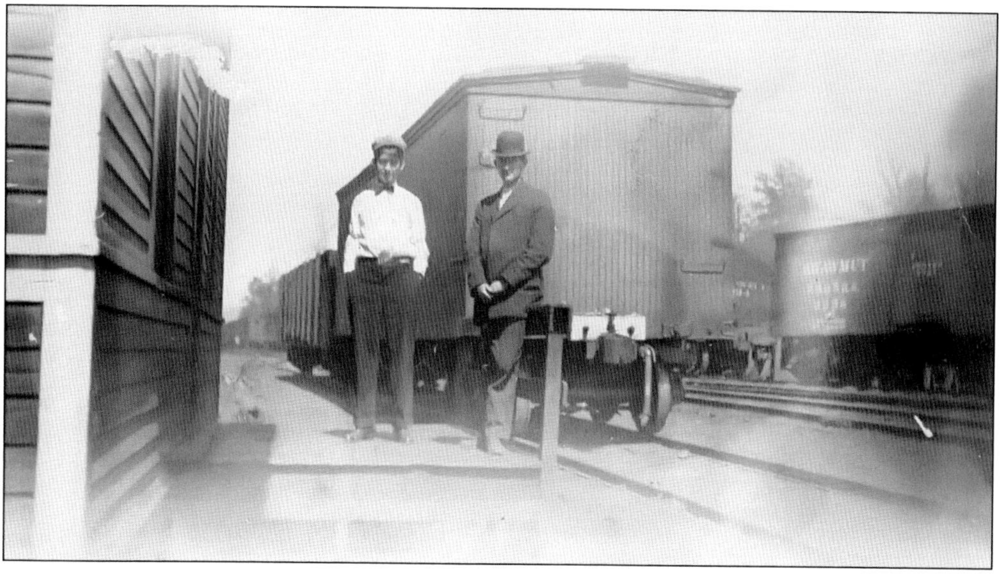

Refrigerator cars of this era, referred to as reefers, were chilled by ice-filled bunkers located at both ends of the cars. Reefer No. 10048, shown above in Smethport, Pennsylvania, was one of 50 cars constructed in 1896 by the Madison Car Company of St. Louis, Missouri, for the Producers Dispatch Line. They were then purchased (as used) by the Shawmut in 1901 for $480 each. They were all scrapped by 1923–1924. Double-sheathed, insulated reefer No. 10086, seen below, was captured in a builder's photograph at the American Car & Foundry Company plant in Berwick, Pennsylvania. Several of these cars were painted as "billboard reefers" proudly advertising their contents as coming from the St. Marys Brewing Company. (Both, SMHS.)

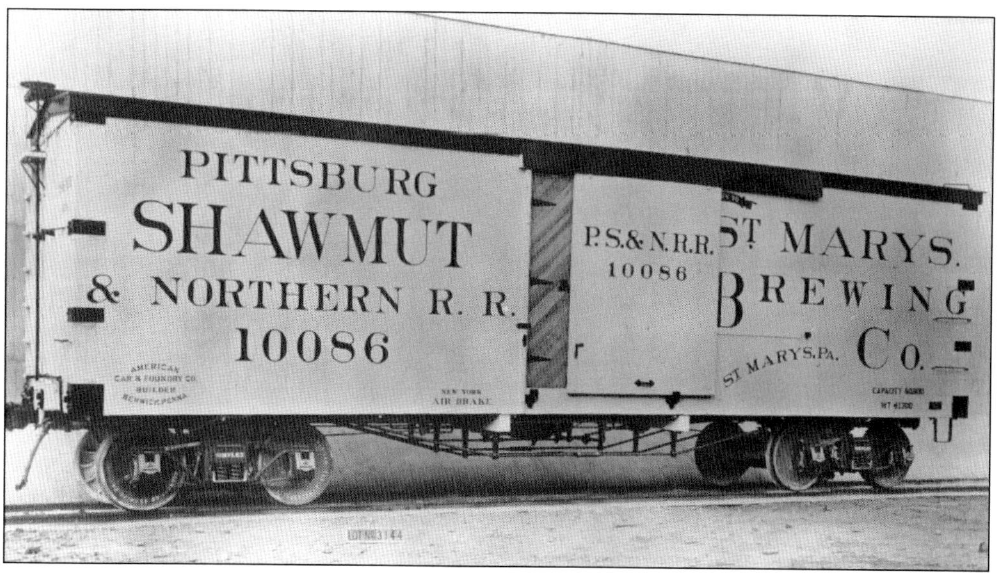

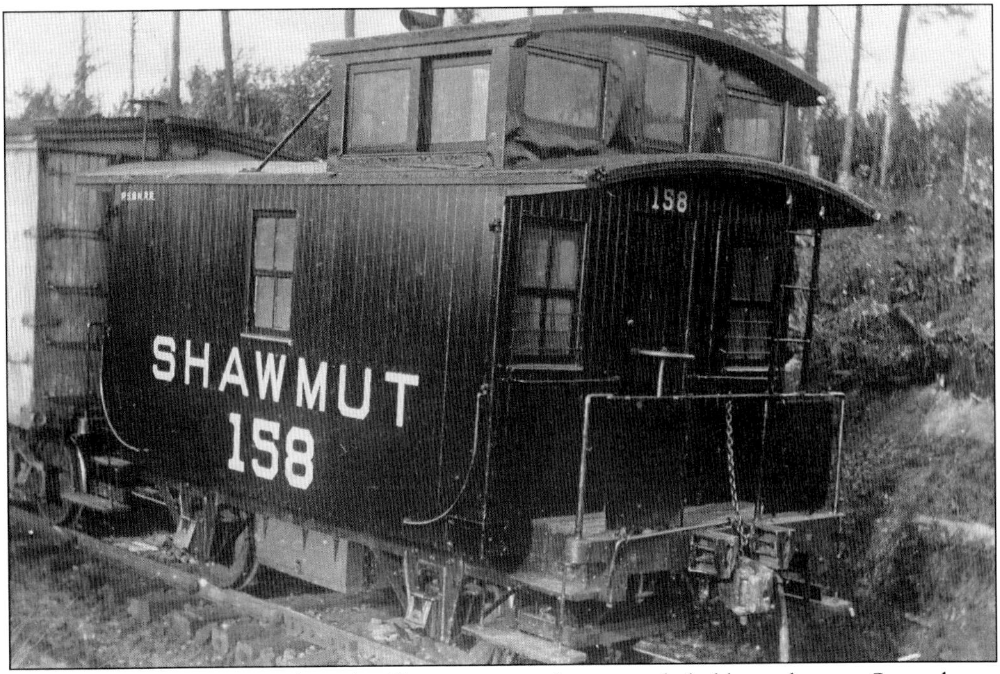

The very first cabooses used on the Shawmut were the two-axle bobber cabooses. Seen above, No. 158 was constructed in the Angelica, New York, shops in 1904. It was constructed to a Delaware, Lackawanna & Western design. It featured an end-cupola and one window per side. No. 173, pictured below, was constructed in the Angelica shops in 1910. It too was constructed to a Delaware, Lackawanna & Western design. However, this design had a higher cupola and two windows per side. Its sister, No. 175, has been preserved at the Pittsburg, Shawmut & Northern Historical Society's museum in Angelica, New York (see page 127). (Both, SMHS.)

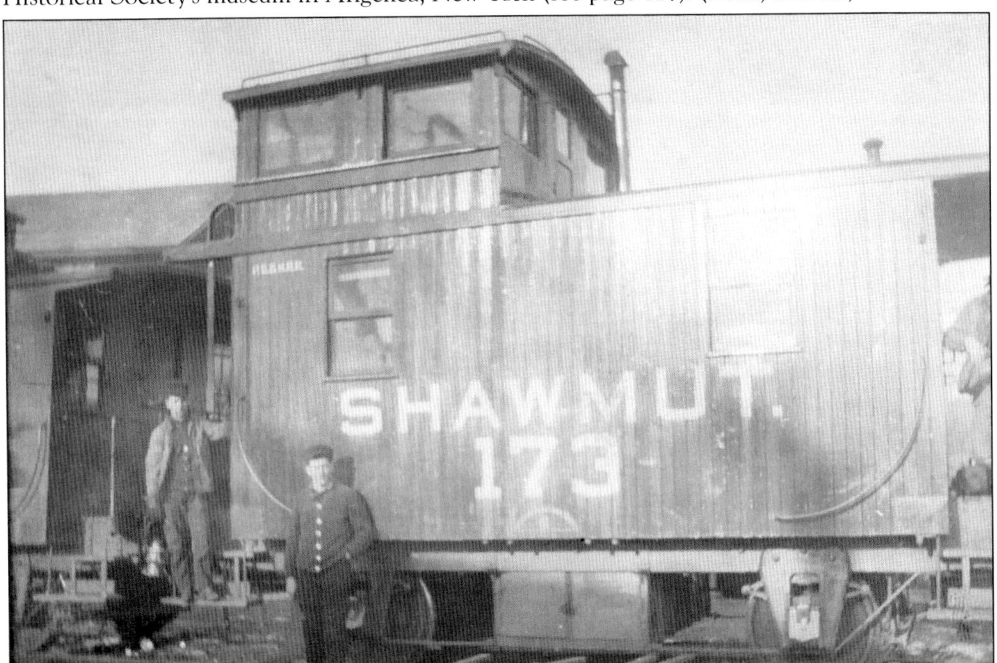

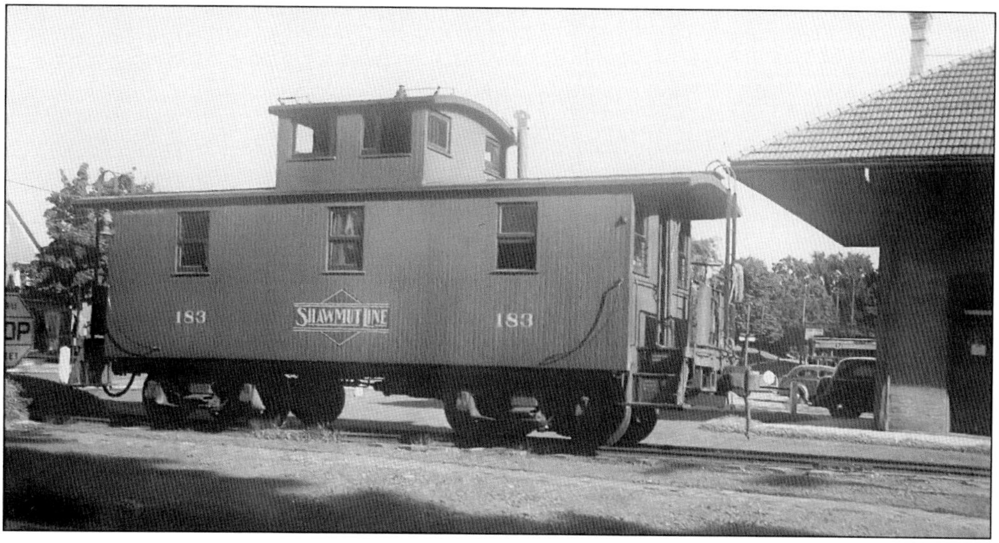

In May 1913, the State of New York prohibited the use of the two-axle bobber cabooses. As a result, the Shawmut commenced construction of 11 eight-wheel cabooses, numbered 183–193. Due to limited shop space, all but three were constructed by the Russell Car and Snow Plow Company of Ridgway, Pennsylvania. On September 10, 1938, No. 183, pictured above, was in front of the depot in Olean, New York. Caboose No. 188 is seen below in 1940 along Adams Street in Olean, New York. The Olean Wholesale Grocery warehouse on South Clinton Street can been seen in the background, along with the twin steeples of the St. Mary of the Angels Church beyond that. Nos. 186 and 187 have been preserved in St. Marys, Pennsylvania. (Both, SMHS.)

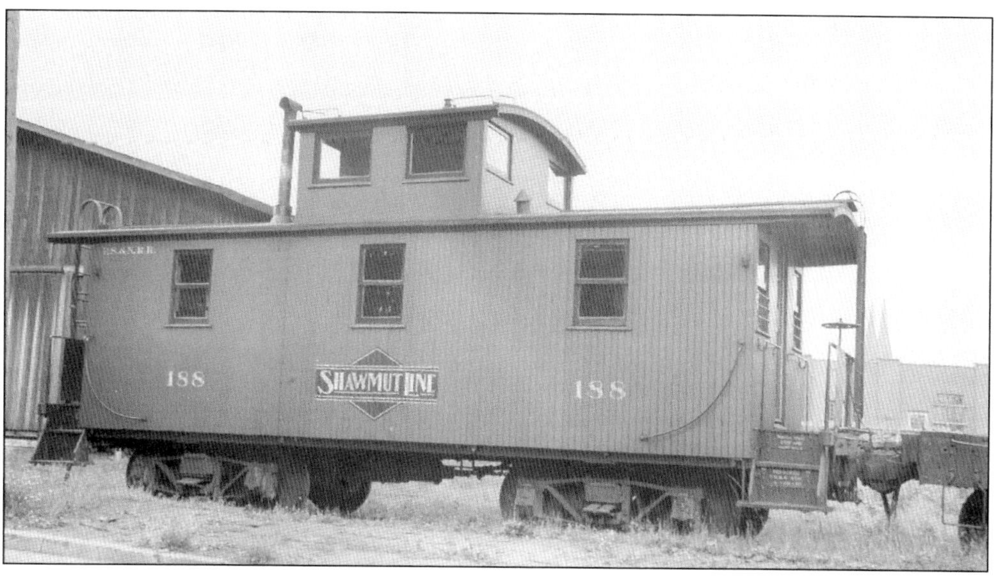

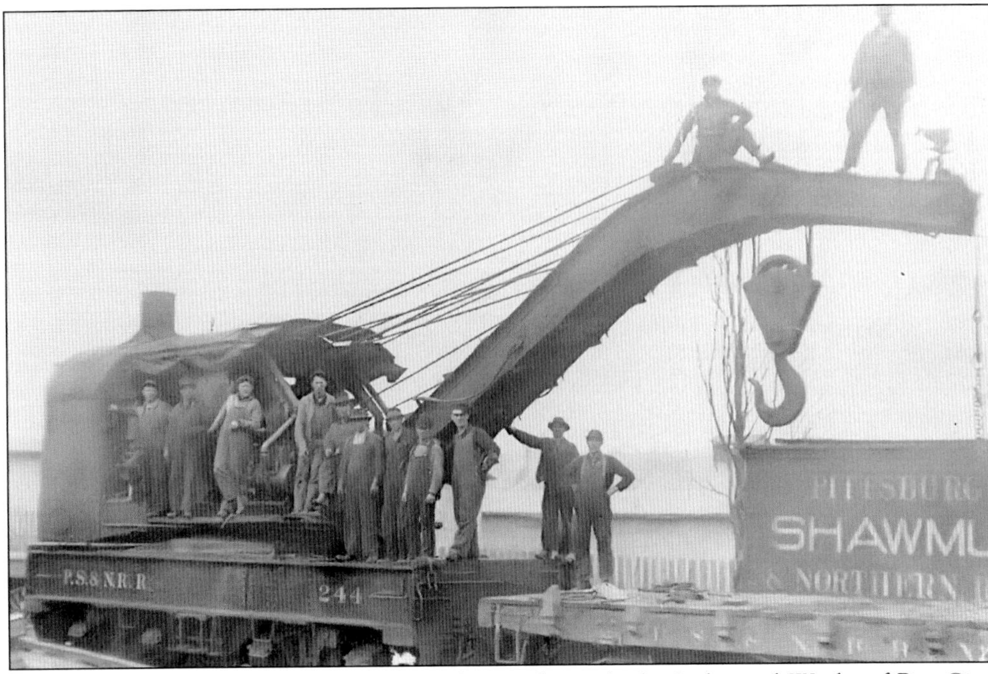

On October 8, 1912, the Shawmut placed an order with the Industrial Works of Bay City, Michigan, for a 100-ton steam wrecker. Known as the "Big Hook" by the crews, it cost $13,850. When delivered, it was lettered as No. 1. This was quickly changed to No. 244. Upon the demise of the Shawmut, the wrecker was sold to the Atlantic & East Carolina Railroad, becoming its No. 44. (SMHS.)

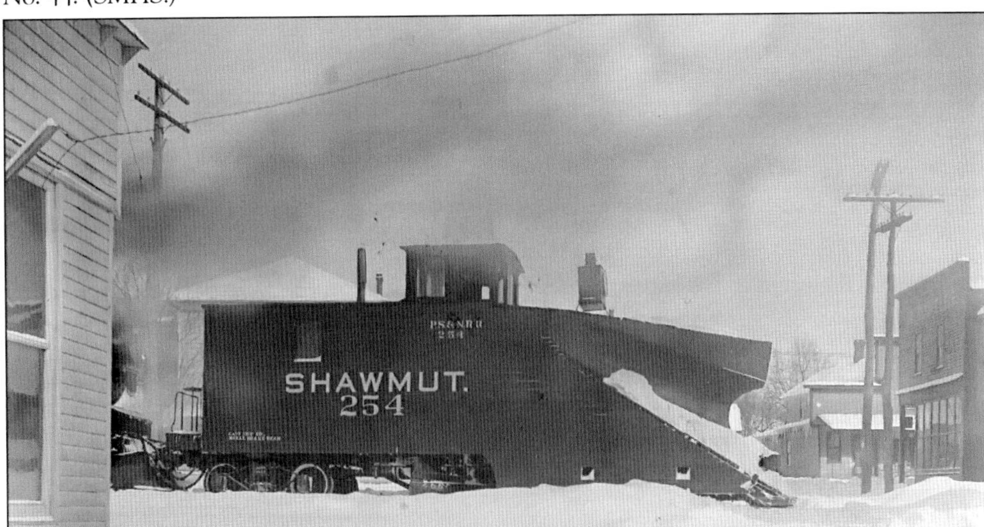

Very early in the history of the Shawmut—the exact date is unknown—the railroad constructed snowplow No. 254 at its shops in Angelica, New York. The plow was a wedge style, meaning that it pushed snow equally to both sides of the track and did not have extendable wings. This undated photograph was taken in Ceres, New York. (PS&NRRHS.)

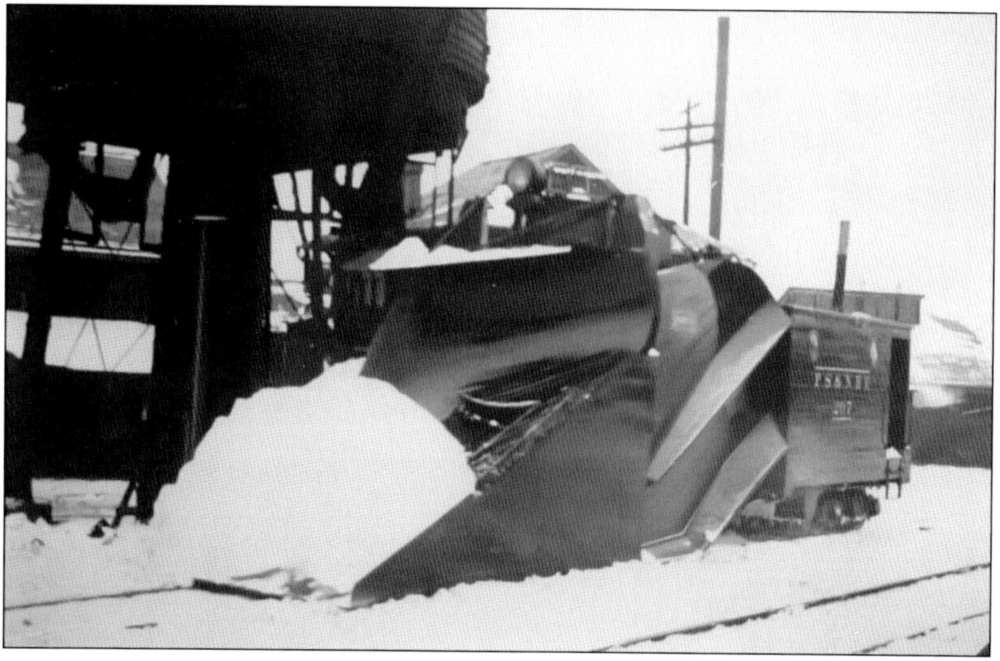

In 1905, with the mileage of the railroad increasing, the Shawmut purchased snowplow No. 207 from the Russell Car and Snow Plow Company of Ridgway, Pennsylvania. This plow had air-operated extendable wings, which allowed for clearing a wider path through the snow. It also included an air-operated flanger. The flanger was a snow blade that could be lowered below and between the rails to clear a path for the flanges of the wheels on the railcars. The undated photograph above shows plow No. 206 at St. Marys Junction. The undated image below shows plow No. 206 leading up a "plow extra" at the coaling tower in Angelica, New York. (Both, SMHS.)

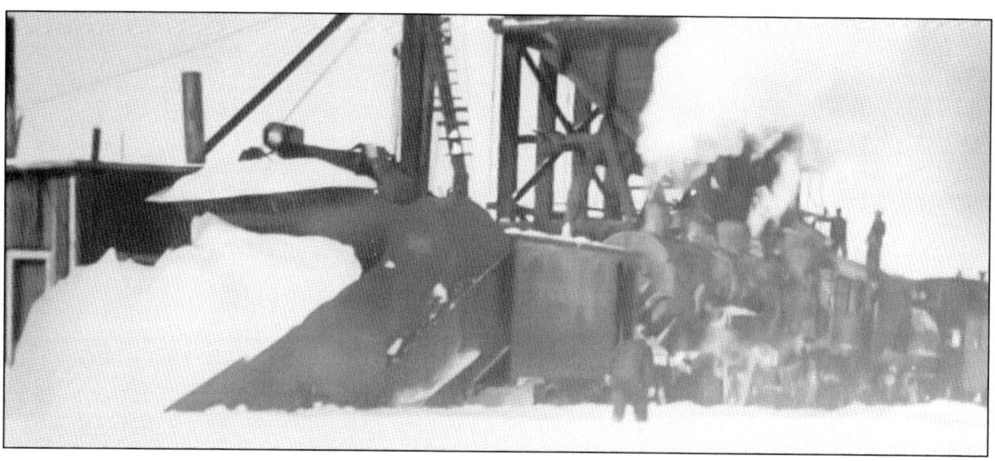

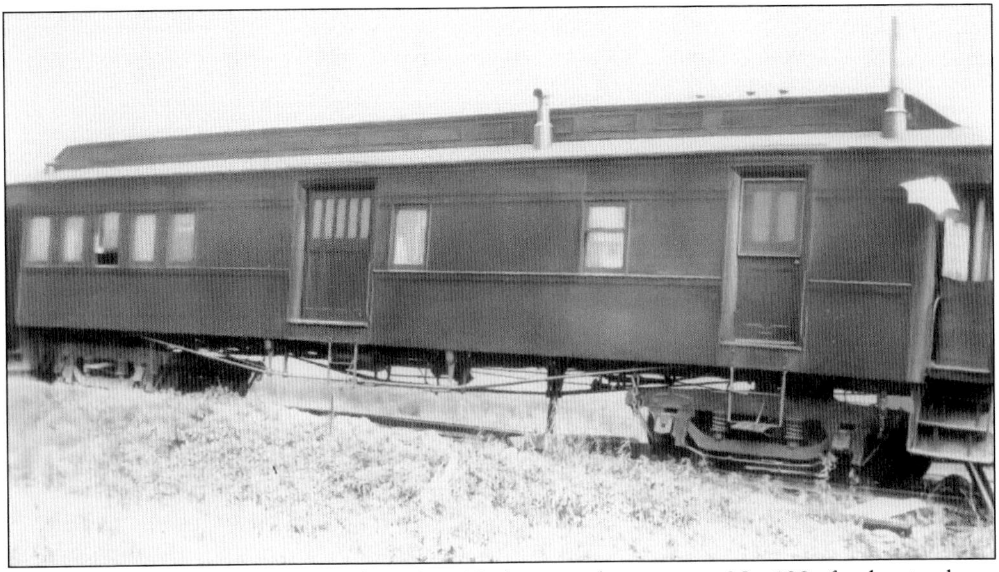

This photograph, taken on November 15, 1920, show combination car No. 128 after having been converted to bunk car No. 262. Bunk cars were portable dormitories used to house crew members who were working at remote sites, typically wrecks and derailments. This photograph was taken at Shelvey Summit, which was located at MP 137.9 on the main line. (SMHS.)

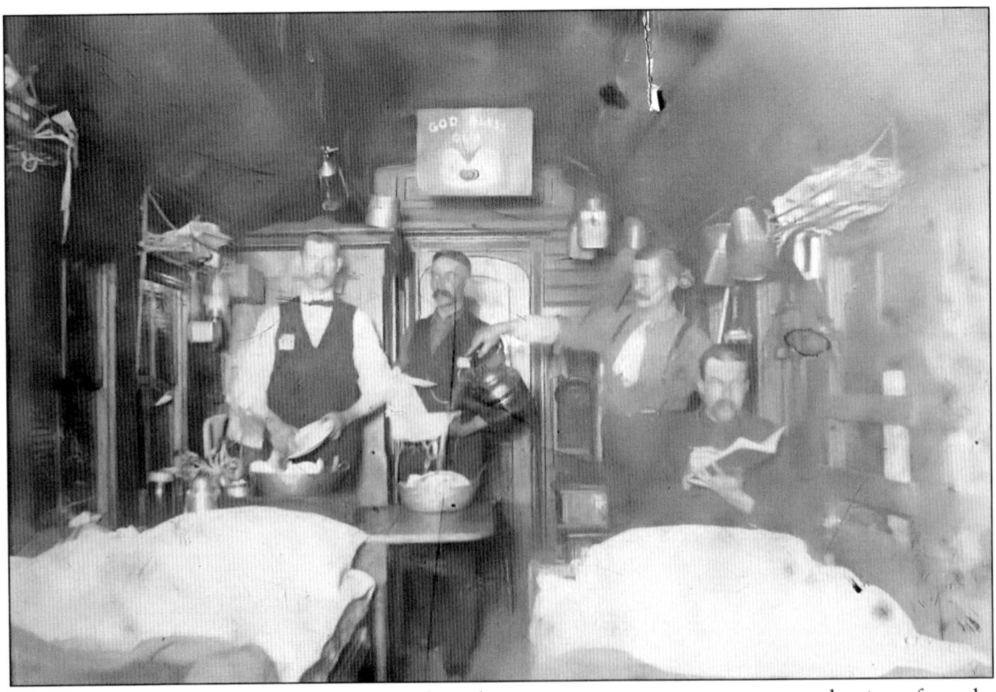

A bunk car is home on the rails for crews when they are out at construction sites or clearing of wrecks for multiple days. From left to right, this 1897 photograph at Swain, New York, shows L. Hopper (engineer), S.E. Heers (engineer), G. Hendershot (fireman), and Joe Way (conductor). (SMHS.)

Four

The Shawmut Mining Company

The Shawmut Mining Company was a wholly owned subsidiary of the Pittsburg, Shawmut & Northern Railroad. It owned 13,750 acres of coal lands having 46,749,061 tons of recoverable coal near Elbon, Shawmut, Drummond, Byrnedale, Weedville, Cardiff, Force, Tyler, and Ramseytown, Pennsylvania.

The oldest workings were in the Shawmut Field, located near the towns of Shawmut and Drummond, Pennsylvania. The 10 mines there go back to the 1860s, when the original Boston investors came to the area. The last mine there, the No. 3, was closed in 1911.

The Elbon Field, located at Brandy Camp and Elbon, Pennsylvania, contained the No. 5 mine. Opened in 1895, it was the Shawmut's largest and most productive mine. Beneath this mine was the older Elbon Mine, originally opened by the Noble Coal Company. Elbon is Noble spelled backwards.

East of the Eastern Continental Divide was the Byrnedale Field, around the town of Byrnedale, Pennsylvania. Named for the first president of the railroad, John Byrne, Byrnedale was the location of the No. 21 and No. 31 mines. West of Weedville on the Browns Run Branch was Mine No. 42. North of Force, up Cherry Run at what was called Cardiff, were the No. 41 mine and the Proctor No. 1 mine. Today, Cardiff is a ghost town.

West of Force, the Shawmut constructed its Mountain Run Branch to Hollywood, Pennsylvania. This was the location of the Proctor No. 2 mine.

In February 1946, a St. Marys entrepreneur named Antonio J. Palumbo established the New Shawmut Mining Company. The above mines were initially leased to and eventually sold to this new venture. Palumbo became very successful, eventually becoming a philanthropist and donating millions to local schools and universities.

The No. 5 mine was closed in 1959. The very last of the old mines, Proctor No. 2, closed in 1967. Palumbo died in 2002. In 2005, the assets of the New Shawmut Mining Company were purchased by Rosebud Coal Sales, Inc. of Kittanning, Pennsylvania; it is an inactive company. The old mines, now silent for nearly 50 years, have been reclaimed and are being remediated for acid mine drainage.

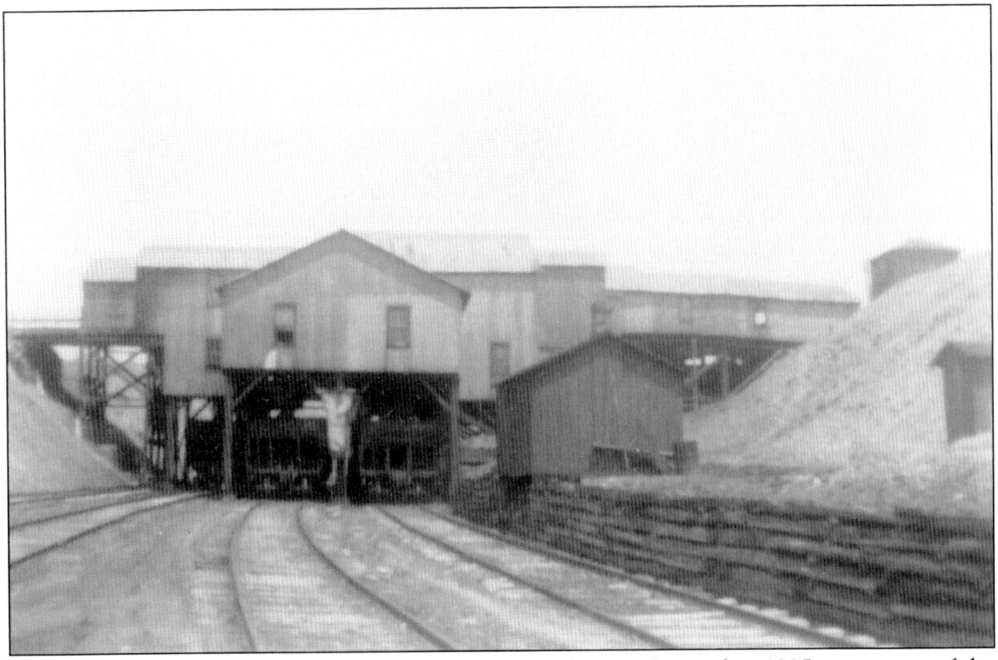

The No. 5 Mine was located in Brandy Camp, Pennsylvania. Opened in 1895, it was one of the Shawmut Mining Company's most productive mines. The tipple included electrically operated screening and sorting equipment. This produced coal that could be sold in differing sizes to meet customers' specific needs. The view in the photograph above, taken in the 1930s, looks east towards the front of the tipple. The two tracks at center loaded coal under the sorting and sizing house. The track to the left was for "mine run" mixed-size coal. At far left was the bypass or return track. The below photograph of the back of the tipple was taken from the top of one of the many slate piles that surrounded the mine. (Both, PS&NRRHS.)

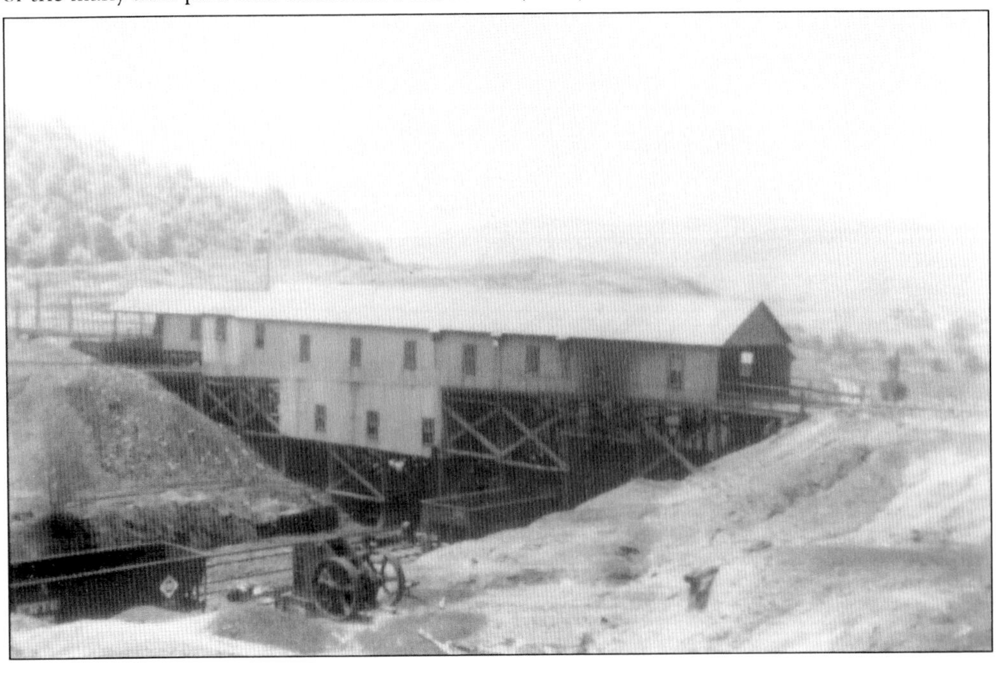

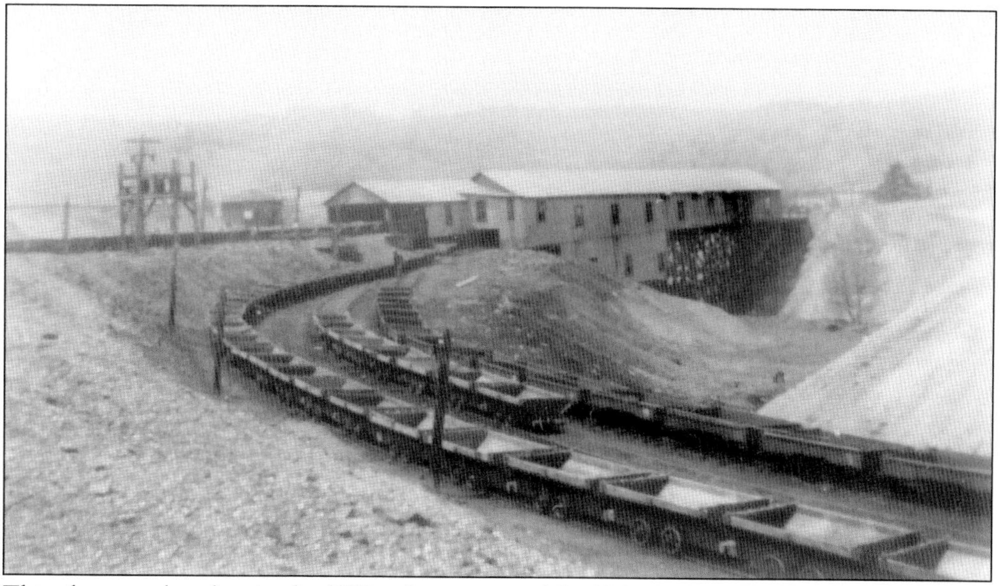

This photograph, taken in the 1930s, shows some of the 738 mine cars used in the No. 5 mine. Loaded cars were pulled by electric mine locomotives into the tipple on the track at upper left. Once emptied, they could roll downgrade on the return tracks in the foreground by gravity. The electrified tracks continued through and beyond the tipple to a coaling tipple that serviced Shawmut locomotives. (PS&NRRHS.)

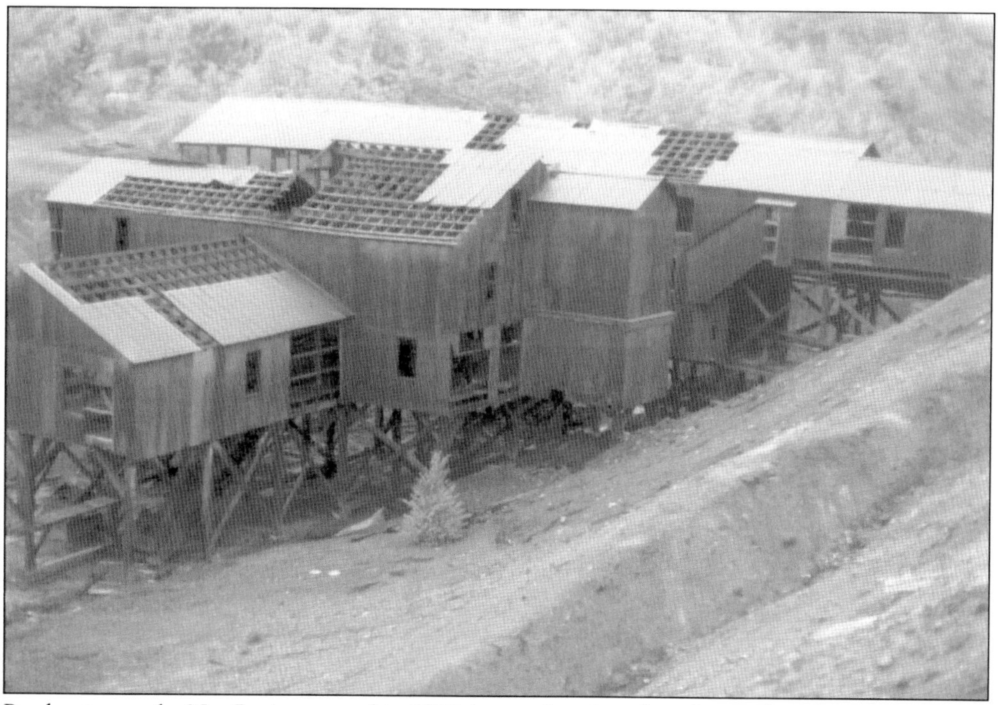

Production at the No. 5 mine ceased in 1959; it was abandoned in place. This photograph, taken in the 1980s, shows how the tipple had deteriorated in the succeeding years: the windows had been broken out and the elements had loosened the corrugated sheet metal that covered the roof and the walls. (PS&NRRHS.)

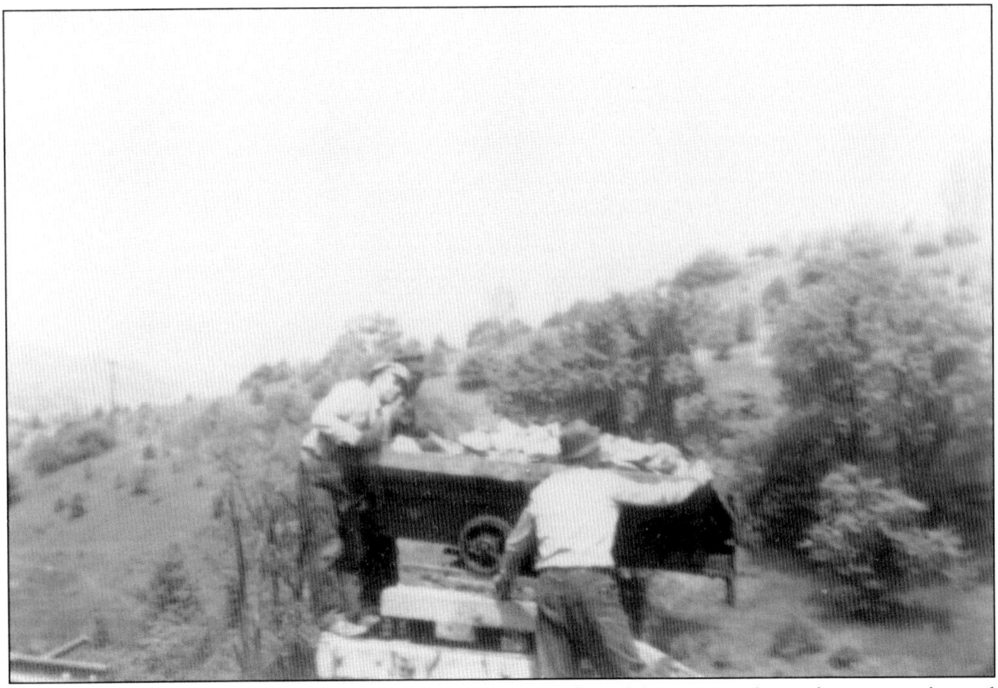

The mines of the Shawmut Mining Company extracted coal from one of two distinct geological seams. Depending upon the location of a given mine, this was either the middle or lower Kittanning seam. These seams varied in thickness from 24 to 48 inches. In order to create enough headroom for the miners, it was necessary for them to remove some of the rock above and below the seam of coal. This rock was referred to as "slate," regardless of the actual type of rock. The slate was brought to the surface in the same mine cars used for the coal. These two photographs, taken in the 1930s, shows the slate being dumped from one of the Shawmut mines. (Both, PS&NRRHS.)

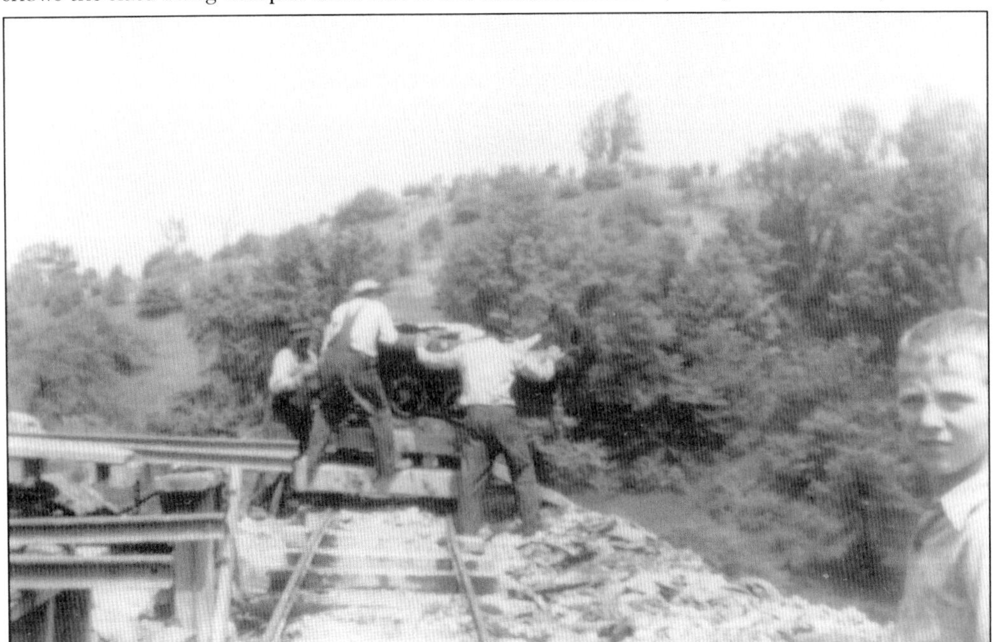

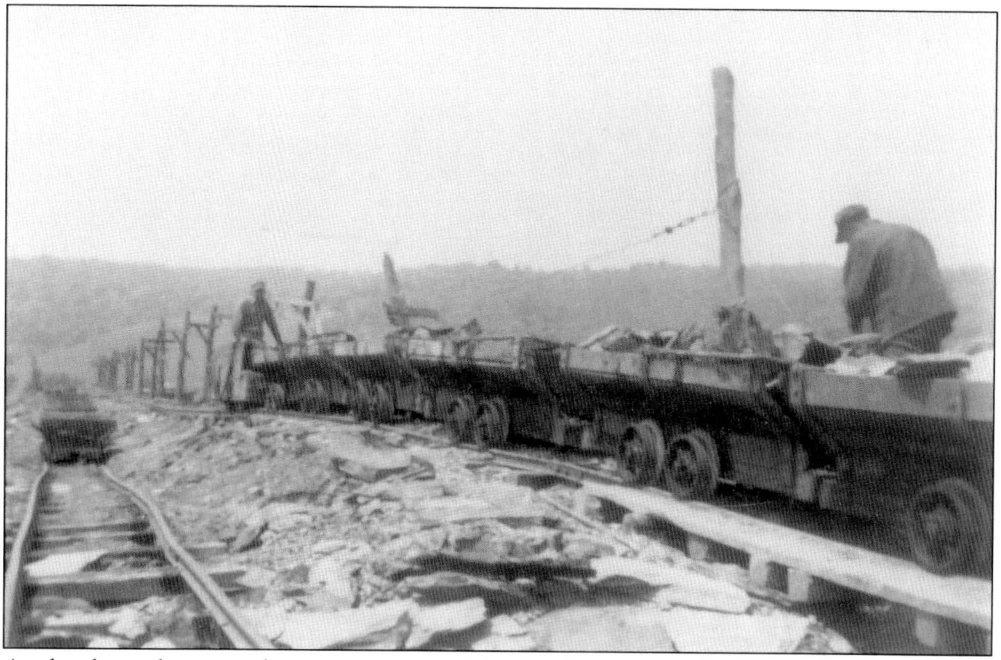

As the slate piles grew, the narrow-gauge mining tracks were simply extended to facilitate the continued dumping of slate. This photograph, taken in the 1930s, shows mine cars loaded with slate being pushed into position by one of the eight-ton electric mining locomotives. Notice how the overhead trolley wire ends near the location of the locomotive. (PS&NRRHS.)

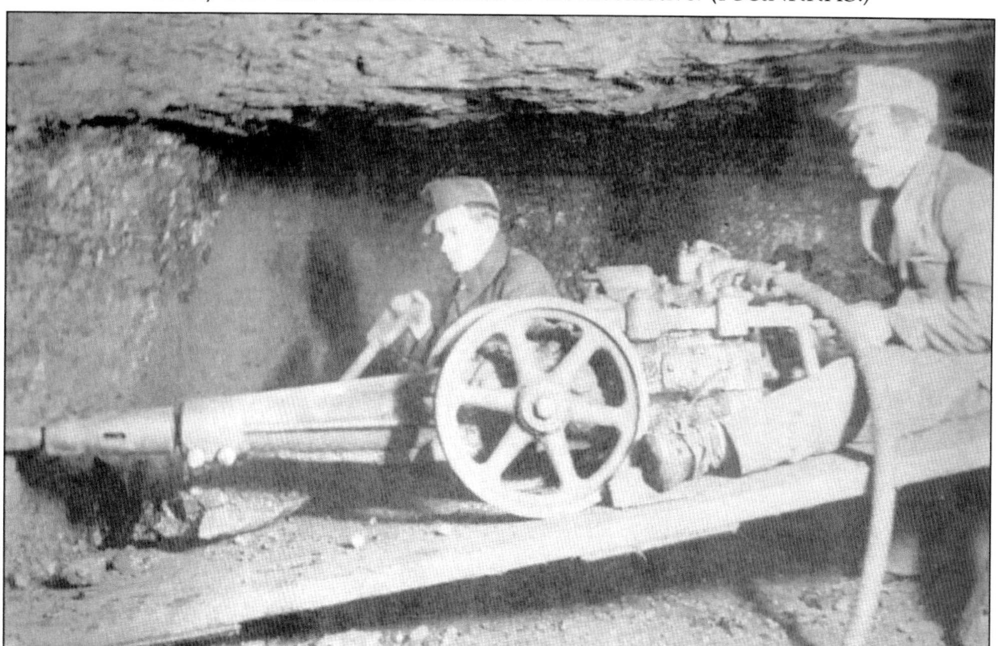

This photograph, taken in 1910, shows the operation of a pneumatic air punch at the mine face deep inside the No. 31 mine near Weedville, Pennsylvania. The machine incorporated a compressed-air–driven piston to which a steel bit about two inches in diameter was attached. Compressed air was supplied by a series of pipes and hoses. (PS&NRRHS.)

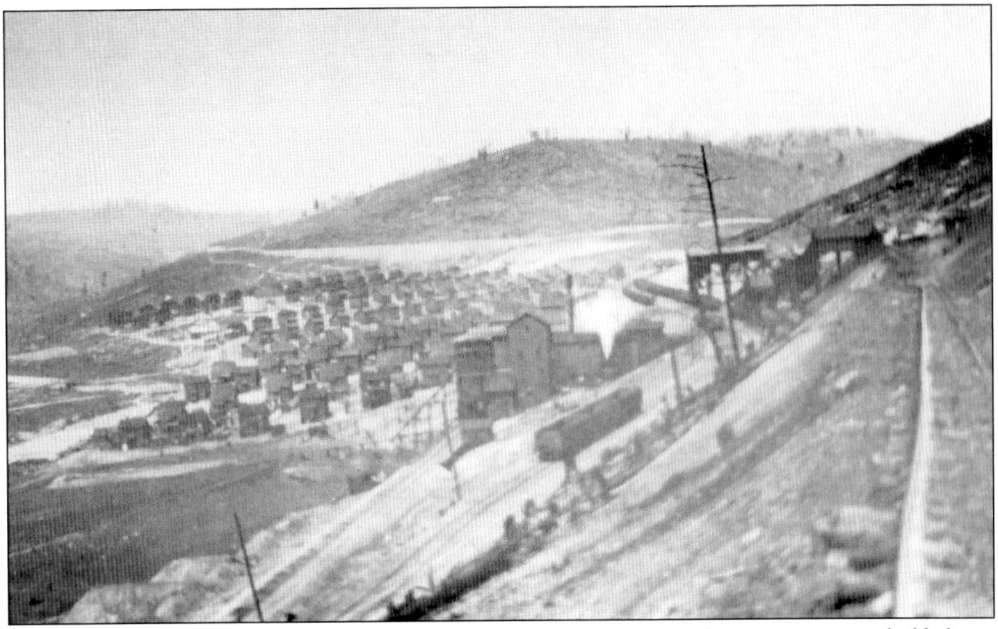

The mine tipple of the No. 21 mine, pictured above, was squeezed onto a narrow shelf above the village of Byrnedale, Pennsylvania. At lower left are the coke ovens. The large building at center is the washing plant, which fed the coke ovens. The Shawmut main line passes through the center of the scene. In the distance at right are the engine coaling tipple and the main mine tipple. At right are the narrow-gauge mine tracks that headed up Caledonia Hollow to the mine entrances. Seen below, the main powerhouse for the No. 21 mine was located at the head of Caledonia Hollow. This mine operated from 1900 to 1918. Both photographs were taken in 1910. (Both, PS&NRRHS.)

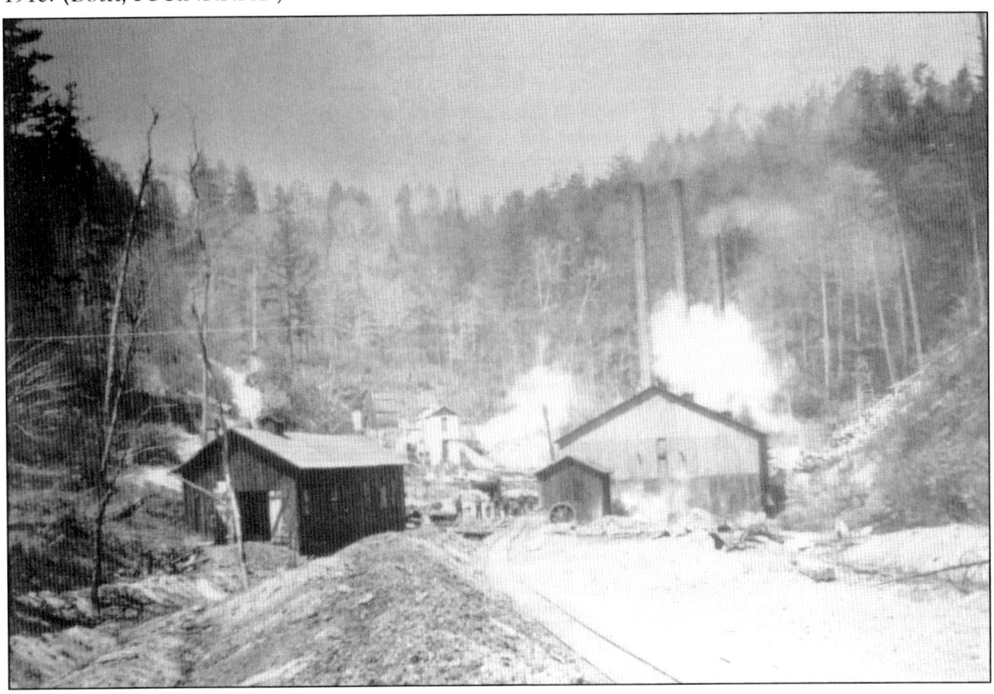

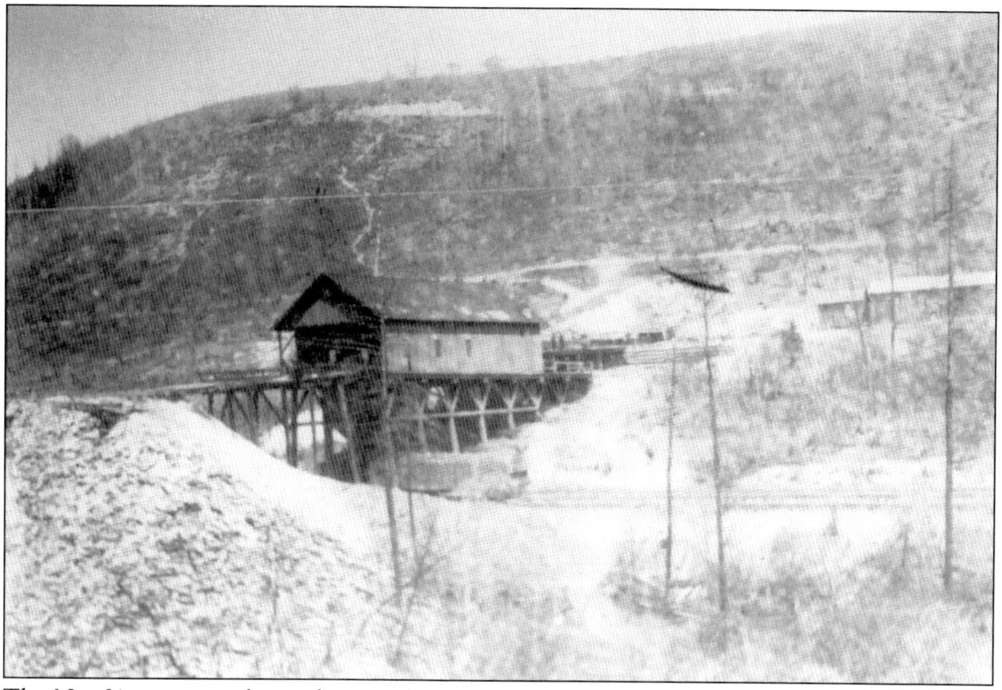

The No. 31 mine was located one mile north of Weedville, Pennsylvania, at MP 141.0. The tipple spanned the narrow valley of Potash Run, a tributary of Kersey Run. This mine was costlier to be operate than the other Shawmut mines. It was closed in 1934 when the tipple burned. (PS&NRRHS.)

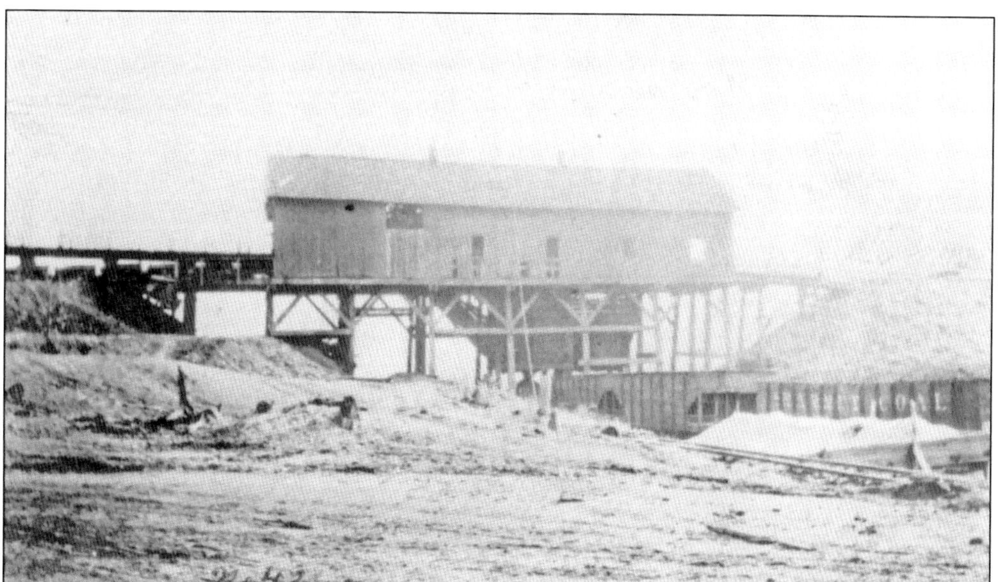

The No. 42 Mine was located northwest of Weedville, Pennsylvania, at the head of Browns Run. The Shawmut reached this mine via its Browns Run Branch. It operated from 1906 to 1953. The mine was electrified in 1918 and had a capacity of 200 to 300 tons per day. (PS&NRRHS.)

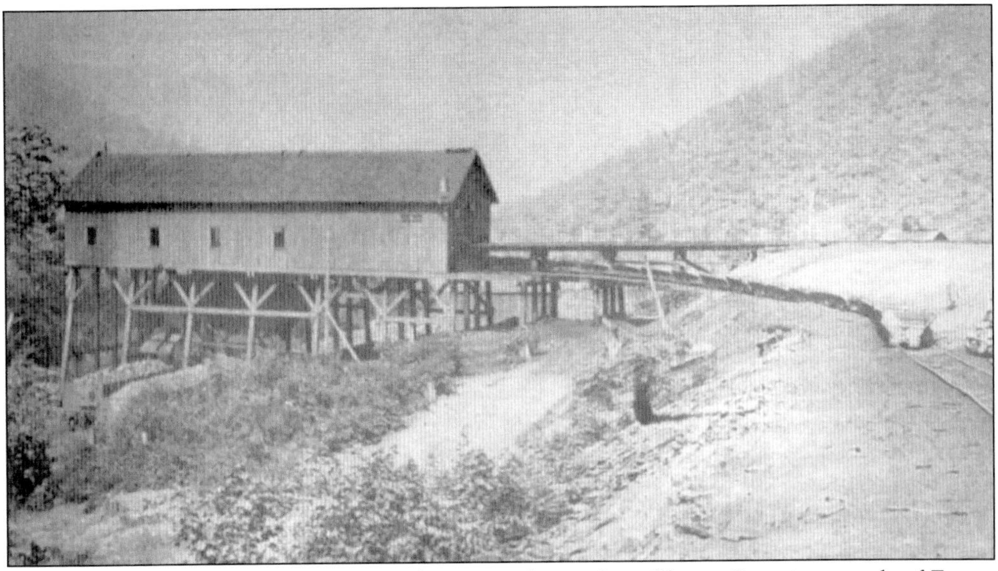

The tipple for the No. 41 Mine, seen above, was located up Cherry Run, just north of Force, Pennsylvania. This mine operated from 1901 until 1922, at which time it was joined underground with the No. 42 mine. From that time on, all production was sent out the No. 42 mine. The company town of Cardiff, pictured below, was located in a side gulley behind the No. 41 tipple. This September 1940 photograph shows some of the company houses and the slate pile from the No 41 mine. Today, Cardiff is a ghost town. There is no indication at this location that a village ever existed. (Above, PS&NRRHS; below, Library of Congress.)

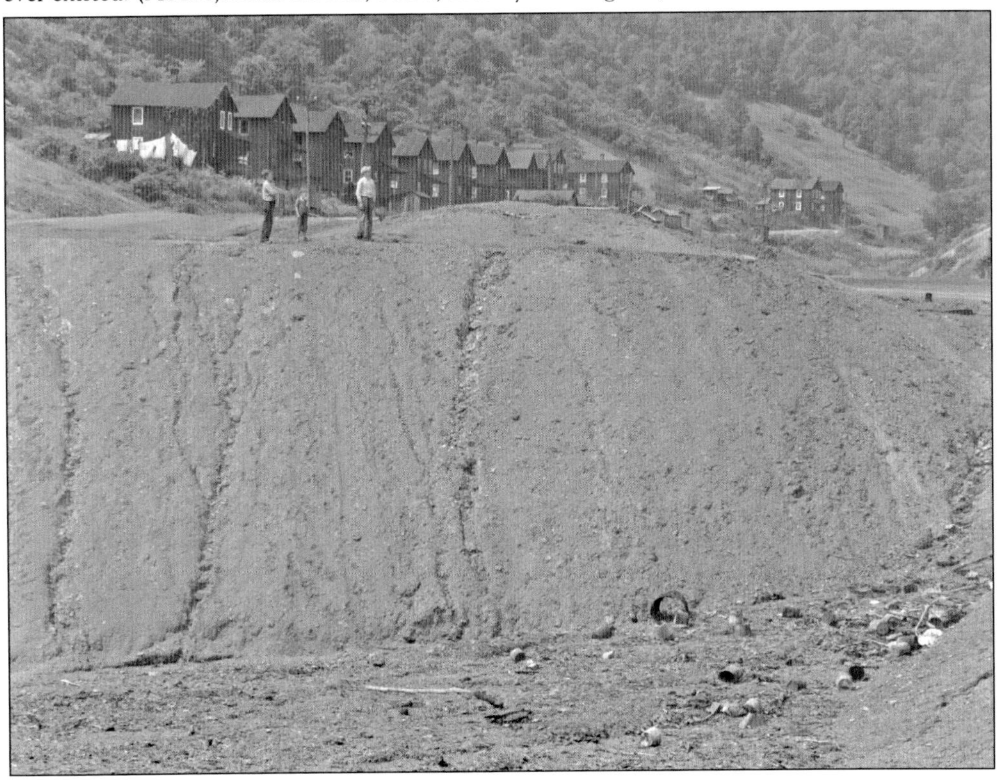

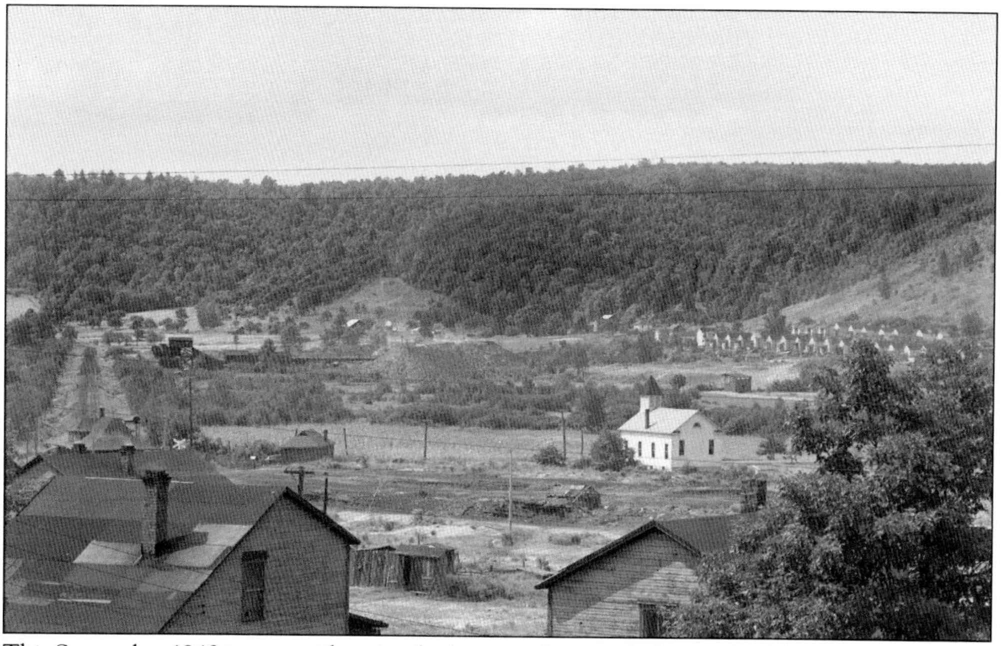

This September 1940 image, with a view looking south towards the tipple of the Shawmut Mining Company's Proctor No. 2 mine, was taken from the mining village of Tyler, Pennsylvania. At right in the distance is the company town of Hollywood, Pennsylvania. The Baltimore & Ohio tracks are at far left. (Library of Congress.)

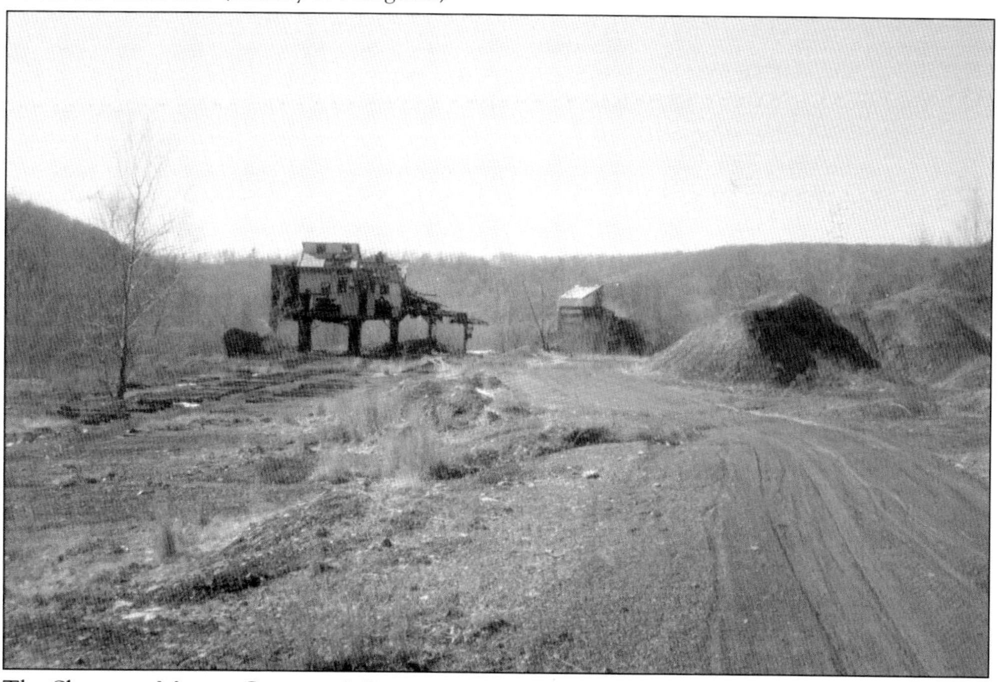

The Shawmut Mining Company's Proctor No. 2 was that last mine opened (in the early 1920s) and was the last mine to close (in 1967). After the demise of the Pittsburg, Shawmut & Northern in 1947, a short connecting track was installed from the nearby Baltimore & Ohio Railroad. This photograph, taken in the 1980s, shows the long-abandoned tipple. (Bill Bauer.)

Bibliography

Clausing, Ernest L. "Olean N.Y., The Way It Was." *Keystone*, Vol. 44 No. 1 (2011).

Cory, Lee. *Stories of the Pittsburg, Shawmut & Northern*. Angelica, NY: Pittsburg, Shawmut & Northern Railroad Historical Society, 1999.

Kilmer, Lawrence W. *Erie Railroad 1863–1976 Bradford Branch*. Olean, NY: self-published, 1990.

Pietrak, Paul. *The History of the Buffalo & Susquehanna Railroad*, Hamburg, NY: self-published, 1966.

———. *The Pittsburg, Shawmut & Northern Railroad Company*. North Boston, NY: self-published, 1969.

———, Joseph G. Streamer and James A. Van Brocklin. *The History of the Western New York & Pennsylvania Railway Company*. Hamburg, NY: self-published, 2000.

Index

About the Pittsburg, Shawmut & Northern Railroad Historical Society

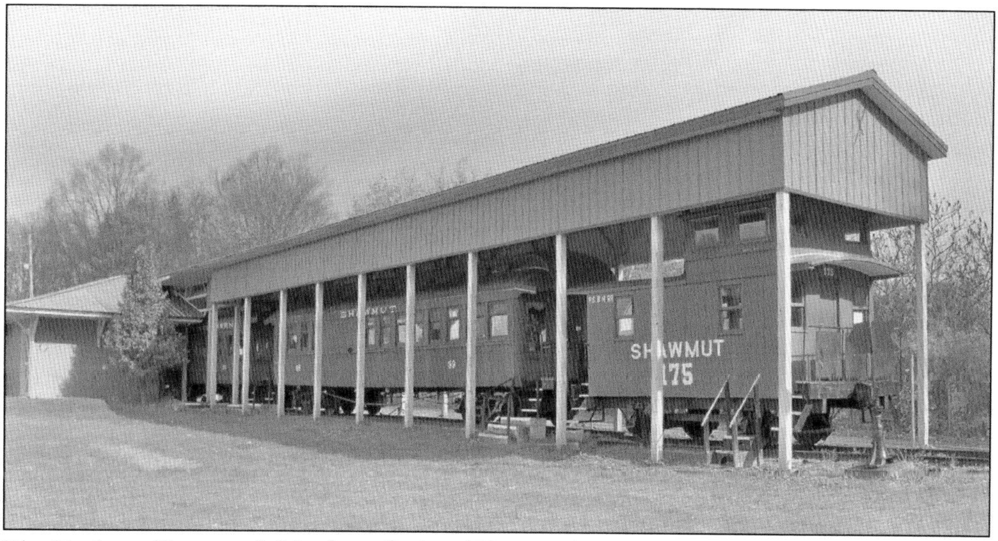

The Pittsburg, Shawmut & Northern Railroad Historical Society is a 501(c)(3) nonprofit historical society chartered by New York State Board of Regents. It was organized on May 24, 1981, as the inspiration of the late Jim McHenry, an ex-employee of the PS&N, and the late Bill Reddy, a railroad employee and local railroad historian.

Over the past 15 years, the society has gained hundreds of members and preserved three authentic pieces of Shawmut rolling stock. Our collection includes coach No. 278, private car No.99, the *Clara*, and bobber caboose No. 175. Our archives and displays are housed in a re-created Shawmut depot.

The society and its museum are located on the Allegany County Fairground in Angelica, New York. The museum is open to the public during certain scheduled events and at any time by appointment.

For information about visiting the museum or to become a member, please visit our website www.psnrrhs.org/ or contact us at:

PS&N RR Historical Society
15 North Street
P.O. Box 222
Angelica, NY 14709

Consistent with our mission to preserve history on a local level, this book was printed in South Carolina on American-made paper and manufactured entirely in the United States. Products carrying the accredited Forest Stewardship Council (FSC) label are printed on 100 percent FSC-certified paper.

MADE IN THE USA